Broken Promises

Broken Promises

Racism in American Sports

Richard Lapchick

St. Martin's/Marek
New York

Design by Laura Hammond

Library of Congress Cataloging in Publication Data

Lapchick, Richard Edward.
    Broken promises.

    "A St. Martin's/Marek book."
    1. Segregation in sports—United States. 2. United States—Race relations. I. Title.
GV706.8.L37   1984   306′.483′0973   83-24803
ISBN 0-312-10592-4

First Edition
10 9 8 7 6 5 4 3 2 1

For Lloyd Sonny Dove, whose life epitomized the struggle of the black athlete attempting to overcome the nearly impossible odds against him. Sonny always fought the odds with a sense of dignity and pride that would have finally brought him home to meet his goals had his tragic death not taken him away at such an early age.

· Contents ·

· Introduction ·

Thirty-five years after Jackie Robinson broke the color barrier in professional baseball, Americans see numerous black athletes being paid more than $100,000 per year to play baseball, basketball, and football. Most thoughtful, intelligent Americans believe that this is a sign of society's progress. Many young men and women, black and white alike, believe that sports is a great racial equalizer.

Born into a great sports family just before the Jackie Robinson era, I too was a believer for most of my youth. Being part of a white middle-class family with a sports celebrity for a father made my early life both easy and happy. I wanted nothing more than to emulate my father's path to athletic glory.

That desire made me oblivious to reality, even to the reality of my own father who was himself a pioneer in bringing about racial change in American basketball. As the country's star pro center in the 1920s and 1930s, his Original Celtics team was among the first to play against the Rens, the nation's first great black team. While becoming one of America's most successful coaches during a thirty-year career, he brought up Nat "Sweetwater" Clifton to the New York Knicks in 1950 to help break the color barrier in the NBA.

By doing so, he became a "nigger lover" to many. Three decades after Clifton came to the Knicks, not only have I been branded a nigger lover for my own efforts to end racism in sport, but my own son Joey has been called a nigger lover because of those he has chosen to play with today.

This book is the story of how I became involved in the struggle for racial equality and why I remain involved in spite of several life-threatening situations. It took me more than three years to be able to write about those life-threatening events, which took place mainly in 1978. The trauma of those times made it difficult to share these experiences with those outside of my immediate family and close friends.

The book is also the story of how little has changed since Jackie Robinson took that courageous first step. America has made many promises to its people. The promise of racial equality is one that has been broken time and time again. Some commentators have said that time is running out, that it is five minutes to midnight. I saw the other side of midnight in 1978. It is an ugly place that I hope my children never see. I have written this book to attempt to see to it that they never will.

· PART 1 ·

The Attack in Virginia

·1·

No Defense

"Nigger, they carved *nigger* on his stomach!" As I heard one of my students say this to his friends while pointing to me, I realized with horror that my life might never be the same again. Still dazed, I tried to reconstruct the night. Within a week I would have to try to reconstruct my life.

It was Valentine's Day, 1978. Early that day, I told my wife Sandy that I had to work late in my college office in spite of our desire for an evening together. There had been little time for such evenings in recent years; the pace of our lives had accelerated too fast. As always I wanted to be with her but my belief that I "had to work" won out in the end.

In the past, such decisions were made compulsively. Now, at least, we had both reached a stage where we felt comfortable with our individual lives and, consequently, with our life together. Sandy, who had retreated from a career as a commercial artist after achieving early success, was now reemerging into the art world. I had somehow learned to balance my life as an academic teaching political science at Virginia Wesleyan College in Norfolk, Virginia, as an activist on civil rights and anti-apartheid issues, and as father, husband, son, and brother.

Previously, I had believed that time given to one cheated all the others. I was beginning to understand that the quantity of time was not as crucial as the quality of that time. So on this particular Valentine's Day, neither of us worried about missing time together.

Several of my students tried to persuade me to go to the basketball game at the college that night. It was almost as hard to say no to them as it was to my wife. This was partially because I would do almost anything to enrich the relationships I had with my students.

On this night I especially wanted to prove to that small part of the world that cared about these things that I was not anti-sport. I was a critic of racism in sport, both in South Africa and in America, and I had heard myself accused of being antisport more frequently during the preceding weekend than ever before. How could I be antisport? How could the son of Joe Lapchick, a legendary figure in basketball, be antisport? When my father criticized basketball for not being integrated, did his contemporaries think he was antisport? That was a question I would reflect on frequently after this night.

But now it was my time to be judged. As National Chairperson of ACCESS (American Coordinating Committee for Equality in Sport and Society), I had been campaigning to end all sports contacts between the United States and teams from South Africa as long as sport and society there were segregated. I had spent two years writing a book on the subject, *The Politics of Race and International Sport: The Case of South Africa*, which was published in 1975 by Greenwood Press, and had already been involved with the issue for eight years. However, at this time, there was a new intensity over this issue in the United States.

The tone of South Africa's press coverage in America and Europe had significantly changed. The South African police were still trying to explain how Steve Biko, the founder of the Black Consciousness Movement and one of the most important contemporary black men in the country, had died in their custody as a result of a crushed skull in September 1977. The Western press could then hardly ignore the October 1977 bannings of most of the other important voices of dissent in that country. News items were beginning to appear about a scandal in the Ministry of Information—a scandal that would eventually bring down Minister of Information Connie Mulder and Prime Minister Vorster with him when it was revealed that huge sums of money were spent to buy favorable foreign opinion.

With its image tarnished, South Africa felt it was even more crucial to successfully stage its Davis Cup tennis match with the United States. Having an integrated team play the matches at Vanderbilt University in Nashville, Tennessee, before thousands of spectators and possibly millions of TV viewers might do for South Africa what a Ping-Pong match did for U.S.–China relations in 1972. If investment dollars, bank loans, and trade, which had been reduced due to anti-apartheid criticism, were to resume on a grand scale, the South African government knew it would have to win this battle in its propaganda war.

Therefore, my visit to Nashville from the tenth through the thirteenth of February was not warmly welcomed by either South Africa or its supporters in the United States. The earlier announcement that the National Association for the Advancement of Colored People (NAACP) would make the Davis Cup a focus of its efforts guaranteed the high level of attention we wanted on what apartheid meant for black South Africans. My visit generated a great deal of attention in Nashville as to why we wanted the matches canceled.

The Nashville sports media and the Vanderbilt athletic department wanted to raise the accusation that I was antisport. However, the news media and the people of Nashville concentrated on what apartheid was about and the oppression it created in South Africa. By the time I spoke at Vanderbilt on October 13, I could feel the momentum shifting. The news that came during my speech that the financial backers of the tournament had pulled out confirmed this. When I flew home to Norfolk that night, I sensed that, possibly for the first time in all my years as an activist in the 1960s and 1970s, I had made a real contribution. Although I was tempted to go to the game, I was secure enough that I had made a contribution that I told my students Sandy would have my hide if I went to a basketball game after I told her we couldn't go out so I could work.

My office was situated on a balcony that circled the main reading room of Wesleyan's library. At about 9:30 P.M. there was a commotion in the library, which began to temporarily fill up with students after the game. When I looked out I saw Lambuth Clarke, the president of the college. I liked Lambuth and had always gone out of my way to greet him. However, I think I gave him a special greeting that night because I wanted him to know I was working late in my office. Although I had no classes to teach on Friday and Monday, I felt slightly guilty that I had been in Nashville and not on campus. We exchanged pleasantries and I went back to my office to work.

At approximately 10:25 I went to the water fountain for a drink. The two librarians still there were about to leave. I told them I would be working late and said good night. I returned to my office and began typing a quiz that I would give to my urban studies class the next day.

There was a knock at my door at 10:45. I assumed it was campus security police routinely checking the library.

Although I could not clearly see who or what stood outside when I opened the door, my life began to change with one rough shove across the room. My shoulder was slightly cut as I landed on one of the railroad spikes that comprised a steel sculpture done by my wife a decade before. As I stared up at the two men attacking me I realized that they were both wearing stocking masks.

I was terrified and confused all at once. Was this a robbery? If so, why would they choose a college professor in his office?

Were these Cuban exiles coming after me because of favorable remarks my students and I had made after returning from two weeks in Cuba in January? I knew that the Cuban exile community of Norfolk was extremely upset, but could they be doing this to me now?

My confusion grew along with my fear as they tied me up in my chair and stuffed one of my thick winter gloves into my mouth. I felt like I was gagging and losing my breath. The first man, speaking without an accent, said "Will you continue doing what you have been doing *now?*" Was it Cuba-related? Had my trip to Nashville provoked this?

The second man, also speaking without an accent said, "Nigger lover, nigger lover." The first man then said, "You know you have no business in South Africa." The confusion about why they were there was over.

All the time the attackers were saying these things, they used the top two drawers of my filing cabinet as battering rams on my chest and face. I did not believe they were trying to kill me; they could have been hitting me with much greater force. Also, they were turning my head from side to side so the blows never hit me squarely and were cushioned by the glove in my mouth. No, it was to frighten me. And they succeeded.

They untied me and one held me up with a hammerlock so I could not move. The hooded hunters were both behind me as I faced the file cabinet. Unable to see them, I listened carefully to their voices. Were they Klansmen? South Africans? All they said were the three phrases, repeated as if they had been rehearsed. They were definitely American though I could not tell where they came from in the United States. Of course, I later realized that if South Africa was behind the attack, the last thing they would do was send nationals with South African accents.

After the file cabinet beating finished, I could examine at least the one man who was not holding me. Beyond the impenetrable stocking, I could tell he was white, about six feet tall, and well built. He reached for the other steel sculpture made by Sandy. I had titled this one *Revolution* since the configuration of the steel spikes appeared to me to resemble a clenched fist. Sandy thought it was a flower. Although always supportive of my political work, Sandy was apolitical—the fist and the flower, we had joked, reflected our outlooks on life. Now the flowers could not bloom so often for her.

The spikes were set in a four-by-four-inch wooden base. The attacker wielded it like a bludgeon, working his way up the backs of my legs to my back and my arms, and all the while the man holding me asked, "Will you continue doing what you have been doing *now?*" His friend said "Nigger lover, nigger lover," and then he repeated, "You know you have no business in South Africa." It seemed so orchestrated, so set. But their fury was genuine and he pummeled my stomach. The ferocity of the bludgeoning and the pain he was causing made me wonder if they were still only trying to scare me. I passed out as the pain and horror became too much.

When I came to, both men were kneeling over me. My shirt had been ripped open and one of the men was using what appeared to be my office scissors on my stomach. I was scared, not knowing what they were going to do. The pain was intense; my terror grew.

I thought I heard a noise from the library. The men pulled me up as if they had also heard something. The one who had been holding me said, "Let's get out of here." That was the only deviation from their script. He was slightly taller and perhaps had broader shoulders than his partner. Also, of course, he was white. He opened my door and was gone. The other pushed me to the floor and, as a farewell gesture, knocked a bookcase on top of me. It hit me in the head and I passed out again.

When I regained consciousness I was in great pain and my head was ringing. The office was dark and quiet. The door was closed. I had only one thought—to get out of there. I could not stand and had to use whatever I could to prop myself up. I half-staggered, half-crawled along the balcony of the library to the stairs, where I began to make my way down until I lost control and rolled down the last eight or ten steps.

Finally I made it to the library desk, where I reached for the phone. I noticed the clock on the wall—it was 11:40. What seemed like an eternity of torture had begun and ended within an hour. I dialed campus security but, amazingly, there was no answer so I called Sandy.

I told her what had happened but that I was not badly hurt, and asked her to call the police and rescue squad. It was obvious that she was worried, but at the same time she was remarkably calm. When we were finished I called campus security again—this time they responded and said they would be right there.

I fell back and rested on the stacks of newspapers that lined the inside of the library desk. It seemed forever before anyone came. At first I was afraid that the attackers were still somewhere in the building. Worse yet, I worried that they or their associates might go to my home.

Our house was always open to students and people from the community, even at late hours; Sandy would never have suspected trouble from anyone at the door. I was glad that she knew what had happened so that she would be more cautious.

I thought of my mother, who was living with us in an apartment we had built onto the house. She had been through this before with my father, who had paid an emotional price for his commitment to racial equality in sports, and with my sister Barbara's second husband, who had been a political prisoner in Uganda.

At that point two members of campus security entered the library. I did not have the strength to yell to them and they seemed to walk around endlessly. Finally, the older man found me. He ordered his assistant, a young black man, to go up to check the balcony. I don't remember him saying anything to me as he scurried around the library desk. I guess he wanted to make sure no one was around; maybe he was embarrassed that this could happen while he was on duty.

"It's a wreck up here," the black guard shouted, but the older man seemed to ignore this. The library suddenly came alive with men from the rescue squad and with students. As I was being examined by the rescue squad, Mike Mizell, a student whom I did not know well at that time, took a long look at my abdomen, which was exposed during the examination. Although I was quite dazed I will always remember the expression on his face, which changed from simple concern to horror. He got up, walked over to his friends, and said, *"Nigger,* they carved *nigger* on his stomach!"* I had forgotten about the scissors but suddenly realized that this was what the attackers must have done with them.

"Nigger lover, nigger lover," began to ring through my head. Images of my children flashed in my mind. Chamy, a soft three year old with a golden Afro, would be sound asleep and was surely too young to be affected. Joey, our intense, high-energy five year old, might not be able to escape being traumatized by repercussions of the attack.

Only one week before he had come to me in my study and asked, "Daddy, are you a nigger lover?" I was stunned until I recalled my own experience when I was his age.

My father, as coach of the New York Knickerbockers, had just integrated the team by signing Nat "Sweetwater" Clifton, who had been playing for the Harlem Globetrotters. We lived in Yonkers in a large old three-story house. Like other children, I loved to answer the phone. I picked up the phone upstairs when my father picked it up on the first floor. Suddenly he began to get a number of "nigger lover, nigger lover" calls. At five, I didn't know what a "nigger" was but it certainly sounded wrong to love one. The callers obviously hated my father. I could not understand this because to me he was such a sweet, gentle man—the center of my universe. Why did he love a "nigger" if it was such a bad thing to do? It hurt to hold it in, but it was half a lifetime before I had the courage to ask him.

I asked Joey, "What do you think a nigger lover is?" He replied, "I don't know. But some mean man on the phone just told me that you were one." I was enraged that people would still play on the minds of children to get to their parents. I didn't want Joey to carry images of doubt about his father around with him as I had done, so I tried to explain to him what I was doing that would provoke racists to call me "nigger lover." Why did a five year old have to understand such ugly things? He would have to know soon enough.

I was brought to Bayside Hospital in Virginia Beach and underwent a number of tests. The doctor in the emergency room was Dr. Martin Lorenz. He was very sympathetic to my injuries and even more so after he heard about the attack.

Sandy arrived and I regained a sense of reality. I felt safe. She said, "Did you know they carved *nigger* on your stomach?" When I said I did, she responded, "Did you know they misspelled it: *niger?*" We both laughed. The injuries didn't seem so bad now and I hoped I could go home. I wanted to teach a class the next day. After the tests were over, Lambuth Clarke, the president, Bill Wilson, the dean, and Alan Stowers, the college information officer, came into the emergency room. Lambuth said, "They misspelled *nigger.* At least we know it wasn't one of our students." I told him it was obvious he hadn't read any student papers recently.

Sandy told me that Dennis Brutus, one of the founders of the movement to end racism in sports in South Africa in the 1950s and still one of its leading voices in exile, had been trying to reach me. Two police detectives entered the emergency room and began questioning me. Sandy excused herself to call Dennis and tell him what had happened. I knew he would empathize; he had suffered tremendously for his work in South Africa— banned, imprisoned, and shot in the stomach by police. I thought that at least here the police would be on my side and would try to help.

They were pleasant enough then and my trusting nature did not lead me to read anything into their questions. I recounted what had happened. They told me they knew nothing of my "political" background and asked a great many questions about it, about my trip to Nashville, about my local involvement with race relations and migrant workers, and about my recent trip to Cuba. At the time, all their questions seemed directed at finding out who might have attacked me. Later, I began to wonder.

Dr. Lorenz returned to tell me that there was evidence of kidney damage since they had found blood in my urine. I also had a concussion and was forced to stay in the hospital for other tests. I began to realize there may have been more damage than I had thought.

One of the detectives stepped out at this point while the other remained to ask me to write out a description of the attack. The one who left went up to Sandy and said, "When we heard who *he* was, we expected to find a screaming, shouting radical. We were surprised to see that your husband is so soft-spoken and gentle." She laughed and took it as a compliment, but it clearly indicated what the attitude of the police toward political activists seemed to be.

The officer returned to the emergency room with Sandy as I was finishing my written account of the attack. I could not understand why they wanted a written statement from me since I was exhausted at that point and had already given a detailed oral account.

I was told, "We don't want this to get into the newspapers. Do not talk to the press under any circumstances." I was surprised at this request and gazed at Sandy, whose expression indicated the same incredulousness. I said, "It's hard for me to imagine how you could keep this quiet even if you wanted to. And why would you want to keep it out of the papers?" I was informed that "We don't want to spoil our chances of catching these men." "If they know what we are doing it would be more difficult," one of the policemen explained. I said I would try to go along with their wishes but considering the national and international implications, it would be almost impossible.

I was then told, "Okay, if the story does break don't, under any circumstances, say they used scissors, or refer to the statue or the misspelled *nigger*. We must keep these clues to ourselves." This made some sense and I agreed.

"I just called Dennis Brutus and told him all those details," Sandy interrupted. She was asked by the detectives to call him back and tell him not to say anything.

It was now 4:00 A.M. Just as the police were about to leave, a hospital orderly came in and asked Sandy to take my clothes home. "Don't you want the clothes for evidence?" Sandy asked the police. Much to our astonishment they said "No."

When Sandy reached Dennis at 6:00 A.M. he had already informed the protest organizers in Nashville. Sandy immediately called Yolanda Huet-Vaughn, a local organizer in Nashville, to be told that they had issued a statement to the *Nashville Banner* condemning the attack. Sandy asked her to call the paper and ask that they not mention that *nigger* was misspelled. Yolanda said she would try. Like so many other seemingly small details, this turned out to be important in the weeks to come.

But now I only wondered if the police would catch the attackers. I was still in a state of shock and could not think of what they would *not* do and what all their innuendos had meant: the lengthy questions about my involvements, their surprise at my demeanor, the request for a written account of the attack at such a late hour, the plea to keep the story out of the press, the lack of interest in the clothes I was wearing. I didn't add these things up at the time. All I could think about was getting my attackers off the streets so I could be safe, so my family could be safe.

By the time I was left alone it was around 5:00 A.M. Exhausted, I could not sleep but finally dozed. An efficient nurse woke me with the stark reality of an enema at slightly after 6:00 A.M.

I called Sandy to tell her I was tired but okay and to find out what happened when she called Dennis. Joey and Chamy were still asleep and unaware of what had gone on that night. The same was true of my mother.

The phone rang soon after I hung up. I assumed it was Sandy. However, it was a Nashville radio station. I was amazed that the hospital switchboard had let the call through at that hour.

"Dr. Lapchick, all of Nashville is appalled to learn of this attack on you," the interviewer said. "You are being called a hero by your admirers here." I told her I was no hero and that I had merely followed my conscience. The Paul Robesons, the Malcolm X's, and the Martin Luther Kings were heroes. They had been long-distance runners whose steel wills and compassionate hearts had been constantly tested by society.

This led to the inevitable, "Will you continue your work now that this has happened to you?" Although it was the obvious question, it stunned me. While she meant it sympathetically, it brought to mind the vision of the hooded hunters eight hours before. I lost control and began to cry. I was not sure whether the interviewer heard me. "How does your family feel about this?" she asked. "Do they want you to continue?"

I remembered my terror as a child when I would fantasize that those daytime/nighttime callers would hurt my father. I wanted to protect him. Now my own son would not only fantasize such fears but would have to cope with the reality of the attack.

What did it all mean? Was it worth it? Had the integration in American sports that happened in the 1950s, 1960s, and 1970s really made life any better for all but the minute fraction of blacks who had made it to the professional ranks? If my work, along with that of others in the movement, did result in the integration of all sports in South Africa, would it really change the lives of people there? Would it lead to the eradication of the heinous apartheid system? Do sports serve as a vanguard for change in our culture? Would I continue now? Who should be asking me this? The attackers? The press? My wife? Joey and Chamy? I was quite shaken now—more so than at any time since the knock on my door.

I replied, "Of course I'll continue. This has only strengthened my resolve to remain in the struggle. It proves that our efforts have been successful enough to provoke an attempt to destroy us. I'll go back to Nashville next week as planned." While I knew I *would* do all of this, I also knew I would have to ask myself all the hard questions I thought about that morning. I knew I would have to confront my values. I would have to come face to face with all the assumptions I made while growing up, about all that my father had taught me, and finally about what I had learned the night before.

· 2 ·

Offensive Attack

The scabs from the carving of *niger* on my abdomen began to come off within a few days after the attack. But the physical scars were there, as were the mental ones that kept me awake at night. Calls of "nigger lover, nigger lover" played over and over in my dreams and wrenched me out of bed. First, my father with the Knicks; now me with South Africa. I knew I had to go back to Nashville to continue the fight over the Davis Cup. It was as reassuring to receive support from people all around the world as it was good to hear from friends around the country. I was told that the attack had resulted in growing support for canceling the matches. That helped ease the pain. The strategy of the attackers was backfiring.

Trying to educate the American people about the reality of apartheid in South Africa had increasingly become my life's work and I was sure that our successes had led to the attack. Sport had become the vehicle for the message.

But it is a reasonable question to ask why, with all the racism rampant in America, and even in sport in America, that I chose to work on the South African sports issue.

Part of the answer is fate. My meeting with Dennis Brutus,

while writing my Ph.D. dissertation on the subject, and the publication of my book led me to confront the enormity of the oppression in South Africa and the role played by the United States in propping up the apartheid regime.

Part of the answer is analytical. I realized that many of the same institutional forces perpetuating racism in America were operating in South Africa. The same corporations that grow rich from the pool of cheap, unskilled, largely black labor in the United States, grow even richer from their operations in South Africa. American corporate exploitation of black South African laborers, who worked for extremely low wages, makes the position of black American laborers even more tenuous as they become increasingly expendable.

In the process, American dollars, through investments and loans, have helped South Africa remain "stable." Stable in South Africa means two things. First, that economic dislocations do not become too severe. Second, that part of the nation's wealth can be diverted to build its aggressive military machine, which in turn attacks its black neighbors to destabilize them.

With only 13 percent of the population white, and with South Africa surrounded by independent black African countries free from minority rule, the future is clear. The forces of history dictate that it is not a question of *if* black South Africans will be free. The question is *when* and *how*.

The situation inside South Africa had come under intense scrutiny by the American press after more than 600 people were killed by the police in Soweto in June 1976. Most of those killed were schoolchildren. The murder of Black Consciousness leader Steve Biko in September 1977, followed by a series of bannings of remaining opposition figures in October, left South Africa's image badly tarnished as the scheduled Davis Cup tennis matches approached. Even the spending of $72 million for propaganda in the previous four years could not help. The Davis Cup was a potential propaganda coup desperately needed by the apartheid regime.

But the time was not ripe for South Africa. Nashville, Tennessee, the scheduled site of the Davis Cup, had many college campuses. And the campuses nationwide seemed to be coming alive on the anti-apartheid issue. The media was predicting—inaccurately as it turned out—that the protest against apartheid would rival that against American involvement in Vietnam. It was in this context that I had gone to Nashville on February tenth.

The Davis Cup matches, in particular, and tennis in general, were the only areas left where South Africans were partially welcome. Successfully staged, the Davis Cup could reopen the flow of investments and loans. Better still, it could soften the image of apartheid and put a silencer on the growing anti-apartheid movement in America. There was a great deal at stake for the Pretoria regime.

However, anti-apartheid groups in the United States were well aware of this and prepared a counteroffensive.

Franklin Williams, president of the Phelps-Stokes Fund and the former U.S. Ambassador to Ghana, took the lead with civil rights groups. He organized the Coalition for Human Rights in South Africa, which included the NAACP and the Urban League. Franklin and I spoke several times soon after South Africa defeated Colombia in Johannesburg in December 1977, "earning" itself a trip to Nashville. We exchanged ideas and materials and Franklin agreed to have the Coalition join ACCESS, the group of which I was chair, to plan the strategy to protest the matches. We both felt that the participation of the NAACP would assure a large demonstration in Nashville.

The creation of the Coalition was a major development. The traditional civil rights groups historically had less involvement than predominantly white groups in the anti-apartheid movement. Their priorities were, justifiably, at home where racism was on the rise. But Soweto, Biko's death, and the bannings were bringing things to a head. Black unemployment in the United States was steadily increasing as corporate dollars went to places like South Africa to exploit black labor there. The same banks that were "redlining" predominantly black and minority neighborhoods by denying them loans were making loans to South Africa. The same conservative politicians that opposed busing and the extension of the Voting Rights Act were supporting legislation that favored white minority regimes in Rhodesia (now Zimbabwe) and South Africa. The same men who fought as mercenaries were Klansmen with expert paramilitary training.

ACCESS had the information on the issue and kept it before the public whenever sports contacts with South Africa came up. We were a coalition of thirty national civil rights, religious, political, and sports groups formed in 1976 to oppose sports contacts with South Africa until apartheid was eliminated.

Our main focus had been on tennis since it was the only remaining team sport in which South Africa competed for the world championship. The U.S. Tennis Association (USTA) had long been a supporter of South Africa's membership in the International Lawn Tennis Federation (ILTF), the world's governing body. But South Africa was becoming more and more of a problem. Many countries refused to compete with them in the Davis Cup (men's) and Federation Cup (women's) championships. They won the Davis Cup in 1974 when India refused to play them in the championship round. As European, especially Eastern European, countries withdrew, the event became more of a farce.

So South Africa was moved from the European to the North American Zone to compete. Most teams in this zone also withdrew except Colombia and the United States. The government of Colombia refused to allow the opening round with South Africa to be played in Bogota so it was moved to Johannesburg.

Thus, the confrontation was set up. We all felt that Vanderbilt University, under the leadership of its chancellor, Alexander Heard, would be the most likely to agree to cancel the matches. We were unfamiliar with the NLT Corporation, which agreed to back the event financially. We had been meeting with the USTA for two years. It had already announced it would press for South Africa's exclusion in 1979, but our concern was 1978. Therefore, ACCESS joined local Nashville groups in putting maximum pressure on Chancellor Heard. He agreed to meet me at the university.

So I began the trip that would turn my life inside out on Friday, February 10, arriving in Nashville in the morning. The issue was catching fire and the exposure I received that weekend was amazing. I spoke on four university campuses, including Fisk and Tennessee State, the two major black schools. I was on two television shows, and did lengthy interviews with the *Nashville Banner* and *The Tennessean.* We held press conferences on Friday, Saturday, and Monday. All three received top news coverage. I spoke at a black church on Sunday morning. We met with local organizers to plan strategy several times.

The only disappointment of the weekend was the meeting with Chancellor Heard and Vanderbilt President Emmett Fields. It was obvious that they were intractable in their decision to allow the matches to take place. On the one hand they said sports and politics don't mix; on the other they said that this was an "open forum" or free speech issue. I had been warned by Vanderbilt's black students that the university's liberal reputation was a false one. My meeting with Heard and Fields accomplished nothing.

Other than this, everything else felt positive during those jam-packed four days. You could *feel* the momentum of the city shifting toward cancellation of the matches. Local organizers had set up an excellent itinerary to maximize the impact of my stay.

On arriving Friday, I perceived the nature of the debate. Opponents of the matches felt that "South Africa is an evil country and we shouldn't play tennis with them," without having a deep knowledge of what apartheid meant on a daily basis for the twenty-plus million black South Africans. Proponents felt that "tennis is a wonderful sport so let's see good competition and keep politics out of it."

This was an issue I knew very well. The combination of being able to bring the information to Nashville, coming from a famous and respected sports background, and having the academic credentials enabled me to effectively deliver my message that weekend.

South Africa saw the momentum shifting and tried to change it by naming Peter Lamb to its Davis Cup team. Lamb was a "colored" (mixed ancestry) South African who was a student at Vanderbilt. He was a good player, but at eighteen was hardly of Davis Cup caliber. Announced on Sunday, February 12, the decision backfired immediately as the press saw it as more tokenism from South Africa. It made me even more critical of Vanderbilt officials for allowing one of its students, who was never meant to play in the matches, to be so badly used. I knew that Lamb would soon find himself in an agonizing position— reviled by black Americans and by black South Africans for being unwittingly used by South Africa.

The element that I didn't recognize at the time was how much white South Africans resented my *whiteness.* I was later told that it was one thing to have a Franklin Williams or Benjamin Hooks do antiapartheid work. It was, after all, blacks who bore the brunt of the oppression. More hated and less understood were whites like George Houser, then the executive director of the American Committee on Africa, or myself. The same was true for white racists in America. It was nigger lover time all over again.

By Monday afternoon as I was about to address students at Vanderbilt, I knew that a great deal had been accomplished. There was an air of excitement, of anticipation. All three local TV stations were there. One technician had a remote system back to the studio. Just as I was about to begin my speech, he told me that the NLT Corporation had announced that it had withdrawn its financial support for the Davis Cup.

I relayed the decision. The hundreds of students and faculty in the audience burst into a sustained applause. They were on their feet cheering for several minutes. I told them "The victory is *yours*. It is only the first." We were on our way to cancellation.

As I began the speech, the NLT decision even made the "Your father is a nigger lover" call to Joey the week before seem more palatable. I told the audience about this incident. Usually a self-assured speaker, my eyes welled up with tears. I had to pause and drink some water. I had never said anything that deeply personal in a speech before. It would not be the last time. However, I caught my breath and went on with the speech. It was more passionate, more alive than the others that weekend.

I was feeling euphoric as I was rushed to the airport. We had the South Africans on the run. A Piedmont Airlines attendant at the gate said, "Well, Doctor, I guess there won't be tennis in March."

I exhausted Sandy with details of the weekend when I got home. Sleep did not come easily that night.

I left at 7:45 A.M. for my 8:30 class on Tuesday. I had three one-and-a-half-hour classes on Tuesdays and Thursdays and usually am fatigued by the end of the day. But on this day I was flying, for it was the day after NLT Corporation pulled out.

The only damper on the day was the word that Norfolk's Cuban exile community was extremely upset about my "biased" reporting of what I had seen with my students in January. Peter Galuszka, a reporter from Norfolk's *Virginian Pilot*, was writing both sides of the story and called me for information. We went out for an hour or so to have a sandwich before I returned to my office to continue catching up on class work. I respected Peter as a journalist and watched how he tried to study the Cuban issue from all sides. Moreover, I liked him as a person and felt a friendship developing.

I opened up to him that night and told him about the call to

Joey and about a series of calls I had received late in 1977. They began after a feature story on my anti-apartheid work appeared in a regional magazine.

I was called three times by the same person. At first I was told I had three weeks to live, followed by the tapping of a metal object—presumably a gun—on the phone. Exactly one week later he said I had two weeks to live. He again tapped the object. Another week passed when the message that I had only a week left came through. The tapping was harder and louder. I slammed down the receiver, realizing that this could be serious.

I told Peter that I went to Bernard Barrow, our neighbor and friend. Barrow was a member of the Virginia House of Delegates. I totally trusted his judgment when he said to hold off calling the police until I returned from a one-week lecture trip. When I told Peter that the series of calls had stopped, I could see relief in his face. Yes, we could easily be good friends.

As I ate the sandwich I could never have imagined the emotional wringer that Peter and I were about to be thrown into together.

Three hours after I left him, the attack began, lasting less than one hour. As it turned out, it only set the stage for the ensuing nightmare.

· PART 2 ·

The Aftermath
of the Attack

· 3 ·
Riding Momentum

There was a sense of total unreality for a minute or two after I was awakened by the nurse. I could see I was in a hospital room. There was a nurse, a bed, and I was in an antiseptic, nondescript room. Yes, it was a hospital.

Slightly dazed, I assumed I must be visiting Sandy. After all, I had not been hospitalized in twenty-five years since a brief bout with polio. There were remnants of my jock mentality left. A jock is invulnerable. My body was now a highly developed, muscular 170 pounds after years of consistent workouts three days a week at a gym decorated to be a "health club."

My mind swirled. I thought of my three most recent visits to the hospital. I came to watch and assist in the births of Joey and Chamy. I came moments after the death of my father. The nurse did, at least, shake me back to reality. It was I who was in the hospital.

I thought of Sandy, Joey, Chamy, and my mother. I thought of last night—of masked men and of the police.

My body literally shook as "nigger lover" rang through my head. But the image was of Joey asking me if I was a nigger lover and not of the hooded hunters of the previous night. Were they the ones who called Joey? Who called me?

I called Sandy. Everyone else at home was asleep. Sandy and I talked briefly about last night, about Dennis Brutus, and about the Nashville press release condemning the attack. Since a press release would obviously bring out the story, I asked her to call friends to tell them I was fine. Included in the long list was Peter Galuszka, the reporter from the *Virginian Pilot* whom I had been with shortly before the attack.

A few minutes later that Nashville radio station phoned and the circus began. Peter Loomis of the *Ledger Star,* Norfolk's afternoon newspaper, called to request an interview. He came and I went over some of the details of the attack, deleting the parts the police asked me to leave out. Then I told him and he wrote that I was "beaten with a blunt instrument until he [I] lost consciousness." I didn't say it was the wooden base of a steel sculpture. He reported that "nigger" (not "niger") had been carved into my stomach "with a sharp instrument" and not with my scissors. He also wrote that I had cuts on my face, chest, and stomach. All he saw, of course, was my face. I wondered if deliberately withholding such details could really help the police to apprehend the men who beat me. I wondered if the detectives were on the case. I realized they were probably asleep after the long night.

Loomis was followed by Peter Galuszka. His was a welcome face, a face that told of his concern for me. We joked for a while, and then he told me he had been assigned to write the story for the *Virginian Pilot.* We talked about the details. He was puzzled when I repeated blunt object, sharp instrument, and "nigger." Peter assured me that the specific details were in the wire service stories already. He knew it was a steel sculpture, scissors, and "niger." I abruptly realized that the Nashville people must have been unable to change their press release.

So I told him the whole story of the attack. By the end of the day I had told and retold the story more than a dozen times. The three local TV channels sent crews. The networks, both TV and radio, did phone interviews as did the wire services and the Nashville papers. Over and over I said I would go back to Nashville, that "as long as I'm able to get out of bed, I'm going to intensify my activities. This has strengthened my resolve." However, seeing the fear in my mother's face that afternoon when she came to visit made me question my bravado, sincere though it was.

Sandy and I agreed not to tell the children what had happened. When Joey called, I told him I was sick. He said that he had heard that "bank robbers got you and cut out your heart and put it in your stomach." I was very upset, more so because I had no time to think. When I wasn't being interviewed I was being examined. Could I really go back to Nashville? Should I take the same risks? Time, I needed time to think.

A Sri Lankan physician, Dr. D. C. Amarasinghe, entered my room and announced that he would be in charge of my case. He gave me a thorough exam and ordered a battery of tests and X rays. When he began to examine me for a hernia I protested, saying I was sure there wasn't one since no one had hit me in that area.

Dr. Amarasinghe patiently explained that such a beating on the abdominal wall could easily cause one. Sure enough, when he said "cough" the bulge popped out. I was impressed by his competence and professionalism but distressed when I learned that I would eventually have to have surgery. The next day he told me that a liver scan showed there were indications of minor damage to that organ. Dr. Lorenz had told me of blood in the urine indicating kidney damage the night before.

Wednesday afternoon was filled with friends. My adrenaline was pumping. Homicide Sergeant William Hayden, who was heading up the investigation, came by to talk. I could tell he was frustrated by having so many people going in and out of the room. When Hayden asked if he could come to my house when I got home to talk without interruptions, I agreed.

Then he asked if he could send the police doctor to examine

me "to make sure you are okay." He had been talking about the massive press coverage the case was receiving and I assumed that he simply wanted another doctor to examine me to be sure I wasn't more seriously injured. I even thought that it was possible that he was concerned that Dr. Amarasinghe was not white and, therefore, somehow less qualified to provide adequate care. I had no objection to being examined again and agreed. I was, however, surprised that Hayden had not talked to either Dr. Lorenz or Dr. Amarasinghe. I had no idea how significant all of this would become in the next few days.

Howard Cosell sent a film crew from New York to do a segment for ABC's "Good Morning America." They arrived late in the afternoon. Much to my amazement, the hospital arranged at that moment for a series of lab tests that lasted an hour. It seemed to create a certain amount of tension among the crew. (I wondered if the black skin of some crew members and the fast pace of the "Yankees" prompted the hospital to insist on the tests then.)

The interviewer was much more intense and insistent than the seemingly more sensitive local reporters. He said he wanted to film the scars on my stomach. I thought he was kidding but he was very serious. I told him I thought this might upset the police so I called Hayden, but he was out. The reporter assured me he would talk to the police before using it. I became really uncomfortable when they filmed the scars of "niger"—it seemed too private.

It turned out that Bob Lipsyte, then a columnist for the *New York Post,* had called Cosell about doing the interview. Bob and I had had a long conversation earlier in the day. I had respected him as a writer ever since he wrote the "Sports of the Times" column for *The New York Times.* One of the nicest things to happen to Sandy and me was that we had become close friends with Bob and his wife, Marge. They were the most honest and forthright people I knew. His sense of humor was devastating. He began the call with "You'll do anything to publicize the cause." Bob and I both assume phone tapping is a widespread practice. We later wondered if his joke gave the police an idea.

One who had many insights was Mike Heaney. Mike was a graduate of Virginia Wesleyan who had joined the Norfolk police and was quickly moving up in the ranks. He came to visit me that evening because, he said, he was upset about the attack. But he was even more upset about the attitude of some of the local police. I had gathered from my conversation with Sergeant Hayden that the police were bothered by the media coverage. I asked Mike if that was it. No—what disturbed him was that some police were saying "you got what you deserved." I was so stunned that I asked him to repeat it. He did, adding that many policemen generally believed that anyone working for black rights deserved to be beaten up.

I remembered the first time I met Mike. He enrolled in the first class I taught on Black Politics in the spring of 1971. By then I had the reputation of being an "activist" in race relations. Students in the class warned me that Mike was a racist. He seemed very uneasy in the class, and the few times we met outside it. My first impression was that he was trying to be defiant, to show me I was wrong. I soon learned one of my first lessons as a professor. Mike had joined the class because he really wanted to shed the stereotypes that are the result of being raised in a racist society. Like others, he only needed to be exposed to the roots and consequences of racism to begin to change.

Mike mostly listened that semester, but you could see confusion, uncertainty, and anxiety melt away. The integrity and the sincerity were always there. In my eight years at Wesleyan, Mike probably grew more than any other student I taught. I don't mean he became radicalized. He became open. He came to look at all situations with an unbiased mind.

Mike was apprehensive one afternoon when he dropped by my office during his last semester. I sensed that something was wrong. Suddenly he blurted out, "Rich, I'm going to join the

Norfolk Police." I said, "That's great, Mike." His jaw, rigid with tension, noticeably relaxed. "Great?" he asked. "I thought you would be angry." He knew I was critical of the police in many areas. But I was genuinely pleased to think of Mike—honest, caring, intelligent Mike—on the police force.

It hurt me to see Mike so tormented by the hatred of his colleagues for me. But I was also grateful that he was there. He gave me a feel for what was going on.

I had had dozens of moving, memorable moments at Wesleyan. That night I remembered what was probably the most memorable. In spring 1976 I taught a senior-level seminar on International Race Relations that compared racial questions in different areas of the world. The seminar gathered the best students I ever had together in one class.

One was Charlie Hatcher. A charismatic man, Charlie had been among those who integrated Norfolk's public schools, and in the process became an all-star basketball player. Although he had had a satchel full of scholarship offers, Charlie entered the army. He was too burned out by the integration experience to do anything else.

Four years later he enrolled at Wesleyan as a twenty-three-year-old man. He quickly became the star of the basketball team. The other students, black and white, admired and respected him. If there was a cohesive force on campus, it was Charlie Hatcher. With two children to support, he eventually had to quit basketball and took a job working with juvenile offenders. I knew he would be late on this particular afternoon because he was to be a character witness in court for two black youths.

Leading the class that day was Leon Donald. Leon was from Milwaukee. Tall and thin, he was another ballplayer. But Leon was more into the black movement than basketball. He had shared with me some touching poetry that he had written about George Jackson, Malcolm X, Franz Fanon, and other important black American and Third World leaders. Intellectually, he was the brightest student in the class. That day he was giving a presentation on Jamaica's Rastafarians.

Listening and absorbing, as always, was Jack Schull. Jack was a frail, quiet young man. He almost never talked in class, but from his writings and outside discussions I knew he was sharp and quick. His shyness prevented others from seeing that he was sensitive and intelligent.

About an hour into Leon's presentation Charlie arrived and, uncharacteristically, said nothing for the next thirty minutes.

During the break we took a walk. I was certain something was wrong. Suddenly he stopped and turned to me. I could see that his eyes were filling with tears. His voice was cracking. This was a different Charlie Hatcher, a man losing control of his emotions. "Damn it," he said, "the judge gave both kids the maximum. Seven years for Bobby and six for Johnny. They're only teenagers. I was sure they would be put on probation. That judge was just another racist seeing two black objects in his court. And I was beginning to believe. It's all the same." He put his arms round me and I held him in turn. His feelings were so intense, so powerful, I could practically feel them through his body.

Charlie insisted on going back to the seminar. He sat quietly, listening to what was a good, academic analysis.

Suddenly Charlie stood up. "I can't listen to this anymore. I have to go now. I appreciate that we can all talk so logically and even care about such problems. But the whites in this room, no matter how much they care, can never know what it is like to be black. Never!"

No one else knew what had happened in court. The class was stunned. No one moved. No one spoke. As Charlie moved toward the door, Jack Schull shouted, "Hold it, Charlie!" Like everyone else, I was amazed.

Jack said, "I appreciate what you said. I even agree with it. I only wish I could know so I could understand better. But you, Charlie, you will never know what it's like to know that my grandfather would have been likely to shoot you dead for being bold. My grandfather. A sweet old man who hated blacks. I have to live with that. I have to overcome that. You can never know what *that* is like."

The other thirteen students were frozen like statues. Charlie stared at Jack, then glanced toward me. Jack was shaking, tears in his eyes. Charlie went over to him, gave him his hand, and nearly crushed his slight frame with a hug.

Almost everyone had tears in their eyes. It was the most electrifying moment of my teaching life. We had always talked about understanding and about trying to understand. But at that moment Jack and Charlie understood, perhaps for the first time.

I thought about this early that evening. The beating I had absorbed and the misspelled "niger" on my stomach had given me something that I thought no one else could ever fully understand. Yet I hoped that my going through it would serve to reiterate that some white people *do* care about blacks and vice versa. Then this otherwise senseless beating would have been given some meaning.

My thoughts were broken by Leon Donald, calling from Milwaukee. He had just heard about the attack on the CBS Evening News. I hadn't heard from Leon since 1977. When the phone rang again, it was Charlie Hatcher, from Chicago. He was flying in to see me the next morning. Ten minutes later Jack Schull phoned to ask if he could visit the following day. It had been a night of remarkable coincidences—proof, if not of ESP, of the sympathy like souls have for each other.

I fell into an exhausted sleep at about 10:30. My last thoughts were of Mike, and the cops saying "he got what he deserved"; about Charlie's agonized "it's all the same," about Charlie embracing Jack.

Early the next morning Sandy arrived with some clean clothes and a robe. She also brought the morning paper. I read Peter's story titled "Masked Men Beat Rights Chief." When he came to visit I teased him about two errors, never thinking them to be important. The first was that I had gone to Nashville "as part of ACCESS's opposition against the inclusion of Peter Lamb . . . on South Africa's Davis Cup team." I told him we were simply against the team playing in the United States, no matter who was on it.

The second error was his reporting of the sequence of events in my office "according to Lapchick and Homicide Sergeant William Hayden." He wrote that the attackers first beat me with the steel sculpture and then beat me with the drawers from the file cabinet, at which point I passed out. Neither of us thought anything of this at the time.

Of all my visitors, the one that came as the biggest surprise was my brother, Joe. We had never quite seen eye to eye on politics, but this time he was on my side. That night he addressed a gathering of some 250 Wesleyan students. He began by saying "The only one who can beat up my kid brother is me." My big brother. I felt secure with him around. We never had to say much to communicate. The Lapchick family bond was still a unifying force.

Ibrahim Noor, a Somali who was the assistant secretary of the United Nations Special Committee Against Apartheid, called to tell me that the U.N. would be issuing a statement condemning the attack. I was still in awe of the U.N. so this meant a great deal to me. I knew it would also help in Nashville. I received a call from Saundra Ivey (who was covering the story for the *Tennessean*) shortly after talking to Mr. Noor. She reported the paper was moving toward calling for the cancellation of the matches. An editorial that day (February 16) had come close:

> There can be no doubt that this community would have been better off had it never heard of the Davis Cup matches. Dr. Lapchick's painful experiences should serve as a stark reminder that the mere debate of racism still has

the potential for violence. At this point, that must be the
real concern of every sane person in Nashville.

Saundra told me that one of the Nashville student leaders
had received harassing phone calls, including a "warning call"
on the night of the beating. This student was the same person
who had taken me around Nashville for the weekend.

I tried to get permission to make a surprise appearance at the
service held for me at Wesleyan although I knew what the
answer would be. Instead, Dennis Govoni, the first faculty
member to visit, arrived. His stay was interrupted by Faruk
Presswalla, who identified himself as the doctor sent by the
police. My initial theory that he might have been sent because
my doctor was not white was instantly disproved. Dr. Presswalla was Indian.

When Dennis asked if he could stay, I eagerly agreed. It was
nearly a month later that Dennis reminded me of it. How
fortunate for me that he was there!

The other part of my theory about why the police would send
their doctor also evaporated during the course of Dr. Presswalla's visit. The examination he gave me lasted no more than
a few minutes and was extremely superficial. He obviously
wasn't there to make sure I was in good health.

However, I didn't make much of this at the time because we
had a good one-hour discussion about politics. He told me of
his involvement in a group called Indians for Democracy. I
discussed my anti-apartheid work.

Then I went over the details of the attack. Dennis listened
with interest. I was surprised that Dr. Presswalla didn't take
any notes, but not as surprised as how cursory the examination
was.

When he asked if I ever thought the attackers would kill me,
I pointed out that they did not use much force with the file
cabinet drawers and that they kept turning my head so I was
never hit squarely in the face. I suggested that when they beat

me in the abdomen prior to my passing out they might have gotten carried away.

After he left, I told Sandy that while I liked Presswalla, I wouldn't want to have him as our family doctor. She went home with the good news that she could pick me up in the morning to bring me home. I slept well that night.

·4·

Hidden Ball

Sandy picked me up on Friday morning. I was feeling great and I was going home. Life would be normal again.

It was a beautiful day and I felt compelled to prove to myself how well I was. Then I began aching after taking a few steps in the front yard.

The day was again a full one with friends, students, and neighbors coming to visit. Sergeant Hayden dropped by in the midst of it all to try to talk. Frustrated but apparently understanding, Hayden asked me if I could come to the police station Saturday afternoon to "quietly discuss" where the case was going.

The best part of the day was being with my family. Although my brother Joe left, my sister Barbara and her daughter Tayu arrived from New York. But the stars of the day were Joey and Chamy. Their presence made life good again.

I called Lambuth Clarke, Wesleyan's president, and asked him if I could meet with the whole student body on Monday rather than trying to explain how I was to everyone individually. He said this was a good idea and we set it up for 11:15, which wouldn't conflict with classes.

Father Joe, the priest from our church, called to say that he was offering masses for me. He said he was proud I went to his parish as I was an example of what he preached regarding social commitments. I told him I attended his church because he was so human and so inspirational. Not many priests had inspired me before and I rarely went to church in Virginia prior to discovering him.

On Saturday, however, my wounds began to ache and my adrenaline decreased. I called Hayden to tell him I had to take a nap and we decided I could come by around 6:00 P.M.

When I awakened, the house was filled. Barbara had gone to the bus terminal to pick up a package from Nashville. I had a fleeting thought it might be a letter bomb, but it turned out to be news clippings sent from Nashville. Barbara had read them and brought me one from the *Nashville Banner.* She was very disturbed.

It was the first article written on the attack and appeared on February 15. Although we had not yet met, Sergeant Hayden was quoted extensively.

The story began: "Authorities said Dr. Richard E. Lapchick . . . was beaten with a wooden statue and the letters N-I-G-E-R were scratched on his stomach with a pair of scissors." I found this quite perplexing since the only "authorities" we met in the hospital had emphatically asked Sandy and me not to reveal any details. As I've said, we took this request so seriously that Sandy called both Dennis Brutus and Yolanda Huet-Vaughn to ask that such information be withheld.

The *Banner* explained that point awkwardly: "Huet-Vaughn's wife, during a telephone call this morning to the *Nashville Banner,* requested an editor to change the letters scratched on Lapchick's abdomen to read N-I-G-G-E-R, instead of N-I-G-E-R, which actually was carved on the victim's abdomen." The article made no mention of why the request was made or that it was the police who had asked us to make it.

As disconcerting as these inaccuracies were, they were nothing compared to the quotes attributed to Sergeant Hayden. First some misinformation—perhaps innocent. "Hayden said Lapchick apparently was assaulted as he walked back toward his office located in the same building as the Virginia school's library. He had gone outside his office to get a drink of water at a fountain and as he returned, he said he was accosted by two men wearing stocking masks." The attack, of course, took place entirely inside my office.

Then the article directly attributed the hold-at-all-cost details to Hayden. "The detective said Lapchick, thirty-two, suffered cuts and bruises when struck about the head and body with the wooden statue and cut on the abdomen with the scissors."

It proved to be only the beginning. "Most of his injuries were not tremendously serious at all," said Sergeant Hayden. First, the two detectives knew of the kidney damage and concussion before Hayden said this. Second, Hayden had not talked to Dr. Lorenz, the only one who examined me, prior to talking to the *Banner.* Third, when confronted with this later, Hayden responded, "The quote is true. Most of your injuries were not serious. I didn't say all weren't serious!"

Then came the clincher. "Hayden . . . said he 'finds it rather interesting' that Lapchick's associates released a press statement before police had an opportunity to hardly start an investigation into the case." The Norfolk police knew exactly how the Nashville people learned of the attack.

I was outraged when I read the story. Nancy Lowe, a neighbor, said that her husband Fred, an attorney, would go with me to the police station to lodge a formal complaint.

We arrived and showed Hayden the article. He excused himself to "make a copy." Since he didn't return for twenty minutes, we assumed he was asking his superiors for advice.

When Hayden returned he apologized and said he could understand why we were concerned. I chose that moment to tell him that I had been told by a reliable source that one of the two detectives on the case was considered to be a racist. We were assured that he was no longer assigned to the case.

Then Hayden asked me to come with him to discuss the details of the attack, telling Fred to stay behind.

I went through everything. At the end I pointed out that Peter Galuszka's article had reversed the order of the events, attributing his account to me and to Hayden. I said that considering what he told the *Banner,* I assumed he was the source of the confusion. However, I still saw no significance in this.

Sergeant Hayden had been very attentive. When I was finished he simply said, "You know, Richard, we have no suspects and leads in this case. I have faith in you, but you should know that it has been raised as a possibility that you staged the attack!"

I might have been calm on the outside, but inside I was stunned and seething. "I want to prove this to be untrue so we can get on with the investigation," he went on. "I want to offer you the opportunity to take a polygraph. It just so happens that our polygraph expert is here tonight and has agreed to administer the test if you accept."

It was an interesting choice of words. He was "offering" me an "opportunity" to prove myself innocent of a crime *that* had been committed against me! I had a sudden flash of insight into how thousands of American women feel who have been subjected to a lie-detector test to prove that they had been raped. I had always sympathized with such women. Now I understood why. For the victim to have to prove she was victimized in such a dehumanizing way is wrong.

If Hayden had looked into my background he could have easily surmised that I would refuse. I quickly realized that this would be an easy way for him to dismiss the case or to discredit me.

I told him I would think about it but was almost totally sure that I would not subject myself to such a test. I suggested it was time for Fred to join us. When he did, I asked Hayden who it was that was raising the possibility of a staging. His response was unambiguous. "The local press!"

"You mean Peter Galuszka and Peter Loomis?" I asked. Hayden said that he could not name individuals.

Fred asked what would happen now. Sergeant Hayden replied no one would know of the "offer" until I responded. If the press asked, he would then have to tell them if I said no. He requested me to sign over the hospital records to the police, and I complied.

We left the police station shaken and disturbed. I told Fred that I was likely to refuse the test because I was the victim and the police were making me the suspect. He said he agreed but warned me that many people would interpret any refusal as a sign of guilt. I kept thinking of all those rape victims.

We arrived home late. We had friends over for dinner, but I was not very good company. I felt I was being set up. But for what?

My physical strength was being eroded. Lack of sleep wasn't helping. My weight at the time of the attack was 170. On Saturday I weighed 160. Within a week it would be 150.

I called trusted friends on Sunday morning. Franklin Williams promised to call other civil rights people. Bob Lipsyte said to refuse the request. Without exception, everyone agreed. Franklin called back and reminded me of attacks on King and Malcolm X followed by police allegations of "staging." Franklin said, "We need to keep you alive!"

I also called Peter Galuszka. I didn't believe Hayden when he said the press had raised the doubts. Peter said he had heard nothing like this. I was glad it wasn't he. However, Peter called back later to say that police had been leaking it everywhere that I had been asked to take a polygraph. They would have to write the story, he said, and suggested he call me later for a statement.

Fred and I got together to prepare it. I called Hayden. He denied that he was leaking the story and said he would try to stop the leaks. I believed him, just as I believed him when he said I wasn't being "set up."

The page-1 story of Monday's *Virginian Pilot* was headlined, "Prof Suspected in His Attack." "Sources" claimed I may have staged the attack, but Hayden wouldn't say I was a suspect. He said I was being very cooperative with police investigators.

The paper printed only two paragraphs of my statement. Curiously, the story did not say the police had requested the polygraph. Here is my statement in full:

> My initial reaction upon being asked to do this was one of shock, dismay, and anger. I asked myself, "Why aren't they out looking for the men who made the brutal attack on me instead of questioning the victim's truthfulness?"
>
> Since Sergeant Hayden has been most cooperative with me on a personal basis, I can only feel that this request made of me arises out of the traditional trend displayed by law-enforcement authorities in doubting those who are willing to take a stand on civil rights issues. More than a few people have suggested to me that the TV broadcast of the life of Dr. King last week may have created a climate for the violence that I was a victim of last Tuesday. I wonder if it also created the climate for the police to attempt to discredit me as they had done to Dr. King prior to and after his assassination.
>
> It is my firm belief that police procedures should not include placing the victim of a crime, regardless of its nature, in the position of having to submit to this type of humiliation. To do so only weakens the entire system of justice and threatens the ability of all people to feel secure with the protection that the police in our society should offer. We are paying the police to catch people who commit crimes.
>
> After consulting all day yesterday with friends, family, and national civil rights leaders, I have decided not to

succumb to the police request for a polygraph. There are several reasons for this: First, police have uncontroverted evidence of the seriousness of the injuries. Second, the two examining doctors have stated that due to internal bleeding, kidney damage, and a hernia, it is virtually impossible for the wounds to be self-inflicted. Fourth, there was absolutely no evidence to contradict my statements. But most important, to succumb would be to perpetuate the police use of this type of negative approach in the cases of civil rights assaults and other assaults such as rape.

As long as people agree to have their veracity challenged in this way, this process and practice will continue. I have decided that in this case it will stop.

As noted, the story quoted only two of the paragraphs. But it did cite Dr. Amarasinghe's "doubts the wound could have been self-inflicted" and quoted Dr. Lorenz as saying that "the only wounds that could have been self-inflicted were the scratches on his stomach."

The *Nashville Banner* story was even more heinous. It quoted at length a "Virginia Beach detective official who asked not to be identified" as saying "This whole thing just did not ring completely true." He added that my refusal to take the polygraph made me the focus of the investigation to see if I "was in on it."

The *Banner* quoted part of my response, then went for the jugular. "Lapchick, who recently returned from a trip to Cuba and has also visited Russia and Red China. . . ." No matter that I had never been to Russia. The truth was receding rapidly into police leaks.

Enter Sergeant Hayden again. "Dr. Lapchick and I had a conversation the other day and that conversation and what took place during our conversation are really between Dr. Lapchick and I," he told the *Banner*. "If Dr. Lapchick wishes to make comments with regard to our conversation, that's his prerogative. I'm not making any comments." The implication was that it was up to me to announce I wouldn't take the polygraph test.

Both articles mentioned that I had been seen by the state medical examiner. Reading this was the first time I thought of Dr. Presswalla since Thursday. Dr. Lorenz was again quoted as to how "the wounds on the professor's stomach could have been self-inflicted."

I was slightly confused by his comments. Saundra Ivey of the *Tennessean* probed him more deeply. "It amazes me that reporters are making so much out of this statement," Lorenz told her. "Obviously, you could inflict almost any wounds, so one could say of almost any assault that the wounds could be self-inflicted. I didn't feel, taking everything into consideration, that the wounds in this case were self-inflicted."

Again, Hayden declined to comment. "The comments you are seeing in the newspaper are not from me, because what I say, I put my name on," he told the *Tennessean*.

All of this had happened by 10:00 A.M. Monday. By the time I got in the car with Sandy to head toward Wesleyan, I realized that I would have to address the polygraph issue with the students when I met them at 11:15. I decided to repeat my statement of the previous night.

My mind was filled with images as we approached the school. Security was tight at the entrance. This hadn't been the case last week. Driving into the parking lot reminded me of being put in the ambulance there, of the students swarming around me late at night, of Mike Mizell discovering the word "niger" on my stomach.

The students were gathering outside Pruden Lounge where I was to meet them. Some greeted us in the parking lot, telling us that the lounge was packed with students and press. I wanted the meeting to be for my students alone, but knew it would become a press conference.

I was weak-kneed and couldn't catch my breath. Like a child wanting to please his parents, I wanted to please my students. I always tried to get them to believe in themselves, to take responsibility for their actions, to stand on their principles, to be proud. They were also my family: Wesleyan had become an extension of my home.

So I worried how the students would react to the morning headlines. Could I convince them that I was standing on principle by refusing the polygraph? Or that I was using good judgment in taking such responsibility for my actions rather than submitting to the police requests? Could I be proud at that moment? Did I really believe in myself?

I grew weaker and less determined as I wound my way up the stairs. I heard one student shout "Here he comes!" and the building filled with cheers. The students were on their feet, shouting, applauding. The TV and newspaper people were everywhere, but all I could see were my students, my friends. I was home.

I began with words suggested to me the night before by Bob Lipsyte. "If you think you might be a murder victim," I told the group, "be sure you cross the city line so the Virginia Beach police don't claim you committed suicide!" The students roared. The ice was broken. I then read my statement. "For the first time, I clearly understood what a woman who has been raped must feel like when asked to take a polygraph." I concluded, "As long as people agree to have their veracity challenged in this way, this process and practice will continue. I have decided that in this case it will stop." The audience rose to its feet and applauded for several minutes.

I felt very good both about what I had chosen to say and the response I had gotten. The press began to ask questions, but I could sense they were not hostile. One reporter, whom I did not know, said, "The police told me this morning that the fact that you have not received any threatening phone calls since the attack is *very* unusual. What's your response?"

More leaks from the police. I told the reporter that the attack was not likely the work of neighborhood kids who then make prank calls, that the business of sports relations with South

Africa was a serious one. I didn't expect such calls. I added that I could not tell whether the Virginia Beach police were trying to discredit me or to close a difficult case in which they had no leads.

It clicked in my mind at that moment that there was no way I could get help from the Virginia Beach police. They had refused to give me around-the-clock protection as I had requested, choosing instead to beef up patrols near the house. We had noticed that even the patrols seemed to stop Sunday night, when the polygraph story was breaking.

I decided I had better consult with some legal experts and that I would follow the advice of the civil rights people and seek the help of the Justice Department.

After a friendly meeting with President Clarke, at which I told him I would ask the FBI to intervene, I taught my Urban Studies class and went home.

Andrew Fine, a lawyer who was an old friend from the Beach, had offered to help in any way he could. I called Andrew and he immediately arranged for a meeting the next day with the U.S. Attorney-General in Norfolk.

The local media was giving the statement I made at the college considerable coverage, although the *Pilot* put it on page B-3 after running the "suspect" story on page 1. The national press began to phone me at home. I was too exhausted to speak at length so Sandy handled most of the calls.

I did speak to Bill Nack of *Newsday*. I felt he and his editor, Sandy Padwe, were two of the best and most serious analysts of the reality of sport as a reflection of society in America. Indeed, he wrote a scathing column on the actions of the police.

Franklin Williams issued a statement on behalf of the Phelps-Stokes Fund, the NAACP, and the Urban League, "deploring the libelous actions of the Virginia Beach police" against me. "Against reason, evidence, or acceptable standards of decency and honor, these authorities have cast doubts on Dr. Lapchick's

veracity in the matter of his own brutal attack by racist terror-
ists. The suggestion that this man of integrity be subjected to
a polygraph test says more about the method and morals of the
police than it does about Dr. Lapchick, a fact that all who know
the man are quick to grasp."

We were receiving calls and telegrams of support for my
stand against the polygraph from all over the country. Several
were from local women who still carried the scars of mistreat-
ment by police after they had been raped and then forced to
take a polygraph.

Andrew Fine and I met with the Norfolk U.S. Attorney-
General on Tuesday at 11:30. I told him that I had lost faith
in the police and that I felt that my civil rights were being
violated. An interview with the FBI was arranged for that
afternoon. I told Peter Galuszka about the morning meeting.
He was anxious to write the story if the FBI agreed to take the
case.

I had some misgivings while we waited for the FBI to arrive.
As a child of the civil rights and antiwar movements, my image
of the FBI was not of Ephraim Zimbalist, Jr., but of J. Edgar
Hoover. The same Hoover who went after Dick Gregory, who
tried to get Martin Luther King, who harassed innumerable
dissenters and protestors, all the while breaking the laws he was
supposed to protect.

I thought, "Times have changed," but then realized I was
living proof that one still could not freely speak out without the
potential of serious reprisal. I thought of the hate calls to my
father and of how he internalized it all. I thought of the modern-day sports critics—Dave Meggyesy, Jack Scott, Tommy
Smith, and Phil Shinnick. All were such threats to our society
that in this February of 1978 they were all virtually unemployable. Harry Edwards was fighting to keep his job at Berkeley.

So I had no illusions as I saw FBI-Norfolk bureau chief
James Healy and his partner drive up to the house. But I had
heard good things about Drew Days, the head of the Civil

Rights Division of the Justice Department, and knew that whatever help I got from the FBI would be better than what I was getting from the Virginia Beach police.

We talked for an hour. I was pleased by their reactions and they said there appeared to be grounds for the Justice Department to take jurisdiction in the case. As they left I asked how I should handle press inquiries. Healy said I could tell them that "the FBI had begun an inquiry."

Sandy and I smiled at each other as the agents drove away. It would be the last smile for a long, long time.

·5·
Injury
Time-out

The phone rang immediately. It was Peter Galuszka. "I guess you called about the FBI," I said. For the first time, Peter was abrupt.

"No. The state medical examiner has just announced that your wounds were self-inflicted. What is your response?"

I had no response. I just sat there, unable to speak. "Richard, Richard?" Peter kept repeating. Finally, I said, "Peter, I am absolutely astonished. How can he refute the doctors who treated me? Dr. Presswalla's exam was superficial. We spent most of the time discussing politics." Naively I asked "Are you going to print this story?"

Peter advised me to call Presswalla, saying he had just spoken to him. He gave me his home number. He agreed not to write anything until I had prepared a response.

Both Sandy and I just sat there a few minutes in a state of shock. Then I called Presswalla. Sandy listened on the other line. His wife answered, pausing when I said who was calling. After a few seconds she said he was not there and that she didn't know where he was. We didn't believe her, and practically begged her to put us in touch with him. She could tell from my voice that it was imperative for me to reach him. She said she would try.

I collapsed on the bed, literally speechless. Sandy moved into action, calling friends, asking them what we should do. Usually we were both at our best in a crisis. She was then. I was useless. I just couldn't believe that this was happening to me.

I was being accused of a sick act of self-mutilation. What could I say? "I didn't do it." There would always be people now who doubted me no matter how much evidence I put on the table.

I knew I couldn't go ahead with plans to go to Nashville the next day. When I called to cancel, my friends encouraged me to come, but were understanding. Bob Lipsyte called back after Sandy had filled him in. As usual, Bob was tonic for me. On this night I needed more than tonic, but still he helped.

"Who is this Presswalla? Was he paid off?" Bob asked. "You can't look back. If you don't go to Nashville, then they will have accomplished their aims. You have to go."

I said I didn't see how I could, but that I would reconsider it.

Then that unwanted call from Peter Galuszka came. I told him Presswalla hadn't returned the call and he said he was on a deadline. He was writing the story with Steve Goldberg, who had also coauthored the "Suspect" article.

Peter gave me the details. Dr. Presswalla based his conclusions on the markings on my stomach. He said they showed hesitation, that is, the person inflicting the wound was cautious not to cut too deeply. An attacker would not do that, but a person would do it to himself. In forensic medicine, such cuts are called "hesitation marks."

Presswalla told Peter that his decision to make his opinion public was based partially on the fact that the FBI had entered the case.

After our conversation ended, Peter called back. He said his editor realized I hadn't said whether or not I had self-inflicted the wounds. I said that the answer was obvious. Peter said, "Then say it." "I didn't do it," I told him. It was hard to utter those words to Peter.

I was talking to Saundra Ivey at about 11:15 when the operator broke in with an emergency call from Presswalla. The timing was not insignificant; the deadline of the *Virginian Pilot* had long since passed. Sandy got on the phone.

My heart began to pound uncontrollably. I asked, "What are you trying to do to me? Do you really believe what you told the press?"

Dr. Presswalla responded that he was sympathetic to me, that as a political activist he knew the importance of publicity for the cause. He added, "What you did is not uncommon in India."

I said that Drs. Amarasinghe and Lorenz had contradicted him, but he quickly pointed to the Lorenz quote saying the cuttings on the stomach *could* be self-inflicted, and said that the doctors had no background in forensic medicine. "In my thirteen years of medical practice, I have never seen an exception to this rule [of hesitation marks]."

He sounded sincere and concerned. I asked, "Couldn't the attackers have made the wounds look self-inflicted?" He said it was conceivable, but the issue now could only be resolved by a polygraph. I should go to another state and be examined by both a polygraph expert and a specialist in forensic pathology, he suggested. After all, he noted, "I didn't say you weren't attacked. You may have been assaulted and carved *n-i-g-e-r* yourself for political effect."

Dr. Presswalla told me he had made his report to the police on Friday, and it was he who had instructed them to give me a polygraph. He said he couldn't understand why Sergeant Hayden hadn't told me this.

Sandy and I hugged each other. Sometimes such hugs give us energy, but neither of us had any at that moment. The phone rang, jarring us. It was Walter Searcy, a local organizer from

the black community in Nashville. He insisted that I come to
Nashville as a testimony to my truthfulness. We went around
and around on this until I finally gave in to him.

The next day I woke up early to see the damage done by the
Virginian Pilot. "Lapchick's Wounds Appear Self-Inflicted,
Examiner Says," proclaimed the headline of a five-column
page-1 story.

The story repeated what Peter had told me the night before
—"hesitation marks," Presswalla's reason for "stepping forward now," etc. It ran twenty-eight paragraphs before saying
that Dr. Amarasinghe stood by his findings that the wounds
could not be self-inflicted.

Presswalla said he was waiting for reports from Drs. Amarasinghe and Lorenz before making a "final statement on the
matter." If he was, in fact, still waiting, then the police were
taking an exceptionally long time in delivering the hospital
report I had released to them five days earlier. I was amazed
to read a newspaper report quoting unnamed sources which
said Presswalla had found "no evidence of serious internal
bleeding, kidney damage, liver damage, or recent hernia," even
though to the best of my knowledge he had not seen the report
nor talked to my doctors.

Then Goldberg and Galuszka set the tone of the debate when
discussing the polygraph: "Lapchick refused and *denounced*
police, who he said were harassing the victim instead of pursu-
ing the perpetrators."

Not only did I never publicly denounce the police but I am
now embarrassed at how naive and reticent I was about their
actions.

Next came more from Presswalla: "I have great personal
support for Dr. Lapchick's cause, and I don't want to harm
him." This was followed by: "Perhaps there is an extra note of
caution [in my report] because I have been in an activist role
myself."

According to the story, he had not wanted to perform the

examination on me because of his sympathy and, when he did do it, he had hoped to "find a graceful way out of the situation" for me.

If Dr. Presswalla thought such statements wouldn't harm me, I wondered what he thought would. If this was his idea of a graceful way out, I wondered what he would do if he were hard-hitting. The answers to such questions were soon to follow.

I was literally sick to my stomach when Sandy came in at 7:30 shouting "Leonard, Leonard—we forgot Leonard!" Of course—Leonard Sharzer, a noted local surgeon, had examined me in the hospital at Sandy's request. Sandy read the story, then immediately called Leonard's wife Lois, a dear friend. It turned out that Leonard was at a conference in Dallas. Lois arranged to put us in touch with him. The frantic search for Leonard began.

Facing my students in my 10:00 A.M. class that morning was terribly difficult. I tried to concentrate on teaching but instead I became unglued. I just couldn't talk about Tanzanian politics.

Karen Gilbert, a good friend who helped me with several programs I ran in the community, interrupted to say that Leonard Sharzer was on the phone. It was the first time I had ever walked out of a class in progress. I didn't hesitate for a second —I had become obsessed with my plight.

Sharzer said he would definitely inform the press that his conclusions supported Lorenz's and Amarasinghe's. As a courtesy he wanted to speak first to Dr. Presswalla to tell him what he was going to say. I admired Leonard for his integrity and professionalism. Now the score was 3 to 1. Certainly the press would now be forced to change its tone.

I ran back to the class and told them, "There is a god after all. A third doctor has just come forth. The truth will soon be known."

Sandy and I were driven to the airport. Ironically, I felt somewhat sorry for Dr. Presswalla. He would have to swallow hard now with three doctors opposing him. The compassion came from a nagging belief that he was being sincere, that he really believed what he was saying. I thought that perhaps my assailants were so professional that they had carved the "hesitation marks" to discredit me. After all, Dr. Presswalla was a "liberal."

I still didn't realize how deep the waters were as we drove to the airport. Kathy Kent, a reporter for the local CBS-affiliate, approached us. "Will you take a polygraph now?" she asked. I said that I was continuing to stand on my principles.

We were met at the Nashville airport by a dozen or so well-wishers. A press conference had been set up there. The theme of it was that I was in Nashville to refocus attention on the Davis Cup. I didn't yet realize how out of focus things had become. I expected many of the questions would be on the attack and Presswalla's allegations. I gave a detailed explanation.

Finally, one reporter asked, "Why not just submit to a polygraph test to clear up any doubts?" I reiterated my reasons, adding, "In many ways it would be easier to do it, but it would also be easier not to speak out against apartheid. I have taken what I consider to be a consistent moral stand."

I did a lengthy interview with Wayne King of *The New York Times*. He questioned me on my athletic background, if I had kept in condition, etc. When I asked why, he responded that it would be very unlikely that someone who took care of and cared about his body would inflict injuries on himself. I sensed that we had recaptured the momentum, that we could remount the protest against South Africa.

We drove to Don Beiswinger's house for dinner. Don was a theology professor at Vanderbilt. I again thought of Presswalla, wondering how he must feel.

Walter Searey, the Nashville organizer, was at Don's with "J.J.," the armed bodyguard hired to protect me in Nashville. It was almost funny watching J.J. dart around the house, checking windows, seating me in exactly the right chair for safety. Some of the pressure was off; we were okay again.

Don asked if we had seen the Nashville papers that day. When he brought them to me, I was devastated. The *Tennessean*'s headline was:

LAPCHICK'S WOUNDS RULED SELF-INFLICTED

The *Banner*'s read:

LAPCHICK WOUNDED SELF, DOCTOR RULES

A TV was on in the other room. We went to see Walter Cronkite's Davis Cup coverage but he had moved to a related item:

> Last week we had a story about Richard Lapchick, the Virginia Beach political science teacher who had planned to protest South Africa's entry in the Davis Cup Match. Lapchick claimed two masked men had assaulted him and carved a racial slur on his stomach. Now a Virginia State medical examiner has concluded that Lapchick apparently inflicted the stomach wounds on himself. Lapchick denied the allegation, but refused to take a lie-detector test.

Everyone was stunned. This wasn't Steve Goldberg reporting but Walter Cronkite. This was the man whom America believed. Someone tried to break the silence with "What was the news about the Davis Cup?" No one had heard it.

Next we were driven to Vanderbilt for my 7:30 speech. J.J., as they say, cased the joint. The only difference was that it was no longer amusing. The balance had shifted again. I didn't feel up to the speech, but I had to give it. Walter Searey, Bob Lipsyte—everyone insisted I had to go no matter how I felt. I would rather have been anywhere else in the world as I walked down the steps of the same auditorium where only ten days before I had triumphantly announced that the NLT Corporation had withdrawn as financial backer of the Davis Cup.

That triumph was a distant memory now as a handful of people in the auditorium hissed when I entered. Ninety-five percent may have applauded; most of them were on their feet. But I heard only the hisses. It was close to being the most humiliating moment of my life. I found it hard to believe that all of this had happened in ten days. I knew then, before I uttered a word, that I would soon have to do something dramatic. *I* was the issue in Nashville, not South Africa.

We were back at Don's by 9:30. When Saundra Ivey arrived, she told me that Presswalla had again gone to the press, saying essentially the same thing but now insisting all the injuries were "consistent with self-infliction." He said there was no evidence that I had been knocked unconscious with the file cabinet drawers as I had "claimed." He added that there were no cuts—save a small one on my lip—on my face and no injuries to my chest. A beating such as I said had taken place would have produced such cuts and injuries. Even though, for all practical purposes, this was the same story as had already appeared, it was again to be page-1 news in Virginia the next day. The story would include the statement of my three doctors, which I had simplistically assumed would be the lead, in the seventeenth paragraph. Presswalla had upstaged Leonard Sharzer by issuing his renewed allegations. I suspected that Leonard's call to Presswalla had provoked him to take action.

Presswalla had told Saundra that clinical physicians such as Sharzer, Lorenz, and Amarasinghe were more concerned with treating patients than with examining injuries in the manner he did and were not adequate judges of whether his conclusions were correct.

Presswalla was absolute in his opinions. There were no more "notes of caution" or "not wanting to harm me." He claimed the wounds were "definitely self-inflicted." He told the *Washington Post* that the hernia "was an antecedent. It was not related to the assault." He said although I claimed resulting internal injuries, there was no evidence of them being caused by the beating. He admitted he still had not talked to Lorenz or Amarasinghe, who had made the diagnosis.

He even implied that he had called me on his own initiative Wednesday night, failing to mention that he was returning my call some five hours after I had made it. He told the *New York Post,* "I'm sure this is going to be ammo for the conservative red-neck types to say liberals are pinkos and liars—which includes me because I am a liberal."

The press loved it. During the six weeks that the case received national attention, I was interviewed regularly, mostly by men. The only women who followed it from start to finish were Saundra Ivey, Athelia Knight of the *Washington Post,* and Ianthe Thomas of the *Village Voice.* Interestingly, it was these women who probed most persistently and deeply.

It was, in fact, Saundra's persistence that first raised my doubts about Presswalla's sincerity. For someone who was so definite in his opinions, he made some curious statements to her.

"I feel sure of what I have said based on my experience but another person may have a different opinion. This is why I have suggested he [Lapchick] consult others in this field and show them photographs of his wounds."

He said he would accept my version of events if I passed a polygraph test "administered by a competent examiner. The only person I knew of who could beat the polygraph is a pathological habitual liar and I'm sure Dr. Lapchick is not a person like that. I have never said he is totally lying, but that I see inconsistencies in the story he has given."

Presswalla told Saundra that it was possible that in an "elaborate plot" assailants could have cut me in such a manner as to duplicate the hesitation marks characteristic of self-inflicted wounds. He reiterated that a polygraph was "the crux of the matter now" if he was to accept my version of what had happened. The *Tennessean* printed all of this.

He had told Athelia Knight, "I'm not saying he wasn't assaulted, but there are some medical inconsistencies."

How could a man of science say I "definitely" did something but would reverse his opinion if I took a polygraph or if another forensic pathologist offered a different conclusion? Could he really believe that someone could be assaulted and while recovering think of carving *n-i-g-e-r* on his abdomen for political effect? Did he honestly believe that I had made up the internal injuries when he had my hospital records in hand? Or that my story of the attack was inconsistent? Did he trust his memory so much that he didn't need to take notes that night in the hospital? Or was he relying on the account mistakenly written by Peter Galuszka in the *Pilot?*

It's true Dr. Presswalla had a great deal of experience— fourteen years. It wasn't until March 21—a month later—that the *Ledger-Star* pointed out that in his years in America I was only the second living patient that Dr. Presswalla had examined (he claimed he had seen living patients in India and Europe prior to coming to America) and that the other case had had nothing to do with self-inflicted wounds. Presswalla claimed it made no difference in interpreting wounds whether they were examined on a living body or a dead one, and that he had performed thousands of autopsies.

Furthermore, it was not until that weekend that I learned that the term "hesitation mark" in forensic pathology refers only to suicide attempts where a person first superficially cuts his wrist or throat to see how deeply he will eventually have to cut. It had no application at all to a carving such as the one on my abdomen.

Nor did I know that the Cronkite story just preceding the one about me was this: "South Africa has quietly ended segregation on its tennis courts, a move that's expected to result in an end to thirty years of sports apartheid in that white-ruled country."

There was no comment—the story was just accepted as fact, although such South African statements were as common as real change was rare. Five years later, South African sports are still segregated. However, on February 24 the one-two punch hurt. First the announcement that South African sports were integrated, then the story that a man associated in the minds of the public with anti-apartheid activities in sports was discredited. Was it a coincidence that Presswalla's first announcement about self-infliction came out within hours of the announcement made in South Africa? It certainly didn't help the next day when the media asked me what I thought of the changes in South Africa. I was not very believable then.

However, I did not know such things that night as I went to bed. I only knew that I was exhausted and humiliated and that I would have to agree to take a polygraph if I was to get the focus back on South Africa.

I met with John Zeigenthaller, the publisher of the *Tennessean,* for two hours the next morning. He recounted problems he had had with a bogus FBI investigation and assured me the truth would come out in the end, that there was no need for a polygraph. While he was saying this, Sandy was on the phone with my sister Barbara in New York and Zeke Orlinsky, a friend in the Washington area, to try to arrange for the polygraph.

The need to do this was again underlined during a TV interview that took place at the Beiswingers'. It was a good free-flowing session but ended abruptly with "Will you take a polygraph?" I replied, "No," since nothing had been arranged. Thirty minutes later Zeke called to say the test was all set for the next morning.

I had abdominal pain all morning and was taken to see a local doctor. It had been suggested that my symptoms sounded like possible spleen damage. The doctor said it was only remaining muscle damage and tenderness. I was actually disappointed.

The obsession with proving that the attack had taken place had grown so great that I had hoped he would discover a new injury that Drs. Lorenz and Amarasinghe might have missed.

The local doctor then sent me to a lab for some tests. When the receptionist called me inside, she said, "I want you to know I believe you." I thanked her, but I realized how awful things had become when a total stranger felt compelled to reassure me. As nice as it was, it furthered the obsession—I couldn't wait for the polygraph.

The anxiety and tension built as we flew to Washington. I felt so nervous and upset that I was afraid my emotions would have a negative impact on the polygraph. We were met at the airport by Zeke and Rebecca Orlinsky. My tension was not reduced in spite of many reassurances by Zeke, who was a lawyer and former prosecutor in Baltimore. We later called Ron Ellison, another attorney who had actually arranged the polygraph. I was wound tight as a drum, and wanted to take a sleeping pill but was told that it might affect the test—no pill, no sleep.

At breakfast, Ron Ellison tried to calm me. At 10:00 A.M. we went to the office of Bob Niebuhr, the polygraph expert. Ron had been careful in choosing him, as we didn't want any doubts raised. Niebuhr was president of the Maryland Polygraphers Association and was also licensed in Virginia, which we felt was important. In the course of his career he had administered 20,000 polygraph tests. Most important, Bob Niebuhr was in no way associated with the left or liberal political causes.

We talked at length about the case. Having read many of the newspaper articles, Niebuhr said he wanted a friend named Al to assist him in preparing the questions to be asked and in evaluating the results. He was cautious, he said, because he recognized the importance of the test.

We went over the questions. Did you ever lie before you were twenty-one? Did you ever lie for personal gain? There were several control questions such as name, place of birth, etc. The big questions were:

Did you cut that word on your stomach?

Did you want someone to cut it?

Did you arrange for someone to cut it?

Did you know who cut it?

I felt like I was on trial even though Bob and Al were sympathetic to my state of mind. Taking the polygraph was among the most humiliating and nerve-racking experiences I ever went through.

Niebuhr saw that I was convinced that the machine couldn't compute my frenzied emotions. They ran a control series to prove I was wrong. They said to pick a number from one to seven. I picked five and wrote it down. I was told to say no every time as Niebuhr asked "Was it one?" "Was it two?" etc. He went from one to seven, then from seven to one. Then they showed me the charts with marked differences each time I said "no" on number five. I felt more at ease, and we went through all the questions for the third and last time. When the wires were removed from the various parts of my body, I went into the other room to join Sandy, Rebecca, and Zeke.

Ron Ellison, Bob Niebuhr, and the mysterious Al met in the other room. They called me back in and asked me who I thought attacked me. I said I couldn't be sure but felt it was either a Klan member or a South African. With this, Bob Niebuhr glanced at Al and then turned to me. "The test proved you were truthful," he said.

I broke down. The emotional pitch had racked me. Bob Niebuhr said the FBI might ask me to take another polygraph test. If they did I would "feel like an old friend was giving it to me," he assured me. He looked at Al as he said it and I finally realized that he must have been from the FBI. Al was not there officially, so I couldn't reveal this at that time. With a tear in his own eye, Al hugged me and said "God bless you."

We all went to the Orlinskis', sharing the sense that the agony was over at last. I called Andy Fine in Norfolk. He was, of course, thrilled by the result and said he would drive directly over to tell my mother so I wouldn't have to call her. Even Andy was sure the phone was tapped and we didn't want the police to know about the test. We also called my sister, who insisted that we come to New York City. She said a group had formed there that wanted to help us.

Zeke and Rebecca were the perfect people to be with that night. We had met them on a charter flight to London and had instantly become friends. Zeke didn't practice law anymore but had bought the *Columbia Flyer,* a dying newspaper he then successfully rebuilt. Zeke and his wife Rebecca shared a marvelous wit. We gorged ourselves on food and drank a lot of wine. The lives we had led up to February 14 seemed ready to be resumed. Our sleep was long and deep that night.

The next day we took the Metroliner to New York. Barbara's apartment was half filled when we arrived. Roy Brown, Barbara's first husband, Sam and Helen Rosen, whom I had known for three years, Jack Geiger of the Medical Commission for Human Rights, and Florence Halperin were all there. All were from the New York medical community.

They had read the Bayside Hospital official report and were outraged by what Presswalla had said. They said that the internal injuries diagnosed in the report proved that the wounds couldn't have been self-inflicted. They were even more sure when they saw the n-i-g-e-r on my stomach. The consensus among them was that Dr. Presswalla had been used by the police to set me up. They felt that as doctors their profession had been misused.

They decided to form a committee and to hire an attorney to investigate. Everyone agreed that Paul O'Dwyer, the former New York City Council president, was the best choice. He agreed to drive in from his country home that night to meet us.

I sensed I was somehow losing control of the situation. Others, who either believed in me or in civil or human rights in general, had taken command of my destiny. So I was reassured when, much to my surprise, my brother Joe arrived.

Barbara, Joe, and I went to Franklin Williams' apartment. He offered us all the facilities of the Phelps-Stokes Fund—an office to use and any other practical help we might need. He liked the idea of the committee and of retaining Paul O'Dwyer as counsel.

We met Paul as planned at 9:30. He was an impressive man whom I had admired for several years. As president of the City Council he had helped pass a resolution against South African tennis players competing in New York–area facilities. We gave him all the details and he said he would let me know by Monday afternoon whether he would represent me.

We all went back to Barbara's. Jack and Roy had prepared a statement for the "National Committee to Protect Civil Rights." Both the statement and title seemed too broad. We settled on the "Committee for Justice for Richard Lapchick" with a more tailored statement. Paul O'Dwyer had stressed that the word "Defense" should not be used because it implied a defense was necessary. Barbara, Joe, and I stayed up and talked until 1:30. They were both great. Barbara had been through this and worse with the arrest of her husband Rajat in Uganda in 1968. Joe, a political conservative, had not only never experienced anything like it but I don't believe he thought it was possible for it to happen in America.

Dr. Bernard Simon, a prominent New York City surgeon, examined me early on Monday. He was more thorough than any doctor who had examined me since the attack. His conclusion was that the wounds could not possibly have been self-inflicted.

Momentum was building. I couldn't wait to get back to Virginia with this mess cleared up. I was beginning to miss my students, and I took it as a positive sign that I was able to think about them again.

Bob Lipsyte drove into the city to meet us. It was the first time I saw him in person after thirteen straight days of encouragement and help on the phone. We discussed strategy. Bob felt strongly that we needed a knockout offensive. He said we should announce a $1-million libel suit against Presswalla and the police. Bob argued that simply saying "I didn't do it" would be a page B-10 story while Presswalla's accusations were all on page 1. My only misgiving was the lingering doubt that Presswalla believed what he said. Others suggested that, if anything, the police might have misled him.

Paul O'Dwyer called and agreed to take the case. That evening I was to see Dr. David Spain, the top forensic pathologist in the country who dealt with civil rights cases. The only bad news was that O'Dwyer couldn't go to Virginia until the following Monday, meaning we could not hold our press conference until Wednesday—nine long days away. I knew we had run this risk when we asked someone as well known and in demand as Paul O'Dwyer. Nonetheless, it was frustrating.

Dr. Spain conducted a lengthy examination, having already seen the hospital report. He was critical of Presswalla, reiterating what others had said about hesitation marks only applying to suicide attempts. He said the marks were obviously made to make the letters stand out.

This ended any sympathy I had for Presswalla. While I never reached a firm conclusion about his motives, all the evidence led most of the committee members to believe the worst about him. As evidence mounted, I agreed more and more with them. I wanted to sue him for libel, to make him pay for the suffering he had inflicted on me and my family.

I was honored to be somehow involved with Dr. Spain. He was the man who had done the second autopsies of the three civil rights workers murdered in Mississippi in 1964. He had also done the second autopsy of Fred Hampton, the Black Panther leader slain by police in Chicago, and those of the prisoners killed in the Attica revolt. Of all people, David Spain knew how medical examiners had been used in the past to bolster falsified police versions of happenings. He had always courageously stood up for the truth.

We took a taxi back to Barbara's. I realized that all was now in place—the opinion of one of the nation's most renowned forensic pathologists, a positive polygraph, the testimony of the three doctors in Virginia and several others in New York. And yet I knew I couldn't return to Virginia in the nine days prior to the press conference; we had been advised that the climate would be too hostile before we released the information planned for it.

I tried to call Lambuth Clarke that afternoon without success. I did reach Del Carlson, who taught political science with me. He agreed to cover my Urban Studies class. I arranged for Jim Brown, the African History professor at Norfolk State, to teach my African Studies class and for Bill Wycoff, a former Wesleyan history professor, to teach my class in Third World Studies. Del, Bill, and Jim all said the climate surrounding the case in Virginia was terrible.

Everyone advised me to get my mother, Joey, and Chamy out of Virginia to avoid retaliation. Bonnie and Phil, my sister-in-law and brother-in-law, offered to drive to Virginia, pick them up, and drive them to my brother's house in Media, Pennsylvania. Eight students offered to remain in the house to protect it.

After two days of working on the committee at the Phelps-Stokes Fund with Shelby Howatt of the Fund and Helen Rosen, we all converged on my brother's house in Pennsylvania on Wednesday night. The plan was for Sandy to fly the children to Florida to stay with her parents on Thursday morning.

Both the children were surviving the ordeal and looked forward to the plane ride. I was pleased that they would be with my in-laws. Sandy's father was the ultimate practical man, politically far more conservative than I. I had waited for the call from him for days after the police request for the polygraph, for I was sure he would want me to take it. He never did; that cemented our relationship.

My mother and I drove back to New York on Sunday morning so we could meet with Paul O'Dwyer. He was scheduled to fly that afternoon to Baltimore to meet Zeke Orlinski and Bob Niebuhr, the polygrapher. He then planned to fly to Virginia on Monday morning. Unfortunately we crossed signals and missed each other in New York.

Finally, O'Dwyer called me at 12:15 A.M. to tell me that he was very impressed with Bob Niebuhr.

I spent much of Monday trying to reach Jack Dici, who did press work for Paul O'Dwyer. He had been assigned the task of setting up the all-important press conference, now only two days away. We knew how much was riding on the conference —everything from clearing my name to getting me back to work at Wesleyan and on South Africa and the Davis Cup.

The matches now appeared set. Vanderbilt had obtained new financial backing. South Africa was still scoring public relations points. Peter Lamb, their "colored" player, was being mentioned more and more in Nashville. It was convenient that he had enrolled at the university where the matches were to be played.

Also getting considerable publicity was the announcement by Piet Koornhof, the South African minister of sport, that tennis and all other sports would be integrated inside South Africa. No one would care—or remember—that almost four years later, the new minister responsible for sport, Mr. Gerrett Viljoen, would make the same announcement to cover for South Africa's first major sports tour since 1978—the Springbok rugby tour of New Zealand and the United States.

With the matches set, the dark, unseen forces I had warned against when I was in Nashville began to materialize. Ads started running in the *Tennessean*:

WELCOME BRAVE CHAMPIONS OF WEST CHRISTIAN
CIVILIZATION
PRO SMALL BUSINESS, AND ANTI-COMMUNIST SOUTH
AFRICA

Don Henson, grand dragon of the Nashville chapter of the Ku Klux Klan, announced that the Klan would protect spectators from demonstrators by having between 300 and 500 members present during the demonstrations. When the Nashville police chief said he didn't need their help, a Klan spokesman said it didn't matter since so many Klansmen were on the Nashville police force.

Unknown to me at the time, an officer of the South African Ministry of Information gave a briefing in New York City prior to our press conference. As stated before, news of the so-called Muldergate or Ministry of Information Scandal was just beginning to break in the Western press. In March 1978, we didn't know how bad it would get. But we did know it was bad. By this time I was convinced that the attack and all subsequent events either were engineered by South Africa itself or by their sympathizers in America. To me nothing else could make sense.

The representative of the ministry was asked at this briefing whether or not the Ministry of Information would continue to operate. First, there was Biko's death, the October bannings, and now a major government scandal centering on his own ministry. What good could the ministry do in this climate? The representative said, "South Africa's image is getting better and better. We have already had a number of successes this year." The questioning then went off in a different direction. After it was all over, Richard Walker, the U.N. correspondent of the *Rand Daily Mail,* asked, "What do you consider to be the successes for South Africa this year?" The second success listed was "the destruction of Richard Lapchick."

Richard Walker told me this in late May. I couldn't understand why he hadn't informed me at the time. He explained that it was just so obvious that my "destruction" would be a gain for South Africa that it wasn't worth mentioning.

Yes, these were big stakes. International sports had become South Africa's Achilles' heel. It was clear that these stakes made our press conference on Wednesday increasingly important.

In Virginia Beach, O'Dwyer had met with Dr. Lorenz, Captain Buzzy of the police department, Presswalla, and Wesleyan Vice-President Jim Bergdoll. I was about to call him to find out the results when Helen Rosen informed me that Paul's sister had died in Ireland. Paul would have to fly directly to Dublin from Virginia Beach. When I told Paul the sad news, he asked me to call Jack Dici, his press liaison, to postpone the press conference, which was scheduled to take place within some forty hours at the United Nations Church Center in New York.

When I reached Dici, he replied that the postponement was a good thing since he hadn't had a chance to call anyone yet! Sandy had just returned from Florida and we decided to get additional help in organizing the press conference. A press conference without the press would not do much to get us back on the Davis Cup track.

On Monday night we let Saundra Ivey know about both the formation of the committee and about the press conference, now rescheduled for Friday to allow for O'Dwyer's return. Andy Fine suggested that we also tell Peter Galuszka so he wouldn't feel left out. Sandy called him on Tuesday and read him the release that listed ten of the most prominent committee members. Peter asked if there were any more. Sandy read him some from the master list. Unfortunately, she included Anthony Lewis, the columnist for *The New York Times*. His name had been penciled in for later confirmation.

Lewis had been at a meeting of the Freedom to Publish Committee, convened by Win Knowlton, president of Harper & Row. Of the twelve well-known writers and publishers present, eleven had joined the committee. Anthony Lewis was the only person who did not.

We received a call from him on Wednesday afternoon explaining that he understood why people might have thought he was on the list. He said, however, that his position as a writer for the *Times* meant he had to stay off such committees even if he sympathized with their purpose. Lewis said he had told Peter Galuszka this when Peter called him.

I immediately called Peter to explain. Peter was extremely hostile. "Off the record," I said, "I wanted to tell you what happened with Anthony Lewis." "I'm not talking to you off the record anymore!" he replied emphatically. It was the first time I had talked to Peter since I left Virginia for Nashville fourteen days earlier.

Those two weeks, lengthened by O'Dwyer's circumstances, were the closest I have ever been to "disappearing." We carefully avoided talking to anyone in the media because we did not want the polygraph story to leak out and be lost. We had been told by half a dozen friends that someone called Buzzy Bissinger of the *Ledger-Star* had been calling them in reference to a "sympathetic" profile on me that he was writing. As much as I wanted some sympathy, I was not returning his calls—or anyone else's.

That is why I was both hurt and angered by Peter. I envisioned the next day's headline as "Lapchick Committee a Fraud." Instead, the *Ledger-Star* ran "Pro-Lapchick Organizer Charges 'Witch Hunt.'" In Virginia, that was just as bad. Bob Lipsyte was quoted as suggesting two theories. "One, that the police can't solve this case so they're trying to close it; two, that the police are somehow implicated. I'm not saying either is the case, but that's what jumps to mind. It could be that the sixties are back again, and what's scary about it is that people are a lot smarter this time around. This time it won't be a lot of sweet college kids."

The only good news was the resolution passed by the Wesleyan faculty. It said, "The Faculty Association of Virginia Wesleyan College wishes to express its outrage at the attack on our colleague and to affirm categorically its faith in his integrity and truthfulness."

However, one *Virginian Pilot* story was careful to note that three of the thirty-one faculty members who voted did not favor the resolution. Furthermore, it stated that "Lapchick asked the association to issue a statement on his behalf." In fact, Joe

Harkey, an English professor who headed the FA, had called to ask what could be done to help.

There were rumors that I would be arrested if I went back to Virginia. Many members of the committee warned me not to return until the day of the press conference. They said that if I were in jail the police could do *anything* to me. In other words if the public believed I was crazy enough to self-inflict internal injuries in the confines of my own office, they could be led to believe that I would do much worse to myself when distraught and humiliated in a jail cell. Andy Fine assured me that I would not be arrested, but the whole situation had become so perverted that I just didn't know what to think.

There were also rumors of the convening of a grand jury to investigate. Presumably such an investigation would be into my account of what had happened on February 14. When O'Dwyer was in Virginia Beach he informed Presswalla and the police that I had taken a polygraph and that other doctors had examined me. This seemed to squash the grand jury idea. The police began to leak the information about the polygraph.

Suddenly, the Wednesday issue of the *Pilot* quoted deputy assistant commonwealth attorney Scortino as saying, "We considered the special grand jury, but we decided against it because, frankly, there's not that much to investigate." Alluding to the positive results of the polygraph, Scortino said, "You're not supposed to present evidence to a grand jury that you couldn't present at a trial." Was Scortino preparing the public to discount the results of the polygraph that his local police had asked me to take?

He added that any evidence from other doctors—presumably meaning other than Presswalla—would be improper evidence. "You'd get into a conflict of opinions and not hard facts." It sounded as if he had already discounted the further medical evidence that Presswalla had requested. I wondered how the network that seemed to be setting me up was tied together. Did they act in concert? The police, medical examiner, press, now the commonwealth attorney's office. Or was it all coincidence?

That afternoon I had lunch with Pete Axthelm of *Newsweek*. He was the first person from the press to whom I had talked since Nashville. I had always thought highly of Pete as a writer, putting him in the same category as Bill Nack and Sandy Padwe of *Newsday*. And it was good to talk with someone who was somewhat removed from the event and could look at it with more objectivity.

In fact, the whole atmosphere in New York was much different from Virginia, where many people who had been casual friends for five or more years suddenly pulled away from us. Our neighbor who occasionally wrote for the *Beacon*, a local newspaper supplement, told me that it was "assumed" by the editors that I was a communist. After all, I had gone to Cuba and China. What more proof was needed?

In New York, people rallied to our support. This was true of friends and strangers. Many of them had lived through the McCarthy era. We met most through Sam and Helen Rosen, who had virtually adopted us. It was much easier to put our fate in some perspective in New York. We had felt our world was collapsing and there was not much time left; yet by March 9 we had been in our nightmare only three weeks since the attack on February 14. Some of the people we met had suffered far more than we, and had for years. Knowing they had been able to pick up the pieces of their lives helped us to realize that we could as well.

We finally neared the long-awaited press conference. The pressure was building; the press regularly called my sister's apartment where we were staying. The police had seemingly once again leaked the information that I had taken a polygraph. We were asked over and over again by the press if it were true. All I could say was that all would be revealed on Friday.

Bob Lipsyte, with whom I spent Thursday, decided it would be best if we all left the apartment. We started by taping a fifteen-minute interview for National Public Radio's "All

Things Considered." Bob and I then cohosted Howard Cosell's class on Sport and Society at New York University, talking about South Africa and how it uses sport for propaganda purposes. Bob mentioned the press conference since these were primarily journalism students. Five actually showed up for it the next day.

Our friendship grew as we spent more time together. Bob challenged me as no one else had. His integrity and sincerity, combined with his sharp wit, always kept me alert. He would often criticize what I said, but I never felt put down. He let me be myself but made me a better person all at the same time. I was glad I was with him on this day.

Paul O'Dwyer returned from Ireland and went directly to his office to meet us at 6:00 P.M. The strain of his sister's death was obvious. Exhaustion had slowed his step.

He said we had three choices for tomorrow. First, we could attack the police and Dr. Presswalla. Second, we could announce a major libel suit against them. Or finally, we could simply present the evidence and let it speak for itself.

Paul said his first inclination had been either of the first two choices. He hated to see authorities get away with abusing the rights of individuals. But he added that his trip to Virginia had caused him to change his mind. If we chose to attack or sue, he warned us, we would be subject to incredible harassment and predicted the climate would be so hostile that we wouldn't be able to continue to live in Virginia. I glanced at Sandy, who was weeping. Even after all that had happened, Virginia Beach was our home. Sandy's expression told me she didn't want to move. She wiped away the tears as soon as she realized I saw her. But they had made their mark.

Paul added that if we attacked or filed a suit it would mean prolonged agony for our family. I flashed on UPI's Tom Ferraro asking my mother if she thought I had cut myself. I knew that Sandy and I could get through this no matter what. But I also knew that at age seventy-four my mother had already had several years taken off her life. Could I put her through any more?

Finally, Paul said that an attack or the suit could continue to divert the focus away from South Africa and keep it on me.

My conscience was retreating from the direction I had been sure we would choose when we convened that night. For two weeks, we had discussed nothing but an offensive. At 6:00 P.M. there was no doubt in my mind about what I wanted to do. At 7:30 I asked Paul what he would do. "Present the evidence, return as a hero, and carry on the battle." Bob and Sandy agreed. At the time the decision seemed right. Within days, I think we all had misgivings.

As I lay in bed that night I thought of my father's forced departure from St. John's because of mandatory retirement and how he had left with dignity. I had wanted him to fight to stay, but he had chosen to win the victory on the basketball court. In some ways I saw my situation as a parallel—I was choosing to win my point by helping to build the best possible anti-apartheid demonstration in Nashville. None of us doubted that Presswalla would abide by his word and recant after the evidence we would present at the press conference. We were convinced that this ugly episode would be forever behind us.

·6·
Blocked Shot

Friday dawned bright and crisp. Snow was still piled up in the street, the remnants of a terrible winter storm. We drove to the Church Center for the United Nations where the press conference was to be held. It was a familiar place; ACCESS had been housed there during the tennis protests at Forest Hills in 1977. I was still in awe of the glass tower across the street that housed the United Nations, its flags fluttering in the wind.

I met Buzzy Bissinger who had requested some details before the press conference so he could beat the noon deadline for the *Ledger-Star.* His aggressive style turned me off. He kept assuring me of his sympathy, and how a few words from me to my friends could help him write his feature story. I decided to have as little as possible to do with him.

Buzzy sat with Peter Galuszka during the press conference. The room was filled with a hundred or more reporters and friends. Paul O'Dwyer began the session by releasing the results and nature of the polygraph test and Dr. Spain's report. I made a statement to clarify why I decided to submit myself to a polygraph after first refusing. The emphasis of both statements was that I could now get on with my work.

Mr. O'Dwyer said that the attack was an "insidious one. It beats anything I have come across in civil rights work and that's a lot." He said that the police were making no apparent efforts to apprehend those who beat me and, thus, had put me in a position of having to defend myself.

Most of the questions focused on Presswalla's motivations. Galuszka and Bissinger were virtually the only ones who didn't raise doubts about him.

The New York, national, and international correspondents were more concerned with the broader story—the possibility of South Africa's involvement in the attack, the motives of the police and medical examiner, etc. We were very careful not to condemn them, much as we wanted to. The Davis Cup was the immediate issue.

Feelings were buoyant and hearts were light as the press conference ended. The tension was broken. Nat Holman, the only living member of the original Celtics, came over and gave me a big hug. Franklin Williams said, "You just paid South Africa back for what it has put you through."

As the crowd dwindled, Peter Galuszka approached me. He was more cordial now. I remarked that it was all over, that I was looking forward to returning to Virginia later that day. He said that he, too, hoped it was over.

But when Sandy and I bumped into the correspondent for *The New York Times* on 44th Street, our euphoria became depression. "I have bad news for you," he told us. "I just spoke to the medical examiner and he says he won't change his opinion."

We arrived in Virginia at about 5:00 P.M. Andy Fine and a dozen or so students were there at the airport. It was not exactly a hero's welcome, but I was happy to see them.

The *Ledger-Star* was already on the newsstands. At first glance, I thought Buzzy had missed his deadline, for there was nothing about the case in the main section. Then my fears about him were realized. The story was in section "B" and eight of the first ten paragraphs were on Presswalla's refutations of the polygraph test and Dr. Spain's opinions.

"I am not an expert in polygraphs and have no way of ascertaining what was the significance of it," he stated, and suggested that a medical board of forensic pathologists be appointed to determine if Dr. Spain or he was correct. He then requested that the police release the results of their investigation. I knew this could only mean that Presswalla had seen their report and that it affirmed his conclusions.

Andy drove us home. On the way, we heard the taped "All Things Considered" program and it sounded very good. We arrived at the house in time for the evening news. The local affiliates of NBC and CBS did not even mention the press conference. The ABC affiliate discussed the polygraph but half-dismissed it by adding that it was administered in Maryland where there were no licensing requirements for polygraph operators. I called Jay Moore, the news anchorman, later that evening to inform him that Niebuhr was licensed in Virginia. Moore corrected his mistake on the 11:00 news. But, as usual, the damage had been done. What began as a day to end it all turned out to be just one more day in the continuing drama.

News stories the next day were mixed. Peter Galuszka wrote a very fair one, extensively quoting from Dr. Spain's report. Part of that report mentioned rope burns on the back of my neck and wrist. Rope burns. The police did not find the rope —that alone should have confirmed that someone had removed it from the office and the building.

I caught an early flight to Nashville where I was to speak at a conference on apartheid. This was the conference that Dennis Brutus and I had tried to communicate about on the day and the night of the attack. I picked up the *Tennessean* at the Nashville airport. Saundra Ivey's article was balanced and, like Galuszka's, appeared on page 1. It concluded with Franklin Williams's charge that South Africa was responsible for the attack. The *Washington Post,* which had sent Athelia Knight to cover the story, printed a lengthy and balanced report on the evidence we presented.

I was picked up and taken directly to a friend's apartment where I was to receive a call from Peter Lamb, the colored member of the Davis Cup team.

We soon realized that someone had tried to break into the apartment through the bedroom window. My friend had already received threats after taking a leading role in the local protests. I insisted that she take some clothes and remain with friends until after the anti-Davis Cup demonstration. She had become one of the primary spokespersons for the protest.

She told me that Peter Lamb had told her that he didn't want to return to South Africa and that he was reconsidering accepting the position on the Davis Cup team.

Even in the atmosphere of fear that pervaded the apartment, I could taste victory. Ray Moore, a white South African tennis star, had already withdrawn from the team after being counseled by Arthur Ashe and, subsequently, Franklin Williams. It would be a great boost to our cause if Peter Lamb pulled out as well.

Lamb's call was a great disappointment. Our conversation was pleasant enough, but he gave no indication of withdrawing.

I was driven along the demonstration route to the site of the proposed rally. I was shocked to see that the rally was to be at the Parthenon, the site of the assassination in the film *Nashville*. Assassinations were no longer only movie themes.

It was good to be at the conference among anti-apartheid activists. It was held at Meharry Medical College, one of the nation's leading black medical schools. The media wanted to ask me about the polygraph test and Dr. Spain, but Dennis Brutus and I had agreed to concentrate on the conference. There was excellent information generated about the reality of apartheid in sport and the false messages emanating from South Africa.

I became faint during the press conference and had to be

taken to the office of Dr. Elan, the president of Meharry. I felt too weak to meet the press and John Dommisse, ACCESS's secretary-general, who also attended, brought me to our hotel room.

Sandy called to say how hostile people in the Virginia area seemed to be. She told me of Buzzy Bissinger's follow-up story titled "Lapchick Defense a Media Show." Sandy said she wanted to move away immediately.

I knew things had to be terrible for Sandy to react that way. There were no more flights that evening. Therefore I booked a 9:00 A.M. flight Sunday morning. I didn't want Sandy to feel alone. Several students had arranged a rotating guard schedule so I knew the house was secure, but I worried about her state of mind.

The flight arrived at the Norfolk airport at 12:30 P.M. and I walked to my car. Before leaving Nashville, I had placed a piece of paper in the car door to be able to tell if someone had broken in. There was no need to have done so; the window had obviously been forced open, breaking the window track and leaving it at a sharp angle.

I searched through the engine and under the car for forty-five minutes. I had become so distrustful of the police that I did not want to report it for fear of their saying I had broken into the car myself. Convinced that there were no bombs, I drove home.

Sandy produced an editorial in the Sunday *Virginian Pilot*. It called for a special grand-jury investigation of the case now that "the dramatics of a private investigation had been completed," and claimed that I had denounced Dr. Presswalla at the New York press conference, which was absolutely untrue.

"Of three private doctors who attended him [in the hospital], one conceded that the cuts could have been self-inflicted while another disagreed," the story said. "The deputy state medical examiner for Tidewater, Dr. Faruk B. Presswalla, was emphatic. He said one carving was 'definitely self-inflicted.' Dr. Presswalla, a pathologist with ten years' experience in forensic medicine, went public reluctantly; he too deplores apartheid and sympathizes with the professor's cause."

I began to realize what we were up against in Virginia. I called Charles Hartig, at WTAR-TV, the CBS affiliate. I had been on several of his TV shows and trusted him. Charles advised me to "cool it," that is, to keep quiet for a while so that some perspective on the situation could be gained. He acknowledged that there had been rumors that I would be arrested. The rumors were based on the police report, which no one had seen but many had heard about. Charles added that my taking the polygraph and seeing Dr. Spain had undoubtedly cut short any plans the police might have had for that arrest.

We visited Andrew Fine. He had been upset by the *Pilot* editorial and said he would personally go to the paper to defend me. Andy insisted that Sandy and I call Hayden about the car break-in, which we did. But before we could complain, Hayden told us that Dr. Presswalla had been very badly hurt by the national attention given to this case, and urged me to hold a press conference, publicly stating my faith in Dr. Presswalla! Sandy and I stared at each other in disbelief from different telephone extensions.

When Hayden's "investigators" came Monday, they told Sandy the break-in was merely one of many car robberies at the airport. They didn't respond when Sandy pointed out that cash and a tape deck were still in the car when I reached it.

I went to see Lambuth Clarke and Dean Wilson on Monday morning. As I entered, two other administrative officers were in Lambuth's office. They left icily, without saying a word to me.

Lambuth said that I was using the college as a platform for my views. He insisted that I was hurting the college in its conservative Virginia community. Lambuth was a nonconfrontational man who did not like to offend people, but he hurt me badly, and it took me some time to understand how disturbed he must have been and how much pressure he had to be under.

Bill Wilson, who was never as warm and easy with people as Lambuth, questioned my priorities. He asked why I hadn't called him to explain that I would be gone for two weeks from my classes.

I tried to explain, starting from the fact that my colleague, Del Carlson, had been fully informed, and that I had left several unanswered messages with Mrs. Baker, Lambuth's secretary, to say I wanted to speak to him.

I could see that nothing was penetrating. Over the years I had always had the feeling that Bill Wilson tolerated me but never that he supported me so I could easily accept his reactions as normal. But Lambuth, who may not always have understood me, had been consistently supportive. I gravely absorbed his attitude.

"The college is my home and its students my family. I would never do anything to hurt it," I said, and agreed to "resign immediately" if he thought it would help. I had a quick vision of a losing coach going to management with such an offer but expecting a vote of confidence. The vision was shattered when Lambuth replied, "You have until May to decide. Don't make your decision today." I knew it was tantamount to an acceptance of my offer.

I had a few minutes before class so I went to my office. Drawers were open and papers were strewn all over the place. I didn't want to touch anything but instead tried to reach Karen Gilbert, who worked with me on our community programs, and Randy Smith, a student who worked with Karen. Both were in my office frequently and I wanted to be sure they hadn't simply left it a mess, although I assumed it had been ransacked. I was unable to reach them before class.

Being back in the classroom was therapeutic. There were not many friendly faces in Virginia, but my students made me feel relaxed. Teaching was a large part of my life and my blood was, once again, running. Pete Axthelm's favorable *Newsweek* column had just come out and several students commented on how good it was.

I finally reached Karen and Randy after the class. They came directly to the office and confirmed that they had not left it like this. We checked the files. The ACCESS and ARENA files were gone, including our mailing lists. I called campus security and Sergeant Hayden. Both said they would investigate, but I have no reason to believe that either ever did.

I stopped by Andrew Fine's house on the way home. He had met with the editors of the *Pilot,* showed them the police photos of the beating, and gone over all the details. Andrew believed they were much more open after the discussion.

He had also called Captain Buzzy of the police department. Andrew had defended the police in several cases and had a good working relationship with them. He asked Captain Buzzy why Presswalla had not retracted his conclusions since I had done what he had asked. Buzzy responded that he was concerned that I would file a libel suit, and admitted that Presswalla had hired an attorney. Andrew explained to Buzzy that I was worried about my family and wanted police help, especially when I was away in Nashville for the demonstrations. Buzzy replied that if I were really so concerned about my family, I wouldn't be going to Nashville.

Andrew asked me if I would agree in writing that we would not sue Presswalla if he retracted his statement. Of course! I assured him.

Bernard Barrow, our neighbor and member of the state legislature, was going to take over the case while Andrew, suffering from exhaustion and the flu, went on a holiday. I went to his house to tell him the plan. As so often before when things looked bright, a phone message from Steve Goldberg of the *Pilot* was waiting to shatter me.

If timing is everything, then Presswalla was a genius. With each shift of momentum, Presswalla came forward to speak to the press. Did Buzzy tell Presswalla about his conversation with Andrew? Or about Andrew's meeting with the editors? Did Presswalla see the *Newsweek* column or Bill Nack's column in *Newsday,* both supportive of me, and, of course, by implication critical of Presswalla? Was it just a coincidence that Faruk Presswalla's written report on the case was given to Steve Goldberg on March 13 when it was given to the police on March 2?

The *Pilot* story, coauthored by Goldberg and Peter, began, "Richard E. Lapchick's shirt was unwrinkled and untorn and every button was in place when police arrived at Virginia Wesleyan College the night he claims he was attacked, a medical examiner's report says. In a written report on the incident, Dr. Faruk B. Presswalla says information about the shirt was provided him by police investigators. He says it helped him reach the conclusion that a racial epithet carved on Lapchick's stomach was self-inflicted."

Goldberg had called me for a reaction on Monday night, March 13, before the story was to appear on Tuesday. I told him Presswalla had never seen the shirt and the police couldn't have thought it important since they told Sandy to take it home, which the official hospital records confirmed that she did.

I told Goldberg that the shirt was still in the bag that Sandy used to bring it home and offered to bring it to him so he could see for himself. He said he didn't need to see it since the police had confirmed Presswalla's report! The shirt had, in fact, been ripped directly down the middle and the reason the buttons looked intact was that they were still in the button holes—fully buttoned.

Presswalla's report said that a Bayside Hospital physician had said there was no blood. Obviously there wasn't; the shirt had been ripped open and didn't touch my body where the cuts were inflicted.

It was a long day; the atmosphere on campus was heavy. Several students whom I was close to shared with me that there was a rumor I had been fired. Did they know something I didn't? I realized after Monday's meeting with Lambuth and Dean Wilson that it was unlikely that I would return next year. Ironically, I had also begun to think that it would be better to be fired than to resign. In that way I would at least be paid a year's salary under American Association of University Professors (AAUP) rules.

I met Dennis Govoni, who had been in the hospital room when Presswalla examined me, in the afternoon. He was upset by the Presswalla report. He clearly remembered the hospital visit, and distinctly remembered my answer of no when Presswalla asked if I thought the attackers were trying to kill me. Dennis also remembered that I said I passed out after the beating on my stomach. He confirmed that Presswalla was not taking notes.

I called Andrew and Bernard. They agreed that Dennis would be an important witness. Andrew said he had spoken to Andy Evans, the commonwealth attorney. Evans insisted that the police had not asked for me to be prosecuted, despite what I might have heard.

Andrew reported he had unsuccessfully tried to reach Presswalla all day to tell him that the police had misled and misinformed him about the shirt. By that time, I had found Mike Mizell, the student who had first noted the carving of N-I-G-E-R in the library. I asked him if he remembered what my shirt was like. Mike confirmed that it was ripped down the middle and hung at my sides, allowing him to see the carving.

Leonard Sharzer, the third doctor who examined me in the hospital, did meet Presswalla that day. Leonard reported that Presswalla was far less decisive than he had been in print, saying that the wounds could have been self-inflicted or the result of an attack. He said he still believed that I self-inflicted the wounds, largely because of the shirt. Leonard said Presswalla was astonished when told the truth about the shirt.

I spoke with Lew Hurst, the highly respected head of the

Virginia State Crime Commission. Lew was due to appear in my Urban Studies class. We had been together several times at Wesleyan over the years. I brought him up to date and sought his opinion. It wasn't comforting. Lew indicated that Press-walla's statements, even if retracted, would make it a near-impossibility to bring the attackers to trial.

The Davis Cup matches were only four days away and press interest was growing. Doug Smith of the *New York Post* called to do a story on the reported activities of the Ku Klux Klan in Nashville.

Bill Wilson, a producer on the Cronkite show, called to say that CBS wanted to fly a crew to Norfolk on Wednesday. Several church and civil rights groups had protested that Cronkite had not followed up on the polygraph story.

TASS, the Soviet news agency, called. They wanted to use my case to exemplify United States attitudes toward human rights. I told the reporter I would call him back, not knowing what to do. I remembered that TASS had taken up Harry Edwards' battle for tenure at Berkeley and it had brought results. But Harry was in liberal Berkeley, where TASS endorsement would not be as calamitous as it might be in Virginia. I never followed this up.

Zeke Orlinsky called to tell me to get out of Virginia because the police had too big a stake in discrediting me. He hung up and immediately the phone rang again. "If you step foot in Nashville you will never see Virginia Beach again!" a muffled voice warned.

The circus atmosphere—press, police, medical examiners, lawyers, friends and enemies—was alleviated with the late-night arrival of Maggie Kuhn, the founder of the Gray Panthers.

I met Maggie on my 1976 trip to China. I think she was seventy-two at the time. One by one, all the members of the group fell sick under the strain of the constant movement.

Maggie, probably fifteen to twenty years older than any of us, kept forging ahead. It was with that spirit that she had built the Gray Panthers into a powerful coalition working for the rights of old people. It was with that spirit that she brightened our home that night.

Maggie gave a speech at Wesleyan the next day. She was sensational. Now Peter Galuszka was with us trying to get a lead on any lawsuit, but I didn't talk to him about anything but Maggie.

That night Bob Lipsyte called to discuss a proposal for a book called *The Last Olympics* that I was contemplating writing. He had talked to several agents and publishers and said there was real interest in it. Bob joked that if I were killed in Nashville this weekend "you would blow the deal and all my efforts would be wasted."

We were ready to go to sleep when Kathy Kent of WTAR called. She had heard rumors that Wesleyan had asked me to resign. The school denied them. So did I. Kathy asked if I was planning to relocate. I answered that such speculation was premature and that I needed to test the climate in Virginia. However, inside I was increasingly certain we would be leaving.

I drove Maggie to her 7:00 A.M. flight and then went to my office. It was the first time I had been in my office in a deserted library since the attack and I went there more to test myself than to do any real work.

After my first class, I went to see Dean Wilson. We had a good open discussion. He remembered seeing a lump over my right eye when he visited me in the hospital emergency room —and suddenly he was a witness. More and more, I saw people not for themselves, but as potential witnesses. Mike Mizell, Dennis Govoni, Niebuhr, Spain, and now the dean: all would testify on my behalf. I wasn't so sure I would have to leave. The mood of relief, as usual, was to be short-lived.

I was walking to my next class when a call came for me in the business office. "If you step foot in Nashville, you won't see

Virginia Beach again," a voice said. I couldn't tell if it was the same person who had called the previous night.

I taught my third and final class of the day. My thoughts were more in Nashville than in Virginia Beach, as I tossed over and over whether I should go. I knew I was wasting my students' time that afternoon and didn't like myself for it. I promised myself this wouldn't happen again when classes resumed after spring break.

After class, I reluctantly returned a call to Buzzy Bissinger. He said his "balanced profile" on me was ready and they needed some fresh photos. I told him he had enough photos already, and asked him what he meant by "balanced." He said it was not all good. Buzzy read me a section attributed to an unidentified Wesleyan faculty member discussing my use of my personal "charisma" to sway students. He quoted an unidentified Old Dominion University faculty member, who had supposedly socialized with me a dozen times, as questioning my motives—among other things—saying I controlled the Norfolk press. I congratulated him on his balanced reporting, noting that I did not know any ODU professors well, and had never been with one on twelve or even six social occasions. I was furious. This was the third week he had been writing the story. We were later told that his original draft had been rejected as being too bland. It had certainly been spiced up.

I just sat there in my office for a few moments. The phone rang. I didn't answer it. A minute later it rang again, and I picked it up. The voice said, "Are you going to continue what you have been doing now, nigger lover?"

I was stopped by Karen Domabyl, the Wesleyan reference librarian, as I left the library. She told me that a man they had never seen before had entered the library and was obviously watching my office. He had told her he was doing research, but he had never opened a book, and had left abruptly after walking around the mezzanine where my office was located. Karen stopped short: she could see how upset I was.

I was trembling as I drove to Bernard Barrow's office to seek his advice. He wrote down the details of the threats and of the presence of the man in the library and told me to call Hayden from his office so he could attest to their being reported. He had his secretary place the call so Hayden would know it came from his office. We discussed the pros and cons of going to Nashville, but I knew I had to go. I was much calmer by the time I got home. I had accepted this was the way things had to be.

·7·
Big Rally

It is a rule in our house that we never wake up the children early unless it is essential. But at 6:00 A.M. this morning I went to say goodbye, completely forgetting that they were in Florida! I knew that many friends and some family members felt I had gone too far. Ann Lapchick, my sister-in-law, told Sandy that if she were married to me she would issue an ultimatum: either get out of the movement or lose your family. Others expressed the same feelings to Sandy.

There I was in Joey's room trying to say goodbye to a child who was a thousand miles away. I had decided to wake him up because I knew it was remotely possible that I would never see him or his sister again.

I had always believed that I hadn't chosen my work in spite of my family but because of them. It tormented me to read about a white cop killing an innocent black man in Houston or Capetown; it tormented me to know that my chances of achieving success in America were directly related to my skin color; to know that the opportunities for blacks on an international level were deteriorating. I wanted to make some contribution, however small, to changing these things so that Joey and

Chamy wouldn't be tormented by them; so that Joey and Chamy could really be free.

However, at 6:00 A.M. on the morning of March 17, 1978, standing in my child's empty room, I had to wonder if my being in Nashville was worth the risk. The children were already gone because we feared for their lives. We had even sent Penda, our dog, to my brother's to ensure her safety.

Sandy called to me, "You'll be late. You have to go now." Yes, I *had* to go.

Tom Doyle, one of our rotating student bodyguards, and I were met at the Virginia airport by Sarah Oliver, another Wesleyan student. We were all tense as the plane took off. We had lived in "the South" for eight years, but somehow I felt I was really going to the South now. The Klan would be there in the open, and a tennis team from South Africa would be there as welcome guests. I tried to think of what it must have been like for my father to be driving to Louisville as a member of the Celtics for the first game in the South with the all-black Rens. The Rens weren't welcome in the 1930s, the South Africans were in the 1970s. The world seemed upside down.

Tom broke into my thoughts by describing the man in the library on the previous day and what he had done there. Tom had almost bumped into him in the parking lot. As they stepped back from one another, he had asked Tom where the library was.

Ten minutes later, Tom entered the library and saw the stranger sitting at a table in front of the magazine display, his chair angled toward my office. At first Tom sat down at the next table and then moved over to the table where the man was sitting. He held a folded magazine that he occasionally perused, but primarily he focused his attention on my office.

Mike Mizell came up to Tom in the library after the man had been there for twenty to twenty-five minutes. Tom took Mike aside and described the man's suspicious actions. Apparently in response, the man walked behind the periodical guides desk.

Each time Tom looked at him, the man was staring at them.

Mike, never the subtle one, moved toward the periodical guide desk and asked if he was waiting to see me. He answered, "No, I'm here doing research," and abruptly moved to the card catalogue as if to prove that was his interest. But by then he had been in the library for forty-five minutes.

Tom and Mike informed Karen Domabyl about what was happening and went to get help. The man left in the five minutes they were gone.

Before leaving, he asked Karen about a certain book, went upstairs, and walked past my office. He doubled back past me again, and left the library without a book. Karen watched him walk toward the science building and told Tom about his departure when he returned. Tom dashed outside and saw the man drive away in a brown Cadillac Seville with a tan vinyl roof.

I hadn't said a word for five minutes. When the story was finished, I asked what he looked like. He wore a brown leather jacket, white shirt, brown tie, and black pants. He was white, in his early thirties, about six feet tall with a medium to large build, had brown hair, and an acne-scarred face.

I sat quietly for a moment. I didn't know about the acne because of the stocking mask, but the rest of the description could have fit either of the men who attacked me. I tried to be rational, recognizing that it was a description that might fit many men.

I called Bernard Barrow with these details as soon as the plane landed in Nashville. He agreed that the description could be important and assured me he would contact Sergeant Hayden with the information.

We were met at the airport by Mike Mizell, Bob Friedland, and Mary Wells. Mary and Bob were also Wesleyan students who had come down early with Mike to help me.

I taped the "MacNeil-Lehrer Report" that afternoon. Charlayne Hunter-Gault was in the studio and Jim Lehrer was in Washington. The other guests were Bud Collins, the tennis commentator, and Slew Hester, president of the U.S. Tennis Association. I had never met Slew before, although we had exchanged considerable correspondence.

I had assumed that Bud Collins would take a position in support of the USTA, which wanted the matches to take place; however, I was wrong. Hester proved to be very amicable although his thinking on South Africa was, at best, confused. I was impressed by the penetrating questions asked by Charlayne Hunter-Gault. We all felt that the show went very well and served to substantiate our arguments for isolating South Africa.

We drove to the Holiday Inn, where I checked in under the name John Dommisse, ACCESS's secretary-general. I didn't want my name to show up in the register. We had two rooms so several of our student/bodyguards could stay with John and me. A TV bulletin said there were 3,000 demonstrators at Vanderbilt marching in a freak snow storm. Our local efforts were paying off. The demonstrations, which were to be held simultaneously with the matches, were scheduled for Friday, Saturday, and Sunday. The major demonstration was to be held Saturday.

We got to the gym as soon as we could, but the snow and bitter winds had reduced the number of demonstrators to about 500 or 600 by the time we arrived. We were told there were less than 1,000 spectators inside.

We marched for an hour. I was surrounded by Mary, Sarah, Bob, Mike, Tom Doyle, and Tom Hollett, a former student and close friend who had flown down from Washington. The rhythmic chants of the demonstrators let my mind focus on these friends. Whether the threats to me were real or not, they thought they were real and were risking a lot to help me.

As chants of "Sports, yes! apartheid, no! Tennis with South Africa's got to go!" rang through the freezing air, I realized how courageous they were. Their bodies were pressed close to mine to stop a bullet they thought might be meant for me. It was a feeling of dedication and commitment that I had never experienced before and that nothing can ever make me forget. At that moment they made all the Buzzy Bissingers and Captain Buzzys seem irrelevant. If our society was ever to be healed, these would be the physicians. If it would be reconstructed, they would be the architects.

There appeared to be a disturbance ahead of us. Two local demonstration marshalls informed us that our group had been surrounded by Klansmen or what the marshalls believed to be Klansmen. They asked that I leave for my own safety. My thoughts turned to the empty bedroom where I had been preoccupied by such visions twelve hours earlier. What was I doing to my family? "Dr. Lapchick, Dr. Lapchick!" The marshall pulled on my arm, bringing me back to the present. We left immediately and returned to the hotel.

We were joined there by John Dommisse, Lila Miller, and Cary Goodman. Lila and Cary were the first two organizers for ACCESS. The circle of friends and associates was closing. It would be completed within twenty-four hours. We had a quiet evening, sharing a light supper and a bottle of wine. Tom Doyle, Mike Mizell, and Bob Friedland slept in the two rooms with John and me. Unexpectedly, I slept straight through the night, awakened only by a call at 8:30 A.M.

By 10:00 A.M. our rooms were filled with twenty or so people. Another Wesleyan contingent had arrived at 3:30 A.M. after driving through the night to get there. The group made a collective decision that we should not join the march until it reached Centennial Park. The radio informed us that some 6,000 had begun the march to the park.

The plan was for the demonstration to start at the state capitol and march toward Vanderbilt. The NAACP contingent went to Centennial Park opposite Vanderbilt while about 1,000 students went directly to the gymnasium from Centennial Park.

We met the march just as it was splitting up. It was a strange scene that encompassed both generational and ideological differences. The NAACP contingent consisted of mostly black people in their late thirties or early forties—veterans of civil rights marches of the 1960s, marches to protest racism in places like Nashville. But this was a mass demonstration against racism on the international level, and I felt it was a breakthrough.

The student group was racially mixed although predominantly white. They were in their late teens or early twenties and were notably more strident in tone. For them, the action was at the Vanderbilt gymnasium. They wanted to be exactly where the South Africans were. The slogan "The people united will never be defeated" had replaced "We shall overcome."

Raised and nurtured on the civil rights and antiwar marches of the 1960s, I had increasingly been drawn to more direct action in the 1970s. Therefore, I decided I would participate briefly at the NAACP rally and then go directly to Vanderbilt.

Franklin Williams greeted me at the park and accompanied me up onto the stage. I was the only white person up there with Franklin, Ben Hooks and his wife Frances, Dick Gregory, Joseph Lowery of the Southern Christian Leadership Conference (SCLC), Judge William Booth of the American Committee on Africa, Carl Stokes, Ossie Davis, and Bayard Rustin. To say that I was honored to be in such company would be a great understatement. Dennis Brutus came a few minutes later. I told Franklin that Dennis, of all people, should be on the stage. Franklin agreed and said he would try to include him.

I quickly perceived the importance of the demonstration for the NAACP; speaker after speaker emphasized the need for strengthening the organization. This was Ben Hooks's first big protest as its new executive director. To have agreed to make such a commitment to an African issue was a brave decision for him. A great deal was riding on the day. I began to understand that he wouldn't want to take a chance of spoiling it with a confrontation with the Klan at Vanderbilt.

The spirit of the moment and the tone of the speeches, even if only for a day, recaptured the high pitch of the 1960s. While it was the feeling of the past, it was the substance of its meaning for the future that prevailed. Everyone seemed to pick up on that—students, old people, even the press.

The speeches were forceful, dramatic, and to the point—racism should be attacked wherever it was found. Particularly good were Ossie Davis, Bill Booth, Franklin Williams, and Ben Hooks. Hooks was especially charismatic that day. Dick Gregory, in his own unique way, was not far behind.

About one hour before the rally was scheduled to break up, Walter Searcy reported that the police had just told him that "all hell had broken loose over at the gym." Walter didn't know what this meant or whether it was inside or outside. I was disturbed, especially considering how well the rally was going. We didn't want news of trouble now, only of protest.

As Franklin was starting to speak, he surprised me by stopping and turning to me. "I want to introduce you to the man who first raised the issue of sports contacts between the United States and South Africa," he said. "We might not be here today if it were not for Richard Lapchick. And what was his reward? Thugs sent by South Africa beat him up and carved *nigger* on his stomach. And Richard Lapchick is a white man. How many white heroes do we have? To me, Richard Lapchick is one of them—to me he is a hero. Please stand up, Richard." When I did, the 6,000 or so in he amphitheater also stood up and cheered. I was grateful to Franklin and to the crowd. I was most grateful that our victory seemed assured, and that all the work and suffering had been worth it. It was the proudest moment of my life.

By then Dennis Brutus had finally come on stage. Reports from the gym had made us tense but the speakers were among the few who seemed to have heard that "hell" had broken loose there. I wondered how Hooks would handle it, when it was his turn to address the crowd.

Ben Hooks introduced me again, this time to speak. So much had been said already that I shortened my speech to simply remind the audience that after the representatives of apartheid left our land there would still be much work to do in other areas of the anti-apartheid movement. I told them that this showing in Nashville would reverberate inside South Africa and would deliver the message that the American people would be tough on apartheid in the future.

Ben Hooks was speaking now, and I decided to hear him from a more protected pocket of the stage. He was worth waiting for. He urged the crowd to disband in an orderly fashion and not to go to the gym. This upset some people who were unaware of what we thought were threatening circumstances. In spite of my original inclination, I decided that in light of threats being relayed to me during the rally I would not go there myself. Hours later we discovered that there had been no problems at the gym. I wondered if the threat against me had also been planted to keep me away from Vanderbilt.

The rally broke up. Everyone felt positive, even amid the clouded circumstances of the police reports. I spent several minutes exchanging stories with Dick Gregory, who has always been one of my heroes.

By then I was surrounded by the Wesleyan contingent. They whisked me into a car to go back to the hotel and then straight to the airport. Everyone sat anxiously in the Braniff waiting area until I actually boarded a plane for Washington with Tom Hollett, my former student and now friend. It was extremely painful to say good-bye as we climbed the elevated ramp. My Wesleyan friends had just given so much. The ordeal seemed over, yet deep down I sensed that my career as a teacher was nearing an end. Even though a final decision had not been made, I knew I could no longer be effective in Virginia and the risks to my family were too great. By now Sandy fully agreed. Still, that would be a tremendous price for me to pay. I was going to Washington to meet Sandy so I could look for a new job and we could find a house.

Even as we flew to Washington we knew that the protests had been extremely successful. We outnumbered the spectators over the three days by more than three to one, and the matches were a financial bust. All the manipulating, all the attempts to discredit me and divert attention from the issue were ultimately wasted.

·8·

Final Buzzer

Sandy and I spent the next week in Washington looking for jobs for the following year. It was a time full of soul searching—where did we want to live, what type of job did I want, what could I get?

Sandy returned to Virginia Beach and I went to New York to talk to Gene Stockwell of the National Council of Churches about a job. I phoned her Thursday morning to see how she was. Someone had called her to tell her that there was a show on television about our new home. She turned it on to find a program about a jail.

As I flew back from New York to Norfolk it crossed my mind that people might be waiting to arrest me. Everything was so distorted.

The next day was Good Friday. I got up very early and spent the day writing the proposal for *The Last Olympics.* My concentration was interrupted by a woman on the phone.

"Is this Mr. Lapchick?"

"Yes."

"We are doing a survey. Are you a veteran?"

"No."

"Are you and your wife permanent residents of Tidewater?"

"Yes."

"Are you sure?"

"Yes."

"Do you both have a cemetery plot?"

"No."

"You will need one soon."

Sandy's parents arrived with Joey and Chamy on Saturday; I had already come home. Suddenly our lives seemed much more normal. Joey and Chamy were tanned and beautiful. There was no way to see then the deep scars Joey was bearing beneath his external beauty. That pain would gradually emerge later, but for now all was well. (When we eventually got to New York Joey spent a good part of our first year seeing a child psychiatrist. It took the psychiatrist only one hour to conclude that Joey's aggressive behavior was a defense mechanism. As a then five-year-old, he closely identified with his father. To grow up to be like his father meant that he, too, would be attacked. That is a lot for a five-year-old to handle.)

We tried to pretend that all was well now that the children were home and I was teaching again. However, we were still receiving threatening calls, and we still had people living with us as bodyguards. Andrew Fine was still gone and Bernard Barrow had not been able to see Presswalla.

Then, our ultimate vulnerability was exposed. That Friday, at 5:00 P.M., the phone rang in my office. I answered it routinely by saying "Rich Lapchick, hello." The caller said, "Hi, Rich," and I assumed it was a friend.

He continued, "It must be good to have the kids home." By then I knew it had to be a friend since only a few friends and the police knew we had sent them away and fewer still knew they were back.

Then he said, "It may not be for long!" I panicked. "Who is this? Who is this?" I frantically demanded. The only sound was the dial tone.

I immediately called Sandy and asked to speak to Joey. She said she thought he had gone somewhere with a neighbor. I drove straight home without telling Sandy of the call, since I didn't want to alarm her. I was there at 5:30. No Joey. I combed the neighborhood but no one had seen him. I called Sergeant Hayden. He was not there so I told the person who answered to get him because it was an emergency, a possible kidnapping. Sergeant Hayden returned my call two weeks later.

I ran through the neighborhood again. By then it was 6:00 P.M. and I had to tell Sandy. She was not at all certain now about the neighbors whom she thought had Joey. It had been two hours since she had seen him. We really didn't know these people well. They had lived across the street for only a few months and now they were moving away. Our state of fear even drove us to conjure up thoughts that these people were part of our nightmare.

I went to Bernard Barrow's at Sandy's suggestion, while Sandy remained home to wait for Hayden or his call. There was nothing else to do but wait. As the minutes dragged on, my insides were being torn apart. 6:15, 6:30. Bernard and I walked through the neighborhood again. It was starting to get dark. Joey had never been out of the neighborhood this late. I was becoming convinced that we were about to pay the ultimate price. As we sat there in silence in Bernard's living room I could think of little else but the refrains of unsolicited advice from friends and family that I get out of this work.

My father had prayed when I had polio that if God would deliver me back alive he would do whatever it took to make me whole again. At 7:00 P.M. I found myself offering up the same prayer about Joey. I didn't know what I meant by it. Would I actually stop working in the area of race relations? Would we leave Virginia immediately? Something drastic had to be done. And soon. Every fifteen minutes I called Sandy to hear what Hayden had said or to see if Joey had called. All blanks.

We went outside again at 7:30. It was almost dark now. We

stood on the side street between the Barrows' house and that of the neighbor whom we hoped had Joey. Cars drove by, their headlights making it impossible to clearly see who was inside. As none of them stopped, the terror grew. Sandy had joined us, having abandoned any hope of Hayden's help.

I was so distraught as I turned back to Sandy that I was very confused when I saw her starting to run. I turned again and saw the neighbor's car pulling up. Joey seemed to be out of the car before it stopped.

He was in my arms and I buried my face in between his head and shoulder so he wouldn't see the tears. I hoped he hadn't seen the terror and panic on my face. Sandy was jumping all over us, soon joined by Bernard. The worst moments of our lives were over, but the memories of them may never fade. That was the one price I knew I could never ever pay.

We had arrived at a new low point. We had been wrong time and time again for six weeks. Wrong about not going on the offensive versus Presswalla and the police; about the effects of the polygraph and Dr. Spain's report on clearing the deck in Virginia; and especially in thinking that the harassment would end after Nashville.

It was a weekend spent questioning everything; no assumptions went untested. The nightmare with Joey had underlined our vulnerability. With a hostile police force, we knew there would be no safety. With a hostile press, we recognized I could not be politically effective in Virginia. We felt as though the entire community had us in a slowly closing vise. What we needed to know was whether life and work would be better elsewhere. Was all this happening because I was in the South?

This reflective period abruptly ended on April 6 at 9:30 A.M. Ibrahim Noor called from the United Nations Center against Apartheid. Ibrahim has become one of my very closest friends. As much as anyone else, he helped nurse me back to being a whole person again. But in April 1978, he was Mr. Noor, from the United Nations.

He asked me if I would be willing to come to New York to work for the United Nations for three months. I tried to be cool on the phone but there was no way. As a student of international affairs, as an activist against apartheid, it was almost too good to believe that I would work for the United Nations Center against Apartheid.

An hour later, I received a call from Nashville. I had been chosen for the Coalition's humanitarian-of-the-year award. That same morning, Pam McAllister called to say that the Federation for Social Action of the United Methodist Church had decided that I should receive their humanitarian-of-the-year award. The contrast in our emotions at 9:15 A.M. and 12:30 P.M. further underscored the mercurial nature of our lives in the recent past. We had run the gamut from despair to hope, from uncertainty to certainty, from painful rejection to warm acceptance. The constant shifting had taken its toll on all of us —our nerves were raw.

Four days later I flew to New York for my three months at the United Nations. I knew I could not return to Virginia for pleasure, that I could not remember that seven and a half of our eight years were very happy. No, this was the South and I was going home to the North. Racism was there, of course, but at least not the racism that deals blows to the body and the mind.

I couldn't know then that those three months would become five years at the U.N.; that the emotional scars were so deep that I wasn't back to full strength until late 1980; that Joey's pain would affect so many aspects of his development; that Sandy would gradually partially withdraw from me to protect herself from the presumed eventuality of my death. No, all I knew on May 15 when the jet lifted off the ground in Norfolk, Virginia, was that I was on my way home. The relative safety of working for the United Nations was a great security blanket, a warm womb that could protect us physically, emotionally, and financially.

*   *   *

The womb seemed to explode again in the fall of 1981. The South African Springbok rugby team was set to tour the United States. I became deeply involved in the efforts to stop the tour.

Those 1981 events forced us to see what we had begun to suspect. What had happened in 1978 was not necessarily because we lived in Virginia.

The new trouble began on September 4, 1981, within hours after the city of Rochester became the third city to cancel a game with the Springboks. It looked like the whole tour was about to collapse. Our coalition members were ecstatic when I announced this at our regular weekly Thursday night meeting.

I arrived at our apartment building at 9:30 feeling very good, only to find Sandy darting frantically about the lobby. Our apartment had been broken into. Valuables, including a camera, watches, jewelry, and cash were untouched. None of Sandy's, Joey's, or Chamy's things had been disturbed. My things had been thoroughly searched, and, for the most part, ransacked. Nothing had been taken. The nature and timing of the break-in convinced me that it was politically motivated.

The police sent three separate squads that night and they were very deferential. I am sure the fact that I worked at the U.N. set their tone.

Before I went to work the next morning I went to see our new car. We had bought a 1968 Mercedes for $1,000. Sandy had picked it up the night of the robbery. It looked beautiful to me that morning and soothed some of the pain of the previous night.

People at the U.N. were upset about the break-in and the day was spent dealing with both that and the Rochester victory. It was all shattered when Sandy called from Kingston, New York, to say that, as she was driving to Woodstock, the engine of the Mercedes had been destroyed. The oil gasket had apparently been loosened and all the oil had drained out after ninety miles.

The mechanic who worked on it said it almost surely had been tampered with by someone. I was frightened.

However, I was not as scared as I was on the following Tuesday when Sandy called to say that our old Volvo had had the grill pried open and the hood was ajar. We had the bomb squad test it, and all was okay. But all was not okay with the Lapchicks. Five days, three major incidents, all discovered by Sandy! She was losing control and the bodyguards who by then were living with us only served to further unnerve her. The last thing we wanted was publicity since we didn't want either the children or my mother to know of the danger. The worst of it was that we were now in New York. We could no longer blame it on living in the South. At least the authorities were more responsive to us in New York.

The events of 1978 and later, of 1981, led me to reflect more on my life, especially my childhood and the various influences in it: the events that took place, both within my family and in the outside world, the influence of my education, of my friends, and of the individual members of my family. The chance to write this book enabled me to go deeply into that period.

· PART 3 ·

Growing Up in Sportsworld

·9·

Child of Sportsworld

My father always teased me that I was born under the wrong star. My mother was forty-one and he was forty-five when I arrived, surely not a birth according to the prescriptions of Planned Parenthood. Furthermore, almost at the same moment, the United States detonated its first atomic bomb in New Mexico. It was July 16, 1945. Perhaps the upheaval of the earth during my birth planted the antiwar seeds that grew in me twenty years later.

Sports marriages are never easy and my parents' was no exception. Basketball was my father's life for at least six months of every year. As a player with the Original Celtics and as coach of St. John's, he was as frequently on the road as he was at home. Paradoxically, he was an intensely private man thrust into the public limelight because of his exceptional status as a player and a coach. He hated the attention although he accommodated himself to it well.

At six-five he was the first great "big man" in pro basketball. The teams he played for always won. The Celtics were so good that the American Basketball League broke up the team in 1928 to send players to other clubs. For the previous eight years they averaged 120 victories and only 10 losses each season. He was sent to the Cleveland Rosenblums along with other Original Celtics Dutch Dehnert and Pete Barry. Cleveland proceeded to win the World Championship in the 1928–29 and 1929–30 seasons before it folded the next year due to the Depression.

The Celtics reorganized as a barnstorming team and my father played for them with continued success until 1936, when he became coach of St. John's University. In his first tenure at St. John's, his teams won two national championships and he became one of the winningest coaches in the country.

Used to winning, Joe Lapchick became intolerant of losing. His fame on the court increased his time away from home. My mother, Elizabeth, felt abandoned. She began to withdraw emotionally and became a "basketball widow." Wary of the enormous attention given to her husband by the press as well as the local adulation accorded to all famous athletes, she focused her attention on her thirteen-year-old son, Joe, and twelve-year-old daughter, Barbara. Ironically, my father hated the adulation and looked to his home as a refuge from it. Sensing his wife's withdrawal but not realizing why, he felt he was losing in life.

Both parents viewed my birth in 1945 as a way of renewing that life. They lavished love and affection on me. As I grew older and began to sense the importance of the role I was playing, I felt an enormous burden. By the time I was five, my brother and sister were both in college and rarely at home. My parents' love was so great that I could not let them down. When I did, the guilt was tremendous, though it was always self-imposed. Somehow I thought that if I could be a great basketball player I would fulfill their needs. It was a major misreading of those needs.

But such a misreading was understandable. Joe Lapchick had become the coach of the New York Knickerbockers in the early years of the National Basketball Association. The Knicks had been formed in 1946 as part of the Basketball Association of America, which merged with the National Basketball League in 1949 to become the NBA. There were no black faces in either league.

Away from home more than ever with the Knicks, his infrequent moments at home were treasured by me. At age five, I began to be brought to Knick games. In the same year, 1950, he signed Nat "Sweetwater" Clifton, the first black player for the Knicks. Occasionally after the Knick games I would descend into the inner sanctum of the old Madison Square Garden on 50th Street and Eighth Avenue. I actually *knew* Nat, Carl Braun, Harry Gallatin, Vince Boryla, and all the stars. It was a high-altitude world for a five-year-old. I would do anything to be around it and constantly fantasized about being part of it someday.

But still something was wrong. For all the glamour and fame, I saw the turmoil and agony my father went through in thinking about each game before he drove to the Garden. Sometimes I would wake up in the night to see him sitting in the chair in my room or hear him walking through the house. He would later tell the press that he lived a thousand deaths in defeat. Late at night, I saw many of them. I always knew when the Knicks lost.

Something else was causing him anxiety: the "nigger lover" calls. I didn't know what a nigger lover was but I was sure it couldn't be good if so many people disliked him because of it; I did not connect Nat Clifton to the calls. When I was in the locker room, Nat Clifton was "one of the boys." I didn't know that once outside the locker room, he became one of a different set of "boys." What I did see was how each call would eat my father up. My brother and sister were both in college and never knew of this. The only reason I did was because I would unsuspectingly pick up the phone upstairs. In the beginning I would go downstairs to see my father after the calls. He had invariably retreated to the living room and was doubled over in a chair. He never saw me look in and I never said anything to anyone. It was a secret that I shared with him, although he didn't know that I shared it until I was grown up. The confusion was tremendous. As a five-year-old I wondered what awful sin this man had committed to make so many people hate him. He was soft and gentle to me. What must this other side of him be if so many people thought he was so horrible? I didn't really want to know for fear I might hate him too.

Later, when I realized what the calls were about, my feelings of alienation from the racist segment of American society began to grow. My father was hated because he loved. At last this dark burden was lifted from my mind and placed where it had belonged all along—on the fears and hatred that are bred so profusely in America.

But as I was growing up, I left unexamined the traumas my father experienced. I buried the pain of the hate calls. Neighbors and friends told me how I would follow in my father's footsteps.

Christmas and birthdays brought gifts of basketballs, baseballs, baseball mitts, golf balls and clubs. Neighborhood fathers wanted to teach me to shoot, wanted me to play with their kids. As I look back, the draw and power of the sports experience seems even stronger if more bizarre. They were doing this when I was five, six, and seven years old. I felt such pressure from them. I had to be good. The only thing I couldn't understand was why my own father, who would spend endless hours talking to me, going for walks with me, playing word and board games with me, *never* played basketball with me. Never even *talked* about my playing basketball.

My meetings with the Knicks made each time I picked up a basketball a vicarious trip down the Madison Square Garden court. It didn't matter that when I threw the ball up it barely reached the basket, let alone went in. It didn't matter because I was Joe Lapchick's son and I was going to be a star. Everyone knew it, everyone told me. And I believed it.

I was seven and enrolled at the YMCA day camp in Yonkers. We were playing all kinds of sports each day behind Roosevelt

High School where the sessions were held. I was in heaven. However, soon after the camp began I got a high fever and had to stay home. Our family physician, Dr. Ahouse, was out of town so they called a different doctor to see me. Everyone was relieved to be told I had tonsillitis. But when the antibiotics and other medication failed to make me better, Dr. Ahouse came.

A warm, wonderful man, he spent an unusually long time with me and then went into the corner of the room to talk to my parents. I remember hearing my mother say, "Oh, my god!" Dr. Ahouse made some phone calls and an ambulance soon pulled up to our house. With tears in his eyes, my father told me that Dr. Ahouse wanted me to go to Grasslands Hospital where they had special facilities to treat polio. I remember he could hardly say the word as he held me. As sick and half delirious as I was, this moment sealed a bond between us. Captured for the first time was that elusive love that comes from total communication between father and son.

The tests confirmed it was polio. When my brother was allowed to come home from West Point to visit me, I knew the sickness was serious. One day a neighbor visited the hospital with the family. "Do the doctors think he will ever be able to play basketball?" he asked my father. Not if he'll be able to walk, not if he'll be able to lead a normal life, but will he ever be able to play basketball. My father was too polite a man to express the revulsion he felt. I was seven years old. I was not a basketball player, I was a little kid.

I don't think he knew that I heard and saw this happen. The next day he sat by my side and asked me if I wanted to play basketball. I enthusiastically, if naively, said "yes." He told me that all he wanted for me was to have a normal and happy life. He said he had prayed that if God delivered me to him in one piece, that he would nurture me back to health, that he would stop everything else to accomplish it. Subsequently, he gave me years of massages and exercise programs.

I realized for the first time that it was unimportant to him for me to be an athlete. Yet, I knew that now more than ever I wanted to be one. Within a year I had recovered from polio. My father's prayers had been answered. Now I had to make my own prayers come true.

As part of my "rehabilitation," my parents bought me a membership at the Jewish Community Center in Yonkers. At the JCC, I was the tall kid with all the potential. I was always high scorer and leading rebounder on the Comets, a club team. My competition was the likes of John Bonito, Fred Fine, and Alan Carmassin, with whom I remained friends for many years. But none of them played in the NBA, or even in college or high school.

My father was doing more and more things with me now. After Knick games he would take me to Mama Leone's restaurant where he would talk about the game with the press. I recall many evenings there, but one stands out in particular. Still unaware of the significance of Nat Clifton in our lives, I couldn't help but be aware of Jackie Robinson. The national sports press was heavily selling his admission into baseball as an indication that sports was the way out of the ghetto for black athletes; it was to become a widely believed assumption about sport and society. By now I was old enough to take an interest in political discussions at home. I had read about Jackie Robinson. I believed sports was the way out for blacks. The press spoke the truth. I continued to believe this for nearly another decade.

While he never discussed racism in sport, my father freely discussed racism in society. I knew it was something he cared deeply about. The Brown *vs.* the Board of Education Supreme Court decision had sparked a major controversy the previous year (1954) when it called for the integration of public schools. It was a decision warmly greeted by my family.

I was relating to sports and not to politics. Anyway, I had read that they didn't mix. Jackie Robinson was much more real and important to me than the Supreme Court. Therefore, when I had an opportunity to meet him at the Garden one day I jumped at the chance. Some sports writers called him "abrasive" and "aggressive." It was only much later that I realized these were code words for blacks that meant they were "uppity niggers." Jackie Robinson shook my hand and spoke to me for two or three minutes. He was neither abrasive nor aggressive, but kind and thoughtful. At Leone's later that night, a member of the press whose name I've long since forgotten asked his colleague, "Did you see that nigger showboating for the crowd?" The friend nodded his agreement. I was nine years old at the time, and my own sports ambitions soon made me try to put this incident out of my mind. But it stuck with me.

My sports progress was measurable. I was euphoric when in the fifth grade I won the school foul-shooting championship; and the Comets and I were tearing apart the JCC League. I was so happy I barely noticed that my father spent day after day in a malaise called losing. Intensely proud, he was about to resign in mid-season, having heard the rumor he would be fired at the end of the year.

My sports development was so good when measured against my competitors at the Jewish Community Center that I barely noticed that the person I wanted to emulate was bleeding to death under my insensitive nose. Sports was so distorting my values that my career as the high scorer among eleven-year-olds at the Jewish Community Center was more important to me than the lifetime my father had given to the sport.

The next year I went to Hawthorne Junior High School. The only way a lowly seventh-grader could survive was by being a good athlete. The competition was better than at the JCC but still I managed to make the seventh-grade all-star team. We were to play the eighth-grade champions. For the first time my father was coming to see me play. He had been rehired at St. John's, and he was more relaxed and not traveling as much as he did with the Knicks. The day of the game I couldn't eat. The way I played I might as well not have eaten the week before. I was awful. My father was incapable of lying so he didn't say anything. I didn't dare ask.

The 1958–59 season, his third back at St. John's, was expected to be my father's comeback year. He had a good team returning plus a sophomore named Tony Jackson, the first black basketball player at St. John's in a number of years. Tony was a poet with a jump shot, and he was to lead St. John's to the Holiday Festival and National Invitation Tournament championships in that year.

Even so, I would hear in private the innuendos from the press and from some other students at St. John's—Tony was lazy, not very smart, shouldn't really be in college. They didn't mention that more than 150 colleges had tried to obtain his services. It was funny that you didn't hear these remarks about white athletes, although my father learned that some of them rarely if ever attended class—an abuse he and his assistant, Lou Carnesecca, quickly corrected. The misuse of athletes was prevalent almost everywhere in the 1950s and is still the norm at many athletic powerhouses. All of this might have been more important in my mind if St. John's was losing. But winning two championships made it seem less significant at the time.

So I vicariously participated in St. John's success. More important, I grew six inches and became one of the biggest eighth-graders in the New York area. Everyone was predicting I would be six-seven or more. I was good for a slow big man and New York high school coaches were looking at me. I leaned toward Power Memorial High School. I liked the coach, Jack Donohue, and they always had an excellent team.

Everyone in the family pushed me toward Manhattan Prep, which was on the campus of Manhattan College. It had the reputation of a fine academic school and attracted many of New York City's brightest students. I didn't care that much about being a good student. In my own mind I was convinced I would be a very good player. With hindsight, I now realize that *all* ballplayers believe this; even ones who aren't particularly good overestimate their talent.

In trying to prove my ability I was forced to confront racism for the first time. I had made friends with a few of the black ballplayers who tried out for scholarships at Power Memorial. I was drawn to them because they were ignored by the white players when they were lucky; despised and decried when they were not. I think it was at age thirteen that I was, for the first time, embarrassed to be white.

My new friends invited me to their neighborhoods to play that summer. Those neighborhoods, of course, were mostly in Harlem. My white friends from Yonkers told me smart whites didn't go to Harlem. I didn't claim to be smart but I knew I could play good basketball there and that my days with the Comets and Hawthorne Junior High were past.

It *was* good basketball. However, when I visited my friends' apartments I had to contemplate why I lived so comfortably, as did all of my white friends, while they did not. All of my developing friendships in Harlem were with people who had few of the physical comforts I had come to expect.

What was it about this society that prescribed such antithetical conditions for blacks and whites? I was deeply troubled by what I was experiencing during that summer. And then I remembered Jackie Robinson. Sports would surely elevate these talented players out of the ghetto. The only difference now was that I was not sure I still believed in the sports panacea. I wanted to; I needed to; but I was not sure I did.

Having acquiesced to my parents' wishes, I entered Manhattan Prep in the fall of 1959. I was ready to make my mark on New York City basketball. I soon learned that freshmen had to pay their dues and I mainly sat on the bench for a good Manhattan junior varsity team. It was one of the better JVs in the city. I became reconciled to my role as full-time cheerleader, part-time player. It was enough for me to send a game against my would-be school, Power Memorial, into overtime with a jump shot. Small things had to carry me then. But I was full enough of myself to ignore the reality of not playing. To be on the team was "manly." I wasn't a boy anymore. To be on the team meant having dates with girls. The two went together. Sports was making my transition to manhood easier.

Manhattan was not the place for a pure jock; at Manhattan, the real "brains" looked down their noses at me. Not only was I an athlete but the curse was already a generation old in my family. For these preppies, sport was the height of anti-intellectualism and was to be avoided. They did, however, have a good biting sense of humor. As we took the floor at our first home game, they unfurled a banner the length of the court that read, "Nobody can lick our Dick."

I was so carried away with sports that I rebelled when my father decided to send me to Europe in the summer of 1960. I wanted to stay in New York and go back to the city's playgrounds. Culture had no appeal. Finally, my mother reminded me that the Olympic Games would be held in Rome that summer. That convinced me to go.

I began to read books about the Olympic Games. What greater honor than to represent your country? What an important role to be an ambassador of peace and understanding. It all sounded so wonderful, so meaningful. Africans, Asians, and Latin Americans could forget the colonial and imperial roles of Western nations. The U.S.S.R. and the U.S. could meet harmoniously. In 1959 it momentarily looked like both "Chinas" might be in Rome. The Olympic Movement was a force for peace.

Seeing Europe helped to challenge my mind—perhaps for the first time. There were no sports to divert me. I wouldn't have imagined that I would ever want to go to an art museum. By the end of the summer I couldn't stay away. Raised as a Catholic, I avoided churches on days other than Sundays. Traveling throughout Europe, I loved to visit the famous and historic cathedrals. Concerts, operas, historical museums. I rarely thought about sports.

Most important was the time I spent with my sister Barbara and Roy, her first husband. They were living in West Germany and we traveled a great deal together. They treated me, the fourteen-year-old dumb jock, like one of their own intellectual friends. We discussed politics. They told me about a senator from Massachusetts in whom they had a lot of faith. I had barely heard of John Kennedy. We talked about Martin Luther King. My friends in Harlem had told me he was their savior, not Jackie Robinson. We talked about Albert Luthuli, the chief of the Zulus in South Africa.

It was at a friend's apartment that I first listened to the singing of a man with a magnificent voice. I heard about Paul Robeson—all that he had accomplished as an artist, all that he stood for as an activist, and all that he had suffered. I wondered if it could be true. How could I not have heard of Robeson? Why did every European white I met speak of him while no white American I knew did? Blacks in Paris and London seemed to be treated differently from those in the United States. Not understanding then the nature of French and British colonialism, I could not penetrate beneath the surface. I knew that all of the blacks I was seeing could not have been former athletes and entertainers who had made it out of the ghetto. Was Europe a model for America?

I returned to New York on the day school reopened with these thoughts buzzing in my head. I would continue in sports, but now life would have more meaning. I began to tell my teammates about Europe. They were bored. I talked to the girls who hung around the team. They found other things to do. When I talked to the intellectual element, they listened, thinking that perhaps I could be "saved" from the morass of sports. But when they listened, a few teammates and some of the girls began to think I was "weird." "Are you becoming a fag, Rich?" I neither wanted to be saved nor a fag, so I reluctantly focused all my attention on the court again. The reluctance soon disappeared. I was starting on the JV. It was now easy to put aside all that I had absorbed that summer. At the end of the year I was brought up to the varsity along with the other JV starters. I was working hard and I was being rewarded for it. My close friend, Billy Jones, had grown several inches while I had not grown a single inch in two years. Now he was the center and I was the forward—the slow forward. But I could shoot. Also, I was studying more and more and had won the academic scholarship awarded to the three students with the highest scholastic average. My family was very proud. My teammates never even knew.

I was also caught up with my father's team at St. John's. Tony Jackson was a senior now and was playing with Le Roy Ellis at center and Willie Hall at forward. Ellis and Hall were both black. It was probably the most talented college team my father ever coached. They were in the Top Ten all year and at one time were ranked second. They played number-one Ohio State in the finals of the Holiday Festival and lost in the closing minutes. We thought they could win the national championship. They didn't. I actually heard St. John's students asking how could they expect to win with three blacks on the front line?

Far worse than this, the second major college basketball point-shaving scandal was breaking. As a pro coach during the first scandal, my father had put together a scrapbook showing how the lives of athletes involved had been devastated. He made each player at St. John's read this and sign for it to acknowledge he read it before the season began.

It was the time for the St. John's Athletic Awards Banquet. Tony Jackson, as a three-time All-American, was obviously going to get the MVP award. I was going to attend and sit with Le Roy Ellis. Le Roy and I had become good friends. He was six-eleven from Bedford-Stuyvesant, one of the poorest and roughest areas in New York. Sports did bring Le Roy and me together and twenty years later we are still in touch.

But on this day two men from the athletic department came to our house and asked my father to go with them. He walked back into the house alone and went upstairs. I went up after a few minutes to find him staring at a wall, his eyes full of tears.

The New York district attorney advised St. John's not to give Tony Jackson the award as he was "more implicated in the scandal than you can know about." St. John's had agreed and sent their delegation to inform my father. He asked for evidence but was given none. He said he didn't believe it, that it was unfair to Tony since there was no evidence, no proof. Whom was he willing to believe, he was asked, the DA or Tony Jackson, a young man from the streets of New York?

Later I heard St. John's students ask how could Tony Jackson do this to St. John's after it had done so much for him. I heard others say that Jackson had been given the chance to get out of the ghetto but that he had blown it. They had already forgotten that Jackson had led St. John's to three great basketball years and had brought in many new fans. His presence had been partially responsible for Le Roy Ellis enrolling, and he had helped revive interest in college basketball in New York City for the first time since the scandal in 1950. All that seemed to be remembered now was the battle to get Jackson into the school in spite of his low high-school grades; the battle to keep him eligible during his four years at St. John's. All too easily accepted then, it was never proven that Tony Jackson did anything wrong. Tony, a likely NBA star, was blacklisted by the league.

Six years later he was allowed to play for New Jersey in the American Basketball Association where he averaged 19.5 points per game and was one of the league's best shooters. But the fulfillment of Tony Jackson's potential ended that day in 1961. The sports world had made a scapegoat of him, along with Connie Hawkins and Roger Brown, two other black New York players merely "implicated by the DA."

As has become frighteningly obvious over the past three decades, but especially in the 1980s with the scandalous revelations about academic abuses in intercollegiate athletics, the

NCAA is incapable of policing itself, for it is not in its self-interest to do so.

The NCAA protects their property by not asking too many questions. How do athletes stay eligible? Would they graduate after four years? Would they graduate at all?

But when the scandals start to leak out, the question of protecting the athletes is rarely raised. Undeniably, the athletes who actually took money to fix scores cheated. They were wrong and should have been punished. Yet the primary motive for the behavior of many of the athletic establishments was simply to protect themselves. The athletes were back on the streets in almost every case. No surprises. Caught in a sports web of cheating, these athletes took the easy way by joining in the cheating. Just more human tragedy. The reality of the sports world was beginning to sink into me ever so slowly, ever so painfully.

I spent that summer at the Friendship Farm basketball camp just being established by Jack Donohue, the Power Memorial coach. There was a big black kid there who was to begin sophomore year at Power in September. It was the first time I had *lived* with someone who was black. He was shy, sensitive, and very bright. He had difficulty handling the racism of some of the others. As he grew taller throughout the summer, racial barbs became more regular. As he began to dominate, there were no more jokes. But one player "niggered" him to death. I got fed up and intervened. Out of sight of anyone else this player decked me. Ashamed of my fate, I never told Donohue. That particular "nigger" is now known as Kareem Abdul-Jabbar, known then as Lew Alcindor. His baiter is now a head coach at a major university. He probably tells recruits of his "friendship" with Kareem to prove how "with it" he is.

I was getting better and better that summer. Playing not only with Lew, but with four others who eventually started at major colleges, I was averaging 10 points a game for the camp team. My only concern was that I was still five-eleven and was now playing guard. I knew I was slow, but hoped my ability to shoot would compensate. Billy Jones was also there and he was growing and improving.

We both came back to Manhattan that fall with high expectations. His were probably real and mine illusory. We both contracted whooping cough before the season began. Billy recovered in time to make honorable mention All-City. I hardly practiced in the first half of the season and became slower and slower on the court. I started to face the fact that I wouldn't be six-seven, and that being Joe Lapchick's son might not be enough to make me great.

I was spending more and more time with Le Roy Ellis. It was his senior year at St. John's and he was about to embark on a fourteen-year NBA career. Usually we discussed basketball, but sometimes we talked about his life growing up in Bedford-Stuyvesant. Without really knowing it, Le Roy had become my professor of race relations. It meant a great deal to me—and I think to him—when we discussed the poverty he grew up in, the loneliness of being black at an almost all-white school, how hard it was for him to deal with his courses after a poor grounding in fundamentals, and how unfair it had been that Tony Jackson was blacklisted by the NBA. My eyes were being forced open as the 1961–62 basketball season was ending. My personal dream had not quite ended, but my belief in the self-proclaimed verities of sportsworld were being shattered.

My own career seemed to be withering away. Suddenly Manhattan's starting backcourt duo became sick before a game with Cathedral. I had brought Janice, my girlfriend and first true love, to the game so that we could go to a party later. It was her first game. I didn't have time to get nervous when told I would start. I scored 18 points and we won easily. Janice was impressed. So was I.

The next day I went to the Manhattan College trainer because I had injured my foot late in the game. He said, "Coach Connington said you played well last night and he wished you weren't so slow so he could use you more." I knew at that very moment that if my coach said this *after* I scored 18 points, I had no future as a basketball player at Manhattan. Maybe I never really had a future. But now I knew. The funny thing was that it didn't hurt at all. From then on I could play for fun. I came out of the closet as a student and stopped hiding my grades from my teammates.

By 1963 my dreams about sports were dying if not dead. In August, as hundreds of thousands of people marched on Washington, Martin Luther King poetically outlined his own dream. Suddenly my experiences in sport—the important experiences —the nigger-lover calls, the games in Harlem, the experiences with Lew Alcindor, Tony Jackson, and Le Roy Ellis—made King's dream the only dream that mattered to me. Le Roy Ellis, by then a pro with the Lakers, had been the only black man in an all-white sea of humanity at Manhattan's graduation exercises two months earlier.

I was speaking directly to Le Roy and my father when I took the platform as the school's salutatorian. I was supposed to greet the people and say some pleasant things about what our experiences at Manhattan meant to us. I did this, but I also talked about all the work we had to do to make our society well again. I talked about racism and poverty to this relatively affluent white audience. I talked about the responsibility of our generation. Then I took my seat to the polite applause of an otherwise perplexed audience. I looked at Le Roy and my father. They understood. I could go on from there. The basketball dream was dead. Dr. King was about to shape a new dream.

·10·

Stolen Ball

I chose to go to St. John's strictly because I was the last of my father's children. My sister had gone to Barnard and my brother to West Point. I knew that I could go to a school with a better academic reputation than St. John's. But I felt that one of us should go even if it was not among the East's academic elite.

When I arrived at St. John's in September I wondered if I would ever want to pick up a basketball again. I had spent the summer as if I wouldn't, working as a lifeguard at the Tibbetts Brook Park Pool, where my father and brother had also worked many years before. I lifted weights all summer, and I was in the best shape of my life. However, it was not basketball shape. I was a very muscular 190 pounds—almost 20 pounds more than I weighed in my junior year at Manhattan. If I was slow at 170 pounds, I was not anxious to know what I would be like at 190.

I met with Lou Carnesecca. He talked to me as if it was a foregone conclusion that I would play freshman basketball. I think he was being kind, for he definitely knew that I was not going to be able to help *this* freshman team. It had been a great recruiting year. There was Albie Schwartz, a Catholic later to be named to the "Jewish All-American" team, Brian Hill, a smooth ballhandler, Billy Jones, and John Zarzicki, a rough aggressive player in the mold of Jim Luscutoff of the Celtics. They were all very good. But the prizes were twin black towers —Lloyd "Sonny" Dove from St. Francis Prep, and Ed Hill from New Jersey. Both were about six-seven. Lloyd, whose life was to end in a tragic car accident in 1983, was already fluid and proficient at age eighteen. He became an All-American and was named MVP in the College All-Star game as a senior. Ed was raw but as time went on showed perhaps more potential than did Lloyd. With such talent on hand, I realized that Lou was trying to be nice to me. I didn't want to expend all the energy practice would take so I could watch the team from the bench instead of the stands. It did not make any sense.

However, four factors made me decide to play freshman basketball. First, I felt a loyalty to Lou, who was treating me so well. Second, I wanted to be around the team to try to better understand what my father went through every day. He would have little to do with the freshman team, but there would be enough interaction. Third, my withdrawal from playing was not going as well as I had thought it would. I wasn't hooked anymore, but I still liked the taste. Maybe I could have fun playing, since I knew I could not compete with the Doves, Hills, and Jones. Finally, being a basketball player—even a bad basketball player—at St. John's was an ego trip. It was the first time I would be a player at a coed school and players were definitely having more fun—more parties and especially more women. I was insecure around women, and the protective shield of "athlete" became my sliding board into the social world of St. John's.

St. John's was hardly a cauldron of progressive ideas. Thomas Aquinas was its intellectual mentor, while at other universities the shapers were Marx, Engels, Marcuse, and Sartre. Yet even Aquinas was in the shadows. Sports, especially basketball, was the major topic on campus. Being a jock meant being macho. Being white often meant being antiblack. Overtly, there were few signs of racism. "The [black] boys" and their "foxes" had their table in the lounge. At the time I guess this was viewed as full integration. Blacks and whites were marching in the South, fighting for integration. Little Rock, Birmingham, Selma, Montgomery—the capitals of oppression were being transformed into capitals of resistance.

We didn't have to resist at St. John's. Lloyd Dove and Ed Hill were freshmen there. Everyone assumed the other blacks were also athletes. (No one seemed to know that most were pharmacy and science majors.) Athletes were the right kind of blacks—they knew their place—the court, the table, then home. All was neatly laid out for us.

Some of my "friends" were taking me aside to say that others were "pissed off" because I was hanging around with blacks too much. It was one thing to pal around the locker room together, another to go out socially. If sports was helping blacks out of the ghetto, it was not getting them much beyond the locker room.

I decided that my interest had to go beyond empathy. I read John Hope Franklin's *From Slavery to Freedom* about the history of blacks in America, Martin Luther King's *Stride Toward Freedom,* James Baldwin's *The Fire Next Time,* as well as other books on race. I tried to discuss the things I was learning with my friends, but the basketball season was about to begin.

The team was required to spend one and a half to two hours each afternoon in a study hall prior to practice. George Lee was to have been the star of the team. With his academic dismissal the previous year, everyone knew they could not slide by only because they were athletes. However, "gut courses" were still available and many players took them. There were professors who were enthusiastic fans—we quickly got to know who they were. They wouldn't have much to root for if the star flunked out.

Getting by was a process of self-education, of the athletes informing themselves how to "beat the system." I cannot remember hearing about a coach turning athletes in this direction. The coaches, in fact, seemed more serious about academics than the athletes. With all the revelations about academic cheating in the 1980s I now realize that, by comparison, St. John's was far ahead of the field in educating its athletes, even in the 1960s.

Then, it seemed the whole institution was involved in athletics. After all, the administration chose to build the gym before it built the library. St. John's, like many other schools, used its national sports reputation to attract students and broaden its scholastic capabilities. The system was working—while I was there, St. John's became the largest Catholic school in America.

So now the athletes had to produce both in sports and in the classroom. Without the books there would be no sports. Without sports, there would be no more books. Without athletes, there would be no major sports program. It was in everyone's interest, including the athletes, to keep the athletes eligible to play. So athletes found the courses, they found the professors; they reduced their academic load to the minimum; they found friendly students to "help" them in their work; and they did study, at least during the study hall period. All of this was necessary because the pressures were tremendous. I am told that 90 percent of St. John's basketball players who played for four years have graduated since George Lee's expulsion. According to most estimates, that is almost double the national average for major sports programs.

At St. John's I was never aware of the additional factor of alumni pressure to win. Since my father was the coach, I am quite sure I would have seen it. However, I had friends in other colleges, as did teammates and members of the varsity, and we frequently heard stories of handsome payoffs from alumni. At the time, most of the money was apparently being given in the Southern and Midwestern schools. One St. John's player had been offered $10,000 a year to transfer to a relatively small school-on-the-make in the Midwest. There were many such stories. Direct payments, clothes, cars, women, jobs for family members. Anything one could imagine. The press seemed to be ignoring it.

Reading my father's scandal scrapbook, as all of us had to do just at the start of the season, I was frightened. I was angry. I knew whom my teammates had to avoid. As I began to learn more about alumni payoffs, about their "support" for intercollegiate athletics, I wondered about the bookmakers on the streets. They were teaching the same values—get what you can. But the bookmakers were more open about it. They were not acceptable. The alumni were "friends." Spending time at St. John's in the 1980s, I see that the alumni gave no "big money," and thus, have a negligible role in the sports program.

We freshmen were ready to play against the varsity in Alumni Hall. We knew we had a good team and could win. The freshmen, however, never beat the varsity. This night was no exception. Our freshman coach was Jack Kaiser, a fine, intelligent man who is now St. John's athletic director. He was also one of the most successful baseball coaches in the country. His philosophy was that the freshmen team would prepare those who would later play on the varsity. That meant Ed and Brian Hill, Jones, Schwartz, Dove, and possibly Zarzicki. Not Lapchick. But all would play that night.

Playing for just the last ten minutes, I didn't do anything exceptional, but I didn't make any mistakes either. Against the St. John's varsity!

The next morning my father said two short sentences to me. "You did well last night. You made me proud." It was only the second time he had seen me play in a game.

Now I was free. I had made *him* proud. I finally realized that although he had never once put pressure on me to play, and in fact had tried to direct me *away* from basketball, the pressure had always been there simply because he was Joe Lapchick. Unknowingly, I had been waiting for this moment.

The varsity started the year poorly but finished strong with wins over Loyola of Chicago, the number-one ranked team, and New York University, our biggest rival. They had an excellent team and were solid favorites. St. John's built a big lead at halftime and my father literally ran off the court at full speed. The team was shedding its washed-up label. He knew it—the packed crowd knew it. They were on their feet when this sixty-four-year-old lean tower bolted for the exit. The cheering went on long after he and the team had disappeared into the concrete corridors. The second half was an anticlimax. It never was a game and St. John's won by 20 points.

The future was bright. Most members of the varsity were returning. Despite Ed Hill having to leave school for personal reasons, the freshmen lost only once. And there was the prospect that Lew Alcindor, who as a junior was dominating high school basketball, would come to St. John's. With Lew and Lloyd, the national championship would be within St. John's grasp. My father was a happy man.

The summer of 1964 was another turning point for me. The civil rights movement was in high gear and students from the North were heading south to help in the Voter Registration Drive. Spirits were high. The March on Washington had electrified the nation the year before. Martin Luther King was rumored to be the recipient of the Nobel Peace Prize. Students and activists were organizing sit-ins throughout the South. But the Voter Registration Drive had the most potential. The ballot was power.

On June 21, 1964, three civil rights workers—James Chaney, a black man from Mississippi, and Michael Schwerner and Andrew Goodman, both white men from New York, were arrested for speeding in Mississippi. Local police claimed they had released them six hours later. Their burned-out station wagon was soon found without them. It was six weeks before their bodies were discovered, but the nation knew their fate on June 21.

For me, this event dictated that I could no longer simply read about black history. I had to become actively involved. Over and over I read Martin Luther King's "I have a dream" speech. One sentence kept jumping out at me. "With this faith we will be able to work together, to pray together, to struggle together, to go to jail together, to stand up for freedom together, knowing we will be free one day."

I was ashamed. Ashamed to have seen what racism could do and not act to stop it. Ashamed that I had thought of myself as being "free" because my father had told me he was proud of how I played basketball; that he was free because St. John's had beaten NYU. Ashamed that it took the deaths of three contemporaries to sufficiently shake me to see how much I had to learn, how much I had to do.

That summer the police tried to obscure what had happened to Schwerner, Chaney, and Goodman. It took Dr. David Spain, a medical examiner from New York, to ascertain the brutality of their deaths.

In 1964 the work I could do was at best token. I couldn't go to the South—and frankly did not know if I had the courage to do so at the time. I was working seventy-two hours a week as both a lifeguard in Yonkers and as an attendant at the New York World's Fair. With little time to myself, I went to Long Island or Westchester three nights a week to collect newspapers that could be recycled to raise money. The money was then sent to help with transportation costs in voter registration projects.

My job as a lifeguard was helping to crystallize my vision of racism in the North. All we read about was what was going on in the South. However, the Yonkersites who were condemning the civil rights murders were also complaining that too many people from the Bronx were coming to swim at Tibbetts Brook Park where I worked. The "too many people from the Bronx" was code for "too many blacks." Disdainful of the blacks earlier in the summer, the white bathers were more respectful after a serious riot in Harlem. Fear bred respect. It was a lesson not lost on any of us. March, sing, parade, and demonstrate—do that all you want and get few changes. But destroy property— and suddenly whites began moving out of your way. Suddenly whites were being taunted and were taking it just like blacks had to for centuries. You could see it at the pool. You could see it in the streets. You could feel it in the movement. The movement was nationwide.

My sister was talking about leaving for Africa, which she did in November 1964. I knew very little about Africa then. The few references to it in textbooks and in high school were to the slave trade and the colonization of Africa, then equated to Europe's efforts to "civilize" and "Christianize" the dark and demonic continent. South Africa—Christian, civilized, indus- trialized, and rich—was portrayed as the hope of the continent. That summer I didn't quite understand why this great hope was being suspended from the 1964 Tokyo Olympics. If they were Christian, civilized, industrialized, and rich, then why shouldn't they play? The press condemned the decision, argu- ing that it was wrong to "mix politics and sport." Most stories explained why. Generally one paragraph near the end referred to the fact that South Africa was expelled because some nations, led by the Communists, felt that it was a racist country. My curiosity was aroused and I began to read about South Africa. The fact that my sister moved to Africa increased my desire to learn more and more. It was in the realm of sports that my education about apartheid had its origin. Many years later I would remember that and try to use it to educate others.

Our family was turned inside out in a matter of hours after my father's annual trip to St. John's to sign his contract. He had always signed one-year contracts. St. John's had been good to him. It had hired him in the 1930s when his playing career was ending. He always said he didn't even know *how* to coach then. And it had rehired him when he resigned from the Knicks. St. John's was about to pay him $12,500 for the 1964–65 season! Yes, St. John's was family. He loved the game and St. John's for letting him play it. But they stole the ball that day.

What he wanted to do most was to help lead it to a National Collegiate Athletic Association (NCAA) title—the national championship. He wanted to give this to his school before retiring. He knew it could be done if he could recruit Lew Alcindor that year. He liked Lew personally very much. Joe Lapchick, the first great big man in basketball, knew what Lew was going through. I counted Lew among my friends. It would be great to see Lloyd and Lew on the same team. There would be no stopping them.

As he was signing the contract, Father Graham, the athletic moderator, said something like, "Joe, we've been proud of our association with you. You've made a great contribution to the school. We hope that your final year will be a great one." He assumed his final year with Alcindor. Of course, it would be a great one. Then they explained to him—for the very first time —that St. John's had set mandatory retirement at sixty-five. Joe Lapchick was devastated.

When I left him in the morning he was buoyant. When I saw him that night he was a defeated and lonely man. I told him we could fight this through the student body. He said no, a rule was a rule. If it had validity, then exceptions should not be made. He called my brother, Joe, who was superintendent of schools in Aspen, Colorado. He told my father that, in general, it was a good rule; in Graham's position, my brother would have done the same thing. For every great teacher over sixty-five there were ten bad ones. Sacrifices had to be made. He only wished it wasn't my father. It was the midnight of my father's life. The man who had spent a significant part of his life fighting for others would not now fight for himself.

He convinced me at the time he was right. The word spread

quickly on campus. I remember Lynn Burke, the Olympic champion turned St. John's cheerleader, coming up to me. She was very upset and wanted to do something. Everyone wanted to do something. Protest at St. John's had not been a major activity. I was pleased to see it might be a possibility. On that day, however, I told Lynn that it would upset my father.

Jack Donohue, the coach of Power Memorial High School, and more importantly, the coach of Lew Alcindor, came over to our house that night. He was an outgoing man with a good sense of humor. But that night he was very serious. I had never before seen him like that. He wanted to talk to my father alone. I had never before been excluded. Something had to be very wrong.

Jack Donohue had been asked if he would be interested in being the assistant basketball coach at St. John's. When Lou Carnesecca joined the staff in the 1958–59 season, my father and the athletic department promised him the head coaching job when my father retired. That job had been taken. Jack as assistant coach? St. John's was a powerhouse again. He could move from there into a good head coaching position. Why was he so serious? This effusive man was so timid. Why? At first, my father couldn't understand it. Suddenly, he couldn't miss it.

He asked Jack if St. John's mentioned Lew Alcindor when they brought up the subject of the job. Yes, they had. What a scenario. One of the most renowned figures in the history of sport, the last of the "pioneers" still coaching, was to be mandatorily retired to make room for this high school coach to become an assistant coach. Lew Alcindor would come with Jack. Joe Lapchick would go home with a $100-a-month pension.

It didn't even make sense. First of all, Jack idolized my father. That is why he was so timid that night. I don't think he would have seriously considered the job because of the pain the circumstances would cause my father. Second, even if he would have considered it, St. John's had offered him several thousand dollars less than he was making at Power Memorial. You didn't have to be a wizard with business figures to know that this did not make sense.

Most importantly, St. John's knew my father had a good relationship with Lew Alcindor and with Jack. Maybe they could have considered hiring Jack as an assistant in addition to Lou. Perhaps that would reinforce any decision by Alcindor to come to St. John's.

What they didn't know and what no one knew except Lew himself, was that Lew Alcindor didn't trust Jack Donohue. As Lew related it in a story in *Sports Illustrated,* Jack had told him he was "acting just like a nigger" at the halftime of one game. For Lew, that was the end of Jack. Jack explained that he was only trying to stir him up to get him to play more aggressively; that he had no racial intention. But for Lew, that was the end of Jack.

When I read this, I wondered how many good players had been destroyed by unthinking statements made in the heat of combat by unthinking coaches. Alcindor was strong and could overcome it. How many didn't?

Many years later, Lew Alcindor, now Kareem Abdul-Jabbar, talked about the possibility of being traded from the Milwaukee Bucks to the New York Knicks. Peter Vescey, a reporter for the New York *Sunday News,* asked Kareem why he wanted to return to New York after he had chosen to leave it for UCLA in 1965. He replied:

> I will say that the only reason I left New York was because Joe Lapchick was forced into retirement at age sixty-five. I wanted to play for St. John's and Mr. Lapchick but for whatever reason he was squeezed out.
>
> I really liked the man and I found I could relate to him as a human being. I used to see him during the summers at camps and he'd never pressure me in any way.
>
> I remember he'd tell me stories about when he was

young and the people in his neighborhood used to gawk
as this tall, skinny kid passed by. They'd call him the
gypsy. He went through the same things I went through
a generation before.

My father had been dead for several years. He didn't know
this. Nor did he know that exceptions to the mandatory retirement rule were made after he left. Maybe St. John's finally
recognized the cruel effects of the rule. Maybe it was merely the
fact that there was nothing to be gained by invoking it.

I could not sleep that night. It was still a month before
practice began, but that night my vision was of a packed Madison Square Garden. St. John's had just won their fourth NIT
championship and my father was being lifted on the shoulders
of a sea of humanity. What a glorious sight. But it was only a
vision.

Without any encouragement from my father, mild protests
took place on campus over his retirement. There was a petition,
a couple of rallies. Lloyd Dove took the podium at a rally on
academic problems at St. John's. He talked about the injustice
of my father's situation. He talked about how much more Joe
Lapchick had to give to St. John's. He asked "if the administration could do this to the best-known person on campus, what
could it do to others?" I will never forget Lloyd for that. Not
only was he a ballplayer—and athletes never dared to challenge
the system in those days—but he was a black ballplayer. It took
great courage. Yet, I will also never forget the reaction of some
in the audience. No comments had been made after any of the
white speakers sat down. But when Lloyd finished, I heard a
group of students saying how disloyal he was to St. John's;
several commented on his inarticulateness. This "boy" belonged on the court, not at a protest rally.

Without my father's encouragement, the protests had no
force. The opening of his last season ended the students' rebel-
lion but initiated my father's own form of silent protest. He was

coaching his heart out, and it almost gave way. Unknown to anyone but his physician and myself, he had two mild heart attacks during games that season. But he couldn't be stopped.

St. John's got off to a great start, including a 75–74 comeback victory over number-one ranked Michigan in the Holiday Festival final. After the tournament each game on the road meant a farewell ceremony for my father. They were all very touching. They were also very frequently followed by a loss. My father attributed the losses, at least in part, to the ceremonies. How could the team fight hard against a school that was being so nice to the coach?

Fortunately, there were no ceremonies in Madison Square Garden during the NIT. St. John's was seeded next to last, yet won the first three games.

St. John's played top-seeded Villanova for the championship, and beat them. For the team, for the crowd, for all New York, it seemed like Joe Lapchick's final game was a crusade. My vision had become reality. Joe Lapchick was riding that sea of humanity. The Garden was in pandemonium. It was the proudest moment of my life. Half of the people must have been in tears. The headline in the next day's *New York Post* was "Joe Lapchick Walks with Kings." He always had. Within a few months he had turned his dismissal from sports into a moment of pure joy, and his tears into his triumph.

Before the end of the season he had been discussing other coaching jobs. He had one offer from the pros and another from the college ranks. I think he probably would have accepted one if he hadn't won that day. But the win simply made him say, "What a way to go!" His intense pride had almost killed him that season, but the victory had made the pain worthwhile.

· 11 ·

Inside Out

My last two year's at St. John's were ones of increasing political
and intellectual awareness. It was a time when the Vietnam
War and the racial situation in America were crying out for
change. At Berkeley I would have been a moderate. At St.
John's I was a radical. In the real world, I was probably a
liberal.

The irony of my father's mandatory retirement was that I
was able to have much more time with him. We would sit and
talk late into the night. He wanted to know what I thought
about the Vietnam War. For him, the war might have meant
losing me and that was enough for him to be against it. The
geopolitical situation was not the issue. He didn't want me to
fight. We watched Muhammad Ali "debate" William Buckley.
At the time they were saying Ali was mentally incompetent but
that program showed how bright Ali really was. When he was
reclassified by his draft board, Ali said, "I ain't got no quarrel
with them Viet Cong." In my senior year of college I was the
sports columnist for the *Torch,* the school newspaper. I wrote
of Ali's courage to stand up for what he believed. My father
thought it was the best thing I had written. White students told

me it was scandalous, unpatriotic; I was mixing politics and sports. Black students said thanks.

We both read and discussed the *Autobiography of Malcolm X* that spring. My father had always disliked Malcolm X while he was alive, believing the press portrayals of him as a violent, white-hating man. The book was a revelation for both of us. Martin Luther King was still the sun, but Malcolm had become a respectable, if distant, star. We were learning together.

In my last year at St. John's I was physically there but felt emotionally removed from it. I shared an apartment with Vincent Ferrandino, probably the most serious and, perhaps, the brightest student I knew at St. John's.

During this time I spent many evenings with Lloyd Dove. We had seen a good deal of each other that year. He was having a great season, leading St. John's to a 23–5 record and an NCAA bid. Lloyd was intelligent and sensitive. He was considered quiet and shy by most students, but this may have been because they were whites viewing a black man in an all-white environment. I had quite a few opportunities to be with him and his black friends, and among them he was a different man.

One evening Lloyd and I went to hear some jazz in Greenwich Village. It was 2:00 A.M. before we headed back to Long Island, and we were both a bit high. I asked him to stay over at my apartment. For twenty minutes he thought of every possible excuse not to. I asked what was really wrong. It was difficult for him to answer, but he finally blurted out that he had never slept at a white person's house before.

Lloyd Dove, sophisticated, intelligent, handsome, All-American Lloyd Dove had never spent the night at a white person's house and, when finally faced with the choice, was apprehensive. I cringed. During my four years at St. John's, I had spent some of my best moments with Dove—double-dating, drinking, listening to music, discussing racism, and sharing feelings. Looking back I think I would rather have been with him than anyone else on campus. Yet here was the bottom line

—he was black and I was white. Because of that difference, Lloyd was apprehensive about staying with me.

As on previous occasions, my consciousness of being white swept over me. No matter how close we had become, Lloyd couldn't forget that I was white and, therefore, a possible racist. I am convinced he didn't believe I was, but there was that hesitation—a self-protective internal mechanism telling black people not to trust white people, not to let the defenses down. I was stunned, and hurt, but in the silence that dominated the end of the ride, the world became more clear to me. That world saw this black man as a jock. As long as he remained a jock, it was color blind. Off court, whether at a white social gathering or at a protest supporting Joe Lapchick, he was invisible. Ralph Ellison, the author of *Invisible Man,* was right.

In the quiet of the car I decided that knowing, studying, and raising money for good causes was not enough. There was too much at stake. I didn't know *what* I would do or *how* I would do it, but I knew then that a major part of my life would be devoted to actively searching for ways to change society. My brother insisted that I was a naive dreamer. Although we were miles apart politically, I had to wonder if he was right.

Lloyd stayed at my apartment that night. We consumed a few more drinks and fell asleep in our clothes at about 8:00 A.M. Poor Vincent. I am sure he must have thought we had had a wild night when he found our bodies strewn about the living room in the morning.

I went home so I could discuss the previous evening with my father. He was sympathetic but not surprised. He mentioned a friend named Bob Douglas whom he knew from his days with the Celtics. They had shared a similar conversation in the late 1940s. Appraising my needs that night, he told me to study— to prepare myself for whatever path I would choose.

Joe and Elizabeth Lapchick had just faced a severe test. Both were Catholics—my mother was devout. Thus it was difficult for them in 1966 when my sister, Barbara, announced that she was divorcing Roy, her Jewish husband.

But the true test came when Barbara introduced her new husband-to-be, Rajat Neogy, a prominent Ugandan literary figure whose parents were Indian. I have known innumerable "liberals" who have balked at sexual relations between the races. For them, any form of integration was positive as long as that sexual boundary was not crossed.

As well as I knew my parents, I did not know how they would react. My father and I watched the sunrise as we talked about Barbara and Rajat. In 1966, such a relationship was virtually unheard of in polite middle-class white society. Then we reached the bottom line. He asked me if Barbara loved Rajat and if they were happy together. I said it seemed so. "Then that's all that should matter," he said. My mother had already given her blessing.

Bill Russell's book *Go Up for Glory* was published in 1966 as Russell's fabulous career with the Boston Celtics was in its final quarter. He would still help the Celtics win more championships, and he had already been a member of the Olympic team and participated in two NCAA championships as a collegian at the University of San Francisco. His Celtics teams won the NBA championships in nine of his first ten years and he was chosen the most valuable player four times by fellow players. He had done everything right in basketball. He should have been lionized.

He should have been—but Bill Russell was black, outspoken, and intimidating. *Go Up for Glory* was, perhaps, one of the first honest sports stories, and these were difficult times to be honest. Protest against the war was threatening all the "yes, sir" people in society, yet Russell criticized America's "yes, sir" mentality. Blacks were rioting in city after city. Respectable black leaders were supposed to calm the waters. Russell wrote about hav-

ing to confront the conditions that had caused the riots. He
wrote:

> The relationship between the white and the Negro is most
> often represented by the police—the symbol of authority
> . . . most Negroes look on the police as the white man with
> a badge, the symbol of the white man's authority. The
> policeman becomes a natural enemy. . . .
> But it is the people—the whites and the Negroes—who
> inhabit the battleground day after day and night after
> night who are the true warriors. Their voices must be
> heard.

Russell also tackled the sports empire. He told story after
story of racism, of quotas in the NBA, of racist fans, players,
and coaches. He even discussed the humiliating segregation of
the U.S. team's domestic tour prior to the 1956 Games:

> It was a hurting thing. Not desperate. We were men. We
> had experienced it before. But . . . it was another scar,
> another slice. We were representing our nation in the
> largest sports event in the world. But in our own country
> we were not equals as citizens.

My father and I both read Russell's book early in 1967, and
when I had finished, I told him—for the first time—about
listening on the upstairs phone when he was receiving the "nigger lover" calls. I told him that I had been frightened for him;
that I had been afraid to ask him for fear that I would also hate
him if I knew his terrible secret. I informed him of how many
times I had been called a "nigger lover" for befriending blacks.
There was a spontaneous yet enormous emotional release. We
wept and embraced each other with a powerful interchange of
emotion. We both accepted the relief of relinquishing our
shared secret. No words passed between us. We understood
each other's pain.

The publication of Russell's book was followed by a public outcry. Critics said that he was only able to write the book because of basketball; he was another ungrateful black man. Russell withstood the attack and grew stronger. But he was, in reality, lucky. If K. C. Jones, for example, a black teammate of Russell's on the Celtics, had written that book he might never have played again. Russell was just too good; the NBA could not afford to dump him. Sports was supposed to be the great equalizer for blacks. Now it was being described as a racist reflection of a racist society.

My father, for the first time, began to open up about his own racial experiences in sport. The Tony Jackson case bothered him more than any other. He mentioned the early days in the NBA, and the signing of Clifton. But it was when he recalled the all-black "Renaissance Five" (commonly called the Rens) that I became most interested. All my life I had heard that the Original Celtics were the greatest team of all time. Now he told me that the Rens were as good as the Celtics by the early 1930s. What had happened to historical accuracy? This was new information for me.

My father admitted that he knew nothing about black people let alone black athletes prior to his contacts with the Rens. Raised in an immigrant family, he had all the apprehensions about competition from blacks shared by other immigrants early in the twentieth century.

The difference was that he was able to have years of contact with the Rens. They played against each other, traveled to the same cities, competed in front of crowds ready to attack these audacious barnstormers, and finally confronted the stereotypes that each held about the other. At first, the Rens couldn't fully trust the Celtics while the Celtics couldn't fully understand the Rens. Time changed that. However, time moved slowly.

All the Celtics knew was that the Rens could play them even, yet they saw the differences in lifestyle. The Rens traveled in a large bus purchased by Bob Douglas, their founder-owner, so that they could avoid confrontations in hotels, restaurants, trains, and public buses that wouldn't allow blacks. There were some towns where they couldn't be seen by day. They couldn't eat, wash, or even purchase gas in some places. When they could find hotels that would take them, they were usually bug-ridden. On the court they faced hostile white fans, yet they played the game straight and with dignity.

Joe Lapchick found it impossible to even share a drink with Douglas in some places. They integrated arenas in several cities, most notably by playing the first interracial game in the South, but they couldn't socialize together outside of New York and a very few other cities.

For years my father was oblivious to racial slights. He finally asked Bob Douglas about them in New York during the off-season. Douglas replied, "Joe, I can't go where you can go. I'm not going to subject myself to rejection and humiliation." They talked for hours that day and my father realized that previously, in spite of admiring the Rens for years, he had never really learned anything personal about them or about Douglas. It had shocked him that, perhaps subconsciously, he had chosen to ignore the racism around him. My father told me that the talk with Douglas was pivotal in his life—a life he vowed to change.

I had been accepted into a masters program in African Studies at the University of East Africa in Uganda. That is where I wanted to go, but I didn't want to leave the country for long because of my father's health. I chose instead to enroll at the graduate school of international studies at the University of Denver, where I would major in African Studies. However, Barbara and her new husband invited me to come to Uganda at least for the summer. I hoped that visiting Barbara and studying even briefly at the University of East Africa would show me how to proceed with my life. It only showed me how much I had to learn.

This was Uganda prior to Amin. 1967 was a beautiful time to be there. Barbara ran the Nommo Art Gallery and Rajat was editor of *Transition,* an influential literary magazine. Both the gallery and the magazine were showplaces for talented Africans, so I was exposed to a wealth of African art and literature. Sitting in their house and listening to Rajat, Barbara, and their guests was a living classroom on Africa. Kampala was an intellectual capital and it seemed as though I met every important African writer and scholar that summer. It makes me ill to think of what Idi Amin did to this beautiful and rich land.

While I had countless extraordinary experiences, two above all have stayed with me. The first related to sports. I hadn't played basketball in two years yet I was drawn to a tucked-away court on the university campus. I was able to talk to the African students in the classroom but outside I was a social outcast. I was not only white, but a white American. Not only racist, but also colonialist. This wasn't a problem with Rajat's friends, but it was with the students. They had seen too many patronizing Westerners who wanted to "help the natives."

I watched the Africans play basketball, day after day in the melting sun. Bad as I was, I knew I was better than the players I was seeing. After all, I had trained for fifteen years while they were obviously newcomers. I had vowed to stay away from sports a few months before, but I was so frustrated by the alienation I was feeling on campus that I had to play. I hated being stereotyped.

What irony! Here I was almost on the equator in blazing heat. Now I was the white man trying to break into African society by playing basketball. It seemed ridiculous but I was desperate. It worked. We played together. We drank beer together. We talked sports and, here in Uganda, sports really did open a door, at least for me.

The second thing I brought home was the African students' perceptions of black Americans. Black pride was rising in urban American cities. Part of that pride was a cultural identification with Africa and Africans. I quickly learned that in June 1967 it was not a two-way flow. I was abruptly stopped the first time I naively referred to an African as "black." "We are not blacks, we are Africans. Blacks are Americans." I was surprised and taken aback. They did not identify with American blacks at all. In fact, the students criticized black Americans for allowing their oppression to continue. It seemed that they felt African independence movements could be analogous to a black revolution in the United States. I disagreed with their analysis just as I would disagree with Andrew Young ten years later when he tried to compare the civil rights movement in America with the struggle against apartheid in South Africa. I unsuccessfully tried to explain the difference in the situations. What was important was not that I disagreed but that this *was* their analysis.

Perceptions changed one July morning. "Black revolt in Detroit" was the headline in *The People,* a Ugandan newspaper. Racial outbursts, large and small, had spread through urban America in the middle sixties. But Detroit was the bloodiest—41 dead and 347 injured—and costliest in terms of property. There was $500 million worth of damage. Some 5,000 inner-city residents were homeless. But what was most meaningful for the African students was that there were 3,800 arrests.

They believed that this was the start of a black revolt, a black American independence movement. The first American magazines to reach Kampala called it a riot—spontaneous and unplanned. The students didn't believe it for a second. American blacks, they felt, were taking control of their destiny.

We spent much of that summer dissecting Detroit and its aftermath. What was nonviolence? When did a riot become a revolt? What was the future of revolt and what were its consequences? Whatever the nature of the conflict, it was apparent that, once again, violence in America was leading to social change. The men who ruled America could listen to Martin Luther King, applaud and go to their white suburbs and forget. They could not ignore a Detroit and would rush to take prompt action to quell the riot/revolt. White Americans seemed seized by fear of a reign of terror; black Americans, to their African brothers, seemed equally seized by a vision.

I left Africa and arrived in Denver still searching for ways to participate, ways to contribute. I marched in all the antiwar demonstrations but knew there had to be more. I was away from St. John's, away from sports. The academic demands were enormous. I was reading five to seven books a week on subjects such as international economics, African studies, political ideologies. I met Sandy on my first day there. She was a graduate student in art, an apolitical woman and a tonic to my deadly serious, highly competitive, very political fellow students. She helped keep me sane.

Professors began to give me direction. George Shepherd taught African Studies; Ron Krieger trained us in international economics; Steve Hunter interpreted diplomatic history. All three were political activists in the antiwar and civil rights movements. They demonstrated that one could be an academic activist. That seemed to be what I should do—teach, work with my students to get them involved, and be an activist myself. All seemed to be settled by the third quarter. I was confident as a student and, for the first time in my life, had a concrete concept of what I would do. Additionally, Sandy and I decided to get married in June.

Then one April evening my confidence crumbled. Martin Luther King was assassinated in Memphis. I was all at once filled with sorrow, fear, and rage. I called home for comfort, but there was none. It was a weepy conversation. The apostle of nonviolence, armed only with moral courage, had met—inevitably, perhaps—violent death. As inner city after inner city erupted, I began to see that revolt just might be underway. I feared for the U.S. for I believed that sustained violent revolt by black America could lead to only one thing—massive retaliatory repression against blacks.

Mostly, I hated America—that is, white America. For King,

the philosophy of nonviolence could only be effective if it pricked the conscience of a moral society. This society seemed to have no conscience and it certainly was not moral. In Asia, we were killing Vietnamese by the thousands to save them from Communism. In Memphis, we had killed a black leader trying to make things better for his people. I wanted to get out. By midnight I decided I would leave the country and join Barbara and Rajat in Uganda. I told Sandy. Always the optimist—at times, annoyingly so—she said I had to stay. "If all those who aren't racist leave, who will be left? You can afford to go to Africa, get your degree there and work. You can do this *because* you are white and have the money. Most blacks in Denver or New York cannot pack up and leave." She made her point.

By 4:00 A.M., I decided to stay and fight. By eight in the morning I had written to Wilt Chamberlain, then playing for Philadelphia, LeRoy Ellis, who was playing for Baltimore, and a host of other professional basketball players whom I knew. I wrote to Jim Brown, the great football player and social activist. I wrote to Coretta King. The idea that I was proposing was to form an organization called PRIDE that would help to introduce black and African history and culture courses into the curricula of high schools around the country. While the time for the idea was ripe, I did not expect a serious response. Then Wilt and LeRoy endorsed the idea. Brown, through John Wooten, his associate, wanted to meet me in Cleveland. I began to see the potential linkup between sports and politics at close range. With the athletes' endorsements, I was able to get Walter Mondale, Jacob Javits, and Hugh Scott, then Senate minority leader, to join PRIDE's advisory board.

That year saw several other linkups between sports and politics. It had been announced in November 1967 that a number of black athletes would boycott the 1968 Mexico City Olympics to protest racism in American society. The efforts were being organized by Harry Edwards, a former athlete then teaching at

San Jose State. Harry, along with Jack Scott, was to become one of the major shapers of the oncoming athletic revolt.

In February 1968, South Africa was readmitted to the Olympics when the International Olympic Committee (IOC) met in Grenoble, France. The reaction was instantaneous. All African nations except Malawi announced they would boycott. They were joined by most developing countries from Asia and some from Latin America. The Socialist nations threatened to pull out. With the potential for racial violence already illustrated by the assassination of Martin Luther King and an attack on IOC President Avery Brundage's hotel in Chicago by blacks, the IOC voted South Africa out again in April.

In both cases, the media criticized the attempts to mix sports and politics. It gave extensive coverage to black athletes like Jesse Owens, who opposed the boycott, and to Brundage, who continued to insist that politics had no influence on the IOC's decision to bar South Africa. Once again, I felt, the press had saved sportsworld from recognizing what it had become.

I returned to New York at the end of May to prepare for our wedding. Most of the daily discussions were of what Sandy and I would do in the future and about PRIDE. After my New York friends had a bachelor party for me I arrived at our house in Yonkers weary from too much to drink. The phone rang late that night. It was Sandy. "Did you hear?" I thought she said "did you hear me" and I joked that I was too hung-over to hear anything. "Robert Kennedy was shot last night in California." Suddenly sober, my body became rigid, my mind became numb. I couldn't believe it.

At the time I was an RFK supporter and thought he was our best hope for real change in America. We had recently met on his campaign stop in Cheyenne, Wyoming. We briefly discussed PRIDE, the concept of which had been endorsed by all the presidential candidates except Nixon. He told me how much he admired my father and wished me luck. I could still feel his firm, reassuring handshake.

I went in to turn on the TV. My father had been keeping a vigil all night. We both broke down in tears. For him RFK was the hope to end the war, to heal the cities, to bring peace to the world and to the country. It was too much to take. When would it all end?

I tried to postpone the wedding date. Not only was it scheduled for the night Kennedy was to be buried, but it was to be held in Rockville, Maryland, just outside Washington. Tent City and the Poor People's March were in Washington. Kennedy would be buried in Arlington. How could we "celebrate" our wedding? But Sandy's parents insisted that the wedding be held as planned, and I acquiesced.

Sandy and I were married in St. Elizabeth's Church. My mother, Elizabeth, liked that. It was about all she liked. Because of our Jewish-Catholic marriage, we found a progressive priest, Bill Talentino. No rabbi would participate. Sandy and I wrote our own ceremony so our Jewish friends wouldn't be offended by an overly Christian emphasis. My good friend, Peter Birdsall, sang folk songs—an uncommon thing for a wedding in 1968. We asked Father Talentino to have his homily focus on Kennedy as a memorial service. Bill, who has remained an inspiration and a lifelong friend, was certainly inspirational that evening. I was very tense and emotional because of what was going on around us. We were seated facing our friends in the church. There I was in a white tuxedo. I started to sob and pulled out an enormous blue bandana handkerchief to blow my nose. Sandy cracked up. I smiled and the somber mood was broken.

We planned to begin our honeymoon in Cleveland. I was to meet Mayor Stokes, Jim Brown, and John Wooten on Monday morning at the offices of the Negro Economic Union, which had been cofounded by Brown and Wooten. But Stokes remained in Washington after Kennedy's funeral and Jim Brown was in Los Angeles. So Wooten and I met to talk about what the Negro Economic Union was doing and what PRIDE hoped to do. We felt that Cleveland might become a test city for the introduction of black history and culture courses in the schools.

Aside from the business aspects of the meeting, I left with a real understanding of the faith of a large part of the black community in the Kennedys. John Wooten, a serious, astute man, talked about looking forward to the Kennedy children growing up and entering politics. In 1968, it seemed like a long time for the black community to have to wait. The black community is still waiting.

Whether it was inspired by or fearfully reacting to the potential of a black Olympic boycott, *Sports Illustrated* published a five-part series by Jack Olsen called "The Black Athlete: A Shameful Story" in July (discussed in detail in Chapter 13). It was the first investigative report I had read on how pervasive racism was in professional and intercollegiate athletics. It confirmed all that I had come to believe about the nature of sports in America, and seemed to add fuel to the controversy about any black role in the Olympics.

Lew Alcindor, along with UCLA teammates Mike Warren and Lucius Allen, had already boycotted the Olympic basketball trials. Up to that point I had not known what to think about the idea of a boycott. However, I respected Lew's judgment enough that I began to support the idea. My father strongly disagreed with me on this, although paradoxically he respected Lew Alcindor more than ever for his decision. He knew it was a decision based on principle and my father thought Lew had made a courageous personal sacrifice.

I watched part of the Olympic Games with my father in New York. Any illusions I had had about the Olympics had been destroyed a long time ago. The pre-Olympic "ceremonies" in Mexico City included a three-day student riot in which thirteen were killed and hundreds more injured. Striking students claimed that the incredibly high cost of staging the games was a national disgrace.

While the boycott itself had been called off, everyone knew

something would happen. The goals of a total boycott were expressed in the simple gesture of two young black men. When Tommie Smith and John Carlos raised their clenched, black-gloved fists on the victory stand, they eloquently expressed what white America had tried to ignore: sport, like society, was racist.

The importance of that gesture became evident in the ensuing reaction. White society was quick to punish Smith and Carlos immediately in Mexico and for many years after as both became unemployable. The sports establishment, from Avery Brundage on down, did everything it could to pretend nothing had changed. In response to a question about how the Olympics could survive as long as politics continued to become more and more a part of the games, Brundage replied, "Who said that politics are becoming more and more involved in the Olympics? In my opinion this is not so. You know very well that politics are not allowed in the Olympic Games."

However, that memory of Smith and Carlos on the victory stand would not go away. It became *the* Olympic picture. Everything had changed. Black athletes were vigorously speaking out. And my father, initially spurred on by Bill Russell's writings, resumed telling me of the forms of hate he had encountered in sports because of his racial views.

For my father, his participation in the integration of the NBA held the most meaning. The door seemed open to integration after the 1947–48 season in the Basketball Association of America (BAA). It was a time of great hope for Bob Douglas and the Rens—a hope spurred on by the hiring of my father as coach of the New York Knicks.

Most importantly, Jackie Robinson had already broken the color barrier by quickly becoming a big star for the Brooklyn Dodgers. The integration of baseball had to make it easier for basketball. Furthermore, the BAA had franchises in cities with large black populations like New York, Boston, Philadelphia, Washington, St. Louis, Detroit, Chicago, and Pittsburgh. Walter Brown was running the Boston franchise and Ned Irish was boss in New York. Both had the guts and foresight to know that blacks had to be admitted into the league.

With Robinson and other blacks established in major league baseball, with boxing long since integrated, and with Lapchick a sure advocate in the BAA's most important franchise, Douglas was most optimistic about the future.

He was informed that the owners of the league teams were going to meet in Philadelphia to discuss admitting the Rens to the then lily-white league. It seemed that the day had finally come when the barriers would fall.

Douglas expected opposition and indeed several owners spoke up to say that the league was in good enough shape without the Rens. Douglas told *Sports Illustrated*'s Bruce Newman, "Joe Lapchick, who was with the Knickerbockers, got up in front of his boss, Ned Irish and said, 'I may lose my job for saying this, but I'd play against the Rens any goddamn day. To me, they're the best.' "

Douglas was asked to leave the room when the vote was taken. The proposal to admit the Rens failed. Emotionally scarred, Bob Douglas was convinced that the door might be forever closed to blacks in the game he loved.

My father considered resigning from the Knicks, but was convinced by others, including Douglas, that it would serve no purpose. On the contrary, Douglas believed that my father could be instrumental in breaking down the color barrier.

The BAA merged with the National Basketball League before the 1949–50 season to form today's NBA. By the next season, the NBA was represented only by major cities having big-league arenas.

The time had finally come. Walter Brown had hired Red Auerbach in Boston. Irish and my father were already in New York. And Brown drafted Chuck Cooper from Duquesne University; Lapchick convinced Irish to sign Nat "Sweetwater" Clifton from the Globetrotters roster. The door had finally been opened. Somehow Douglas had known that Lapchick would be there when it happened.

My father's telling of this story—far more complicated than I have intimated here—was abruptly interrupted by the news that my sister's husband, Rajat Neogy, had been sent to Luzira Prison in Uganda. The date was October 18, two days after the Smith-Carlos raised fist salute. We could no longer think about the Olympics, the Rens-Celtics sagas, or about the integration of the NBA.

Rajat had been charged with sedition. The charge stemmed from his printing a letter to the editor in *Transition,* the magazine he edited, that said that Uganda should Africanize the courts, that is, that the judges should be Africans. The trauma lasted for five months.

The case was clearly racial and political. Rajat was an Asian Ugandan. By 1968, Asians had become scapegoats for all the ills of Ugandan society. The trial became an anti-Asian showpiece and, in the process, Rajat had his Ugandan citizenship revoked. When the jury handed down its verdict, Rajat was ruled innocent. But the mental anguish for my sister continued when he was rearrested at the conclusion of the trial. Knowing that all mail would be opened, she sent a letter back to us with friends. Her baby's nursemaid had turned out to be a police informer. Now Barbara was unable to sleep because each night she listened for the nursemaid's steps that signaled the arrival of the police car to collect the day's information. Joe Lapchick, who said he died a thousand deaths in defeat, was dying once more through the suffering of his daughter. My mother and father drew very close together during this period. The weight of the horror was finally lifted when Rajat was released in the spring of 1969. He and Barbara rushed to leave Kampala and all they had there before President Obote could change his mind and rearrest him. It was over for all but Barbara and Rajat, who had yet to work out their private nightmares and inner fears. Fifteen years later, Rajat still has deep scars.

* * *

The events of the previous four years had a tremendous impact on my father. Joe Lapchick had been known as a man who shaped the destinies of others. He had tried to instill pride in his players—pride in yourself and what you had done, pride in being self-disciplined and honest, and pride in being able to accept victory and defeat in the same way.

The press described him as a humble and self-effacing man. An event in the last full summer of his life underscored this. The Maurice Stokes NBA All-Star benefit game was being held at Kutscher's Country Club.

There were mobs outside the arena when my father arrived. At six-five his head was way above the crowd. No one else in line was connected to the game. He could have signaled Kutscher's employees at the gate, said "excuse me," and gone right through. In spite of wanting to see Lew play against Wilt, he refused to use his influence to go ahead of those who had arrived before him. If you didn't know him, this almost seemed absurd. The first great big man of basketball refused to use his fifty-year-old reputation to obtain a seat to see two of the greatest big men square off. As my father told a reporter that night, "It wouldn't have been right. These people have come a long way to see the game and if I had forced my way in, one of them would have been turned away." He never saw the game.

I spent two weeks at home during the 1969 Christmas holidays. The events of the 1960s were forcing my father to look at the dark side of his life; to acknowledge to himself the cumulative effect of the series of racial incidents he had encountered in sports. In the course of our conversations, it became even clearer that his lifelong friendship with Bob Douglas had been pivotal for what my father did in race and sport. I hated for that Christmas vacation to end. As much as I thought I knew my father, I was learning more and more. Sandy and I were about to move to Washington where I was to do research for my Ph.D. thesis on the racial factor in American foreign policy.

Being so close to New York, I felt I would continue to learn more about him.

Back in Denver to prepare for the move, I met Dennis Brutus at a reception in his honor. Dennis, as I've already said, had suffered for years because of his efforts to end racism in sport and apartheid in South Africa. This meeting took place less than a week after I left my father. Dennis and I talked nonstop for four hours, finally finishing at 3:00 A.M. Race and sport—I couldn't get it out of my mind. I decided to submit a new dissertation proposal, this one on the politics of race and international sport. I never went to sleep that weekend and finished the new proposal early Monday morning.

The proposal was approved and we canceled our plans to go to Washington. Three weeks later we were in London where I did the bulk of my research. By the time I returned to begin teaching at Virginia Wesleyan College, my research had shown to me that racism and politics in sport were not products of American society but were global in scope.

My mother came to visit us in Virginia on August 4, 1970. She was unpacking when we received a phone call from Monticello, where my father worked at Kutsher's. He had had a heart attack while playing golf. The doctor said we should come right away. We drove straight through the night, arriving at 6:30 A.M.

My father was in the intensive-care unit. My mother went in first. Because of the rules, I had to wait one hour before I saw him. His spirits were good but you could see that his body had taken a terrible beating. We joked with a nurse about allowing our dog, Blivit, my father's constant companion, into the room to sleep under the bed. He complained that we had driven there "for nothing." He repeated this when my brother Joe arrived. But he lit up with a broad grin when told that my sister was flying in from Greece, where she and Rajat had been living since fleeing Uganda.

My father seemed to be doing better and there was hope.

Sandy and I were at the hospital most of the day. He was talking about going home. He couldn't wait to see Barbara. She was due in Monticello at about 8:30 that night and he asked that she wait until the next morning to see him.

Suddenly I heard a commotion in the corridor. The door swung open, and the intensive-care unit took on a cocktail party atmosphere. Five or six people entered. One man talked to a nurse on duty. I was incredulous. She looked at me and shrugged her shoulders as if to say "What can I do?" The people, one of whom was carrying a small dog, stood around my father. The man introduced himself as one of the principal owners of the hospital. He said how proud they were that Joe Lapchick was with them and that they wanted a photograph with him. They got it.

Joe Lapchick, a man who sought privacy but was denied it throughout his life because of his fame in sports, was even to be denied it now. Late that night, he took a turn for the worse. By 7:45 A.M. on Monday he was dead.

We were called at 7:15 about his condition. My sister and I rushed to the hospital at 7:30 in the hope of snatching one final moment, one last touch that would have to last a lifetime. We rushed into the intensive-care unit to see his body wrenched across the table with his legs dangling off one end and each arm floating over a different side of the table. His face was frozen in pain. Barbara, who had traveled thousands of miles, kissed him tenderly.

I met with his attending physician in the corridor. He told me they did everything they could, that he was sorry, and then tried to explain the mass visit on Sunday.

They were bracing for a lawsuit. But this was Joe Lapchick, the man who had fought battles for others. Our family would never have allowed the last moment of his life to precipitate a legal battle. He would have been very unhappy.

His death was widely covered by the media. We would go home late at night to see clips of him speaking on the news. We couldn't let go. He was still with us. Hundreds of friends came to the wake in Yonkers. St. Denis's Church was jammed for the funeral. Television crews were there. The stories kept coming. All emphasized my father's qualities as a human being and the contribution he had made to basketball and to his community.

On the last night of the wake I noticed several black men staring at the drawing of my father above the closed casket. The same men were seated together at the funeral and stood together at the burial. I walked over to introduce myself and to find out who they were. The first man I went up to said, "I'm an old friend of Joe's. My name is Bob Douglas." They were the remaining members of the Renaissance team. I was deeply touched. Mr. Douglas took me in his arms.

·PART 4·

There Is a Difference: Sports in America in the 1980s

·12·

For the
True Believer

With more than a decade of experience in the area of race, politics, and sport, I welcomed the request of my publisher to take a substantial look at racism in sports as part of this book.

There is little doubt that sport has become the broadest common cultural denominator in almost all societies. Men and women, blacks and whites, reactionaries and revolutionaries, Soviets and Americans, barefoot village people from the mountains of Kenya and sophisticated urbanites from New Delhi seem to "think sports." The proportion of newsprint devoted to sports is usually as large or larger than that devoted to international events, domestic politics, the economy, the arts, education, or religion. American television, especially on weekends, is saturated with sports events; there are several cable channels devoted to showing sports twenty-four hours a day.

Rabbis, priests, ministers, and politicians use sports metaphors to make their moral or political points. Values taught in sport will make their flocks better Jews, Catholics, Protestants, Muslims, or Americans. Therefore, clergymen don't mind that Sundays are essentially the property of the NFL or the NBA. Religious services have become warm-ups for the bigger game to follow at the stadium. Religion and sport are on a continuum, teaching moral virtue to all who participate.

With so many Americans either playing themselves or watching others play, an enormous subculture has arisen. Many people in the subculture have come to accept a series of age-old verities about sport. I call such people "true believers." Here is their credo: sport can influence everything, for the better. Sport contacts with other nations build friendships, peace, and understanding. Sport has been a major social equalizer in America, leading blacks out of the ghetto through increased educational opportunity, changing attitudes of white teammates and opponents, and increasing employment opportunities at the end of their sports careers. Women can assert themselves on athletic fields in ways that will break down "feminine" stereotypes and, therefore, prepare them to enter executive positions.

But sport goes beyond this; it is an inspiration to everyone. It builds character, motivates individuals, generates teamwork, and teaches discipline through structured and contained competition. Sport is an acceptable outlet for aggressive behavior. Values learned in sport are assets in schools, business—in all phases of life. Good athletes become good citizens and succeed as a consequence of their own dedication and hard work. Those athletes who make the pros have unlimited opportunities when their playing careers end. But, pro or not, everyone benefits from competition; schools, communities, and the nation come together to root for their team.

It is undeniable that there are exceptions to such generalizations but those who have joined the sports subculture see them as only that—as aberrations from the norm. This is because they tend to view society itself as healthy and on the right path. But the draw of sport is so powerful that even many of those who are strong critics of society view sport in the same positive light. The assumptions have been well packaged. Sport is . . . sport does . . . sport will.

Yet obviously, ours is a far from perfect society. And if sport is so good, what went wrong? How have all of us, trained in the value system of athletics, forgotten those values so soon? Could it be that the true believer was misinformed, that sports does not by itself break down barriers? Is it possible that, in fact, we can see a microcosm of the whole society—with all its strengths and weaknesses—in the sports world?

On the international level, sport seems to be as much a source of national friction as it is a source of friendship, peace, and understanding. It is usually benign when we compete with "friendly nations" such as Britain, France, and West Germany. However, since American dominance has shifted in favor of the Soviet Union, Cuba, and the German Democratic Republic, our viewpoint toward them is different. In the late 1960s Americans started to become increasingly critical of the Olympics. We claimed that the Soviets and their Third World clients had politicized the Games that we were trying to protect. The sports media was willing to confirm for us that America doesn't play sports politics, that sports is above politics. How fast they changed when President Carter called for a boycott of the Moscow Olympics in 1980 to punish the Russians for invading Afghanistan. The Carter administration bludgeoned athletes into going along with the boycott, cajoled allies into joining the boycott, and offered incentives to developing nations, especially in Africa, if they would shun the Games. The press, for the most part, tended to ignore the methods being used. Finally, its reporting of the Games tried to paint them as a failure. Yet it is arguable that the Games were a success. Thirty-six new world and seventy-four new Olympic records were set—more records than at any previous Olympics. Eighty-one countries attended. More than 60,000 foreign tourists came to Moscow and an estimated 1.5 billion watched the Games on TV. And the Soviet Union was still in Afghanistan.

Let's examine those instances where America has become openly involved in sports politics. In 1936, we refused to boycott the Nazi Olympics in spite of a massive grass-roots protest against the Berlin Olympics in the United States from 1933 to 1936. In fact, an international boycott collapsed when America agreed to go to Berlin. In the late 1950s President Eisenhower directly intervened when the International Olympic Committee admitted the People's Republic of China (PRC) and excluded Taiwan. The pressure led to another sixteen-year delay in admitting the PRC into the modern Olympics. Throughout the 1960s and into the 1970s, the U.S. government refused visas to athletes from Cuba and the German Democratic Republic. In 1976, President Ford threatened to pull out of the Montreal Games unless Taiwan was admitted. Even so, he refused to go along with the 1976 African boycott that evolved over the racial situation in South Africa. America has never backed any request to boycott South Africa in spite of the fact that the vast majority of nations agreed to end competition with that country as long as apartheid dominates its policy.

What does it tell us when we boycott games to protest communism and do nothing in the face of racism and fascism? A great deal if we look closely.

Women's sports are growing in popularity, and, unlike men's sports, most of them are white dominated. The exceptions are, of course, track and field and, increasingly, basketball. This whiteness helps market sports for television, commercials, and dollars. Most professional women athletes are white and middle to upper-middle class. It isn't surprising that a recent exception to this rule in tennis is Leslie Allen—a beautiful, fashion-designing, magna cum laude graduate of USC in speech communications—the super-black woman.

Certainly there have been gains for women in sports. Between 1970 and 1980, the number of women who competed in high school sports increased by more than 500 percent. So many more women are competing in colleges that by 1980 the Association for Intercollegiate Athletics for Women (AIAW) had more than 800 member schools, when it did not even exist in 1970. Gains have been so impressive that the NCAA, which did not have women's sports in 1970, has now successfully fought for control of them and has crushed the AIAW. This is the same NCAA that not only didn't support Title IX, which called for more equalization between men's and women's sports, but actively opposed it; the same NCAA that still opposes equal spending for men and women in revenue-producing sports. However, it is difficult to believe there will be much difference between whether women's sports are ultimately controlled by the AIAW or the NCAA. The bottom line is that while women pay more than 50 percent of all tuition and fees, they receive less than 20 percent of the school's athletic budget. Once again, this is still a white middle-class problem. The high-school drop-out rate for Spanish-speaking American women is nearly 75 percent and is only slightly less for black women. They won't have to worry about proper implementation of Title IX.

Everyone knows that professional sport is a business like any other, although most sports values are expected to apply. But in colleges, high schools, and little leagues, sport is thought to be pure. We expect dedication and loyalty to the team, hard work, honesty, discipline, character building, and a commitment to winning through excellence and not through destruction of the opposition. Our coaches are to be philosophers and teachers of these virtues and nurturers of their athletes, both on and off the court.

The truth is very different. "Winning isn't everything, it's the only thing," is a reality. Winning at all costs is the philosophy most coaches believe in, no matter what pieties they may utter. Alumni and boosters pay coaches, players, and families of players. Athletes disregard academics and dream of incomes far beyond their ability. Faculties shrug their shoulders while college presidents say they can't expect athletes to take academics as seriously as other students. Sanctions for violations are rare and selective. Ultimately, it pays to cheat. It is a system gone mad. Win at all costs, at any cost. Why is it happening? The answer, of course, is money.

Athletic budgets are soaring to finance dominant teams that will fill arenas and obtain lucrative TV contracts. Major league baseball's 1983 $1 billion TV contract and the NFL's 1982 TV contract, worth more than $2 billion, are benchmarks for college contracts. A top college team today can earn more from one TV game than it cost to run an entire athletic program in 1975. There are now $10 million-plus athletic budgets all over the country and these figures exclude lucrative booster donations.

The abuses of athletes that were revealed in 1980 seemed to shock many people. The extent of the academic/athletic scandal made claims of such abuses by sports critics like Jack Scott and Harry Edwards in the late 1960s seem insignificant.

History should have told us something. The NCAA lists seven football conferences with sixty schools as the most prominent football conferences in the country. *Before* 1980's scandal broke, forty-two of the sixty had received public disciplinary action. That's 72 percent.

Basketball was even worse. Between 1952 and 1980, there were only two schools (Chicago Loyola in 1963 and Marquette in 1967) that won NCAA championships that were not subject to some form of public disciplinary action at one time or another because of their basketball programs.

So the scandal in 1980 was nothing new. The only difference is that there is now more to gain so colleges are taking more chances today. Perhaps most important is that it was the glamour schools and not simply schools-on-the-make that were caught.

These included the University of Southern California, Oregon State, Arizona State, and UCLA. At USC, nineteen football players enrolled in a speech course they didn't attend. USC had to forfeit an NCAA track title because it was revealed that

Billy Mullins, its 1978 sprint star, was accepted on credits allegedly accumulated simultaneously from four widely separated junior colleges. Arizona State forfeited five football wins in 1979 after it was divulged that players were getting credits for extension courses they didn't take. (Earlier, coach Frank Kush reportedly said, "My job is to win football games. I've got to put people in the stadium, make money for the university, keep the alumni happy, and give the school a winning reputation.") Oregon State dropped its only win in an eleven-game season because it used an ineligible player. The FBI alleged that New Mexico's basketball coach arranged to forge a star player's transcript to get him into school. According to a university report, the Portland State basketball coach was accused of both paying players and taking kickbacks. He claimed he took money for the players but not for himself.

An internal investigation at the University of San Francisco, which was partially precipitated by the Quintin Dailey case, revealed lucrative payoffs to athletes and special treatment for them, and led to the university temporarily dropping its basketball program. (The Dailey case has a special significance and will be discussed later in this chapter.)

The most spectacular allegations in 1980 were made against Wichita State, which denied the charges. The *Kansas City Times* reported that a former coed claimed that basketball coach Gene Smithson arranged and paid for her abortion when she became pregnant as a result of a liaison with one of his star players. She was told not to tell anyone and promised a bank job and money if she kept silent.

The mother of basketball player Antoine Carr, who had lived in poverty prior to his enrollment, bought two new cars and a $62,500 house after he chose Wichita State as his institution of higher learning. The woman, who claimed her boyfriend helped her with the finances, made lease payments with fifty $100 bills, then closed on the house with a $7,965 down payment, and bought a new car the next day.

Auguster Jackson received $500 when he was recruited by Wichita State and more later. He said, "That money was so new you had to pull the bills apart—$100 bills I'm talking about— to make sure you weren't giving away two bills for one. And they [the coaches] let you know they had the money. That was the first thing they hit you with." Jackson, Lawrence Howell, Tyrone Augburns, and Richard Williams—all former players —reported they received $4,500 in gratuities from coaches and boosters in the three previous seasons.

The NCAA conducted a lengthy investigation that resulted in a three-year probationary period for Wichita State, including a two-year ban from post season tournaments. Charles Allan Wright, chairman of the NCAA Committee on Infractions, said the NCAA found,

> numerous violations related to receipt of commercial air-lines transportation, cash, clothing, and use of automobiles by former student athletes, as well as promises to make such benefits available to recruits. . . . In light of the serious nature of these violations and the university's past involvement in NCAA infractions cases, the committee concluded a severe penalty in this case was warranted.

University President Clark Ahlberg said, "Each and every allegation reported by the *Kansas City Times* was considered by the NCAA and each and every one of those was refuted." Coach Gene Smithson had called the *Times'* charges "garbage." Claiming that most of the violations noted by the NCAA came under previous coaching staffs, Ahlberg added, "We're delighted the NCAA has confirmed our faith in our coaching staff." The three-year penalty was one of the harshest ever doled out by the NCAA.

In a series of interviews with Jane Gross of *The New York Times,* people associated with Wichita claimed the negative publicity has helped the school. The team went as far as the

1981 NCAA regional finals; fans filled the arena at home; and boosters, who raised only $80,000 in 1976, raised $1 million in 1980–81. Dr. George Farha, the president of the booster club, said the university was the "beating, intellectual heart" of the community. Dr. William Eckert, another ardent booster, noted "The athletic department has, in effect, developed a community semipro team. It's really a commercial venture." Success continued into the 1982–83 season in spite of the NCAA sanctions, which banned the team from post-season competition.

More often than not, the black athlete is the ultimate victim of all these abuses and ends up without an education (as we will see in Chapter 13). However, white athletes are also seriously shortchanged in the process. Both are sucked into the cheating that is so common it seems right. If coaches and athletic administrators are supposed to be their models, then who can fully blame the athlete for taking what must simply appear to be his piece of the pie?

Are players on scholarship "student athletes"? That is what the NCAA calls them. However, evidence shows that high-level players are really athletes first and students second.

William E. (Bud) Davis, president of the University of New Mexico, told *Newsweek*'s Pete Axthelm, "Our recruits were recruited to be athletes, not students. There was never an expectation that they'd get their ass out of bed at eight o'clock to go to class and turn in their assignments."

A report signed by University of Southern California President James H. Zumberge said that between 1970 and 1980, 330 athletes were admitted who did not meet the school's minimum requirements. He said decisions were "based chiefly on athletic prowess as judged by the athletic department, and without normal admissions office review." USC Athletic Director Richard Perry, replying to the charge that only slightly more than half of the athletic team members graduated from USC between 1964–77, noted, "I didn't know of anything that says the purpose of higher education is to procure degrees."

Bill Wall, who was the president of the National Association of Basketball Coaches, said, "I know some coaches who couldn't stop cheating if they wanted to because their alumni and boosters wouldn't let them."

Under tremendous pressure to produce, many coaches opt for the simple answer: do everything possible to get star athletes for their team. This applies to recruiting and to keeping the athletes eligible to play.

Auburn football coach Doug Barfield told Pete Axthelm that the choices of a losing coach are limited. "Go on as you have been and eventually get fired. Cheat more and survive. Or quit." Auburn was on NCAA probation at the time. Tates Locke explained to Axthelm why he violated the rules at Clemson before it was put on probation and he moved on to the University of Jacksonville. "I did it because I wanted to win. There were a tremendous number of people doing it then. And there are more now."

The extremely high turnover rate for Division I basketball coaches indicates the extent of the pressure. A *Washington Post* survey showed that between 1970 and 1980, forty-nine schools had at least three basketball coaches in the last decade. The sampling came from 110 major schools in the eleven most powerful basketball conferences, plus fifteen other powers. More revealing was the fact that only 10 percent of the coaches at Division I basketball schools in 1970 were at the same schools in 1980. UCLA, the most glamorous school of all, had four coaches in ten years.

Remarks by the presiding judge in the Norm Ellenberger trial gave chilling testimony to the situation. Ellenberger was convicted on twenty-one of twenty-two counts of fraud and making false public vouchers. The judge deferred sentence for a year and said that all counts would be dropped at the end of the year. He was not asked to make restitution and was placed on one year of unsupervised probation.

The judge explained his reasoning prior to announcing the sentence.

> I'm being asked to sentence a man who was only one cog in the entire machine called college ball. I'm being asked to sentence a man because he got caught, not because his conduct was unacceptable. The question is how fair is it to incarcerate a man for doing what almost everyone in the community wanted him to do—namely, win basketball games at whatever cost.

The judge added that "Naturally, rules and laws were broken. Is anyone really surprised? This is a problem that probably exists at every major college and university in the country."

The chain of corruption, commercialization, professionalism, and dehumanization starts early. Parents push their children in the Little League and Pop Warner League. The pressure starts there; the position specialization starts there. The dehumanization starts there. The end of most athletic careers starts there. Parents don't want each child to play in each game. They want *their* child to play the whole game. When the Little League and Pop Warner football instituted a rule that every child had to play, 1,800 teams withdrew from the league. Families move near schools with better athletic programs. Parents in Georgia and Texas are now arranging for their children to repeat the eighth grade to increase their chances for college scholarships five years later by giving them one more year to mature.

Dr. Thomas Tutko, a leading psychologist dealing with children in sports recently told Emily Greenspan, writing in *The New York Times Magazine,* "I'm concerned with how many good athletes have been scarred by injury or burned out psychologically by the time they were fifteen because they were unable to meet the insatiable demands of their parents, their coaches, or their own personal obsession."

The pressures get worse in high school. Many teenagers already have gone through a recruiting process to get there. Coaches even help their families relocate nearer to the school. In December 1980 a father allegedly went to a Michigan coach's home and assaulted him because his son wasn't playing enough. High school teachers regularly "pass on" illiterate players to keep them eligible and the seemingly easy ride to the top has begun. In November 1980, the principal of an Idaho high school punched a referee in the stomach and knocked him down after he thought the ref missed a couple of calls.

For those whose eighth-grade dreams are still alive in the twelfth grade, the good life continues unabated. College coaches offer players a variety of inducements to come to their school. Payoffs have included jobs, housing, cars, clothing, meals, transportation, and direct cash handouts. Frank Lollino, the high school coach of star basketball player Mark Aguirre, told reporters that Aguirre was offered cash, cars, and trips while Lollino was offered cash, trips to Hawaii, and better coaching jobs if he could help get Aguirre. He claimed he was offered $10,000 in cash and $15,000 later if he could deliver Eddie Johnson, Aguirre's teammate, to the recruiter's school. Lollino calls recruiters "bagmen."

Between the athletes and the coaches are the boosters and alumni. Together, they now contribute a significant portion of the athletic budget and almost all of the bagman's money; they have a great deal of control. Through 1980, over half of the actions taken by the NCAA Committee on Infractions have been against booster-related offenses.

Many administrators appear to condone departures from the rules. Some encourage them. After all, a winning team enhances the school's prestige even if it is at the educational expense of the same student-athletes responsible for that prestige. A winner brings in TV money and exposure, gate receipts, and at private institutions, it can mean a drawing card for new students, thus more revenues.

Then, of course, there is the faculty. Many have suggested, even expected, that they obtain more critical academic control as kind of super ombudsmen of athletic practices. However, the reality is they tend to be either fans themselves or feel themselves above sports, thereby absolving themselves of any academic responsibility for athletes.

So who or what is left to make things right? It appears to be the National Collegiate Athletic Association (NCAA), led by Executive Director Walter Byers. The NCAA tells us it is organized solely for the benefit of the amateur student-athlete who participates in sport "for the educational, physical, mental, and social benefits he derives therefrom and to whom athletics is an avocation."

Yet, George Sage, the highly respected sports scholar, writes that the NCAA is a "business organization that is part of the entertainment industry whose product is competitive intercollegiate sports events." He argues that it is a cartel that has a monopoly on the production and sale of the commodity and controls the wages of the labor force. Universities are member firms with no choice but to join if they have big-time programs, for the NCAA runs all national championships and controls all TV rights.

The NCAA regulates everything regarding athletes, who make up the largest single group of employees. It maintains an artificial low wage for them. The "transfer rule" of one-year mandatory ineligibility restricts mobility if a player changes schools; the "five-year rule" allows colleges to red-shirt players; that is, to allow them to sit out a year and defer eligibility, and the "freshmen eligibility rule," which allows freshmen to play varsity sports right away, reduces costs for member firms. All these rules maximize the profits of the schools and dovetail nicely with professional rules by delivering mature athletes to the pros.

Finally, the NCAA is its own police force and penalizes those who violate NCAA rules and regulations. With more than 725 members, the NCAA controls major sport.

With all its power and profit, the NCAA, if it wished, could really come down on corrupt athletic departments, finance a substantial investigation unit, and clean up college sports in a hurry.

However, with its power comes self-interest and self-preservation. If the NCAA went after as many of the major colleges as are suspected violators, there would be few teams eligible to compete for the national championship. They tread gingerly. Newspapers and the FBI have been uncovering more dirt than the NCAA Investigation Unit.

But where does that leave us? Time-Life ran a major series as President Reagan came into office called "American Renewal." Articles on this theme were included in Time-Life publications such as *Fortune, Money, Time, Life, Discover, People,* and, of course, *Sports Illustrated.* The *SI* piece examined the "elusive topic of the country's moral fiber," looking "at competition in America and its importance not only in sports but in all areas of life." It accepted as fact many of the problem areas that have developed in sport. But like the conservative politicians, its prescriptions for change to decades-old, complex problems were almost unbelievably simplistic.

The formula was that colleges should stop "toadying to the pros," stop carrying athletes who are poorly prepared academically just to win and make money. When that's done, high schools, in "an interesting side effect," will have to prepare athletes academically. If they can do it, "a whole generation of better prepared players-for-life, not just sports, will emerge."

As for coaching corruption, we should severely limit recruiting and give coaches job security. Coaches could then be teachers again and stress team play, require self-sacrifice, insist on striving for excellence in performance and not just victory. If these prescriptions could be implemented, then many of the problems discussed could be solved. However, the simplicity of the prescriptions doesn't account for the deep-rooted nature of the problems. Answers that address the surface can't penetrate to the core. (Several substantial reform proposals are offered in the Conclusion.)

Although black athletes are clearly affected by the fact that time-hallowed assumptions about sport are not as incontrovertible as they once seemed, it is still assumed that black athletes become immune from racism simply by participating in team sport. As we will see in the following chapters, this is the least true of all the verities.

·13·

Educate Thyself

If Bob Douglas were to return, he might easily believe it was the 1920s instead of the 1980s. The Klan was publicly on the march; there had been a significant increase in racial violence against blacks; the courts still weren't convicting many whites accused of racial violence; federal agents again appeared to be involved in provocative racial incidents; and the Reagan administration had either swept away or emasculated most of the social programs designed to aid the poor.

As bad as he thought things were for blacks then, they are worse now. But he might assume that, at least, he wouldn't have to endure any more racism in sport. All those barriers were assumed by society to be gone.

Unfortunately, such assumptions are far from reality. Ask James Cuba. In November 1978, he was ordered by his DeKalb (Texas) High School coach to go to the locker room because he wasn't giving 100 percent. According to Lee Balinger in his book *In Your Face,* Cuba turned his back and threw down his helmet. His neck was then broken when two coaches tackled him.

Or perhaps we should consult Darryl Williams. A fifteen-year-old from Roxbury, Boston's Harlem, he caught a pass that gave his Jamaica Plain High School a 6–0 halftime lead over Charleston. It was his first varsity start. September 1979 seemed like a good time for Darryl. He probably had visions of being on his way to the NFL. As Jamaica Plain gathered in a huddle before the second half, a sniper made sure his dreams were finished. Darryl's career was over, but at least his life was saved.

A cross burned during the halftime festivities of a football game between black and white high schools in Durham, North Carolina, in the fall of 1980.

The publicity director for Monticello Raceway, a harness racing track in the Catskill Mountains, invited the Pennsylvania Klan leader and his followers to take advantage of the raceway's "group party plan package" to hold a 1980 meeting there. This was the same man who announced that Soviet horses couldn't run in Monticello after the invasion of Afghanistan. Forced to fire him for the KKK incident, the Monticello president still called him "aggressive, hard working, and imaginative."

A group of black football players at South Miami High called several of their white assistant coaches "honky crackers" after they lost the regional championship game, on November 28, 1980. They wouldn't even listen to their white coach when he tried to talk to them after the game.

Two black members of a Catholic high school golf team in Louisiana were not allowed to participate in a twelve-team tournament because it was being played on a segregated private course. Even so their school went ahead and competed without them. The commissioner of the Louisiana High School Athletic Association shocked some when he said, "Unfortunately, every school and every area doesn't have a municipal golf course. Some schools wouldn't have a team if they didn't use the private clubs. This is true even in tennis and sometimes swimming. So we don't knock the local clubs that cooperate with the high schools." The principal of the school, a Catholic nun, added,

"It's not that big an issue, and there's no reason to keep badgering us about it."

While the above examples are minor racial incidents taken by themselves, the following demonstrates they are part and parcel of the totality of racism in American sport today.

Still, many maintain that blacks are lucky to have sports as a way out of the ghetto. To them the above examples are only "aberrations." The true believer knows that sports have led blacks out of the ghetto even if the quality of life for most American blacks isn't much different than it was in the sixties.

By 1970, black athletes had power on the playing field. Their numbers were increasing at all levels in basketball, football, baseball, boxing, and track and field. As the mood of the country shifted slightly toward giving blacks more educational opportunities, coaches with an eye toward the scoreboard took advantage of "open admissions" policies. White coaches, and administrators, boosters, and players had to adjust. If they had been racist before, they would have to tone it down.

Take the case of the University of Texas at El Paso. Jim Bouden, then its assistant athletic director, painted for Jack Olsen a picture of racism at UTEP so deep that Olsen devoted one part of his five-part series in *Sports Illustrated* to it. In 1966 UTEP (then called Texas Western) beat all-white Kentucky for the national basketball championship with an all-black starting team, and blacks across the country thought that athletics had enabled them to take one more step forward. Blacks celebrated and cheered, but once again they were betrayed; the five black starters never graduated. UTEP's racism surfaced again and again. Then Bouden told Olsen, in referring to his boss, Athletic Director George McCarty: "This is the first institution in Texas —right here!—that had a colored athlete. George McCarty's done more for 'em than this damn guy Harry Edwards. . . . George McCarty's done more for the nigger race than Harry Edwards'll do if he lives to be a hundred." By the 1980s, UTEP recruited most of its black athletes from Africa and the Caribbean while Kentucky started five blacks.

Yet, even in the 1960s there were plenty of white coaches trying to deal honestly and fairly with blacks. Dick Hays, who had been the Kansas coach, told Olsen after he left Kansas:

> Sure we broke down some of the physical segregation. . . . We did all the formal things, but the times called for more than that. What I wanted to do was reach the minds and hearts of my white players so that they would become determined not to permit the Negro to be anything less than a complete human being. What I had hoped was to use the basketball to turn out a bunch of white college graduates who would walk that extra mile for some Negro because of the experiences they had as members of an integrated basketball team. I don't think I produced even one such white man.

Hays actually quit his job when he was pressured not to play four blacks at once. This was a man of principle and commitment. Yet his case points out one of the real problems that persists today. Hays told Olsen that his only "integrated player" was Maurice King. Hays meant it as a compliment. But listen to him: "There must have been something exceptional about him [King] because he got along so well with the others. The rest of the Negroes spent their time off the court with other Negroes." King was willing to hang around with whites and they let him. But that is precisely the problem. White coaches, no matter how well meaning, naturally view events from a white perspective.

When Kevin Porter was hired to coach at St. Francis (Pennsylvania) in the spring of 1983, he became only the fifteenth black coach at a major college. With blacks dominating the sport, how are the white coaches going to develop the sensitivity to understand black players? The older coaches probably didn't play with blacks. They didn't have a Bob Douglas to teach them. Some major schools have black assistants, who should help with the problem, but their primary purpose is to help recruit more blacks. There is some hope that the younger white coaches, who played with blacks, will be more sensitive to their needs, but this has yet to be proven.

One of the most hallowed assumptions about race and sport is that athletic contact between blacks and whites will favorably change racial perceptions. The jury is still out on that question. Coach Hay's experience says it won't. So does Bill Russell's. In *Second Wind* he points out the same problem from the other side.

When he joined the Boston Celtics in 1957, he was the only black and had no social contact with the white players. "Exactly twenty years later I was coach and general manager of the Seattle Supersonics, which had only two white players on the team—and they were excluded from almost everything but practice and the games." Russell argued with his players, but they ultimately said that "white players are just too different."

Predominantly white campuses, like corporate boardrooms, naturally reflect the value system of the dominant white culture. They are not equal meeting grounds for white students and blacks, whether from the ghetto or the farm. Blacks start out on the campus as they have been all along—as something less than whites.

Bill Russell described the feeling many years ago. "You are a Negro. A living, smarting, hurting, smelling, greasy substance that covers you. A morass to fight from." While the militancy and struggle of the sixties and seventies have reduced the negative self-perceptions of most young blacks, the stereotypes still exist for whites—the stereotypes and all the taboos that go with them.

White and black athletes meet on campus carrying a great deal of racial baggage. Their prejudices are unlikely to evaporate with the sweat as they play together on a team. First, any display of negative behavior is likely to reinforce existing biases. If the whites happen to take to a black athlete, he is likely to be viewed as an exception.

Chances are that competition at the high-school level bred hostility. There it is usually white teams against black teams, reflecting the city's residential housing patterns. There is virtually no playground competition between blacks and whites as few dare to leave their neighborhood. For some, games become racial battles.

On a college team, blacks and whites are competing for playing time, while in the society at large, black and white workers compete for jobs, public housing, even welfare. A primary difference is that whites are apt to accept blacks on the team since they will help the team win more games, get more exposure, and, perhaps, get *them* more exposure.

It is easy for even racist white athletes to accept blacks on their team for two other reasons. First, they need not have any social contact with black teammates. As Russell pointed out, off-the-field interaction is rare. Sports that blacks dominate are not sports like golf, tennis, and swimming where socializing is almost a prerequisite of competing. Players need not mingle after basketball, baseball, or football. More importantly, black male players need not mingle with white women after those games. Housing on campus, and social discrimination through fraternities and sororities, further protect the purity of the whites.

Second, now that the physical dominance of blacks has been accepted in so-called black sports, whites can explain away that success with racist theories about genetics. Isn't it strange that we never explained white sports dominance in the 1930s with reference to white physical characteristics? But then all-black teams began to beat all-white teams. The Rens took the Celtics in basketball. According to John Holway, author of *Voices from the Great Black Baseball Leagues,* teams from the Negro baseball leagues beat white major league teams in over 60 percent of their 445 games before Jackie Robinson broke the color bar in 1948. Joe Louis became an acceptable black champion after he beat Max Schmeling; Jesse Owens was an acceptable black star after he won big for America in Berlin.

Suddenly we had genetic theories. The Germans claimed Owens and other black Americans were successful because of their peculiar bone structure. An English report charged that the blacks had leg operations to increase their speed. The American Olympic Committee was attacked for bringing "black auxiliaries" to the Games. The late Avery Brundage, long-time International Olympic Committee president, added later that "one could see, particularly with Jesse Owens, how the Negroes could excel in athletics. Their muscle structure lends itself to this sort of competition."

The South Africans openly deprecated the achievements of the blacks. In 1968, three decades later, their white Olympic chief, Frank Braun, said, "Some sports the African is not suited for. In swimming, the water closes in on their pores so they cannot get rid of carbon dioxide and they tire quickly."

The University of Southern Cal's track coach, Dean Cromwell, wrote in *Championship Technique in Track and Field,* "The Negro excels in the events he does because he is closer to the primitive than the white man. It was not that long ago that his ability to spring and jump was a life and death matter to him." That book was published in 1941.

Things were more serious when blacks were not only playing but dominating sports in the 1970s. M. Kane's assessment of "Black Is Best" for *Sports Illustrated* in 1971 brought nods of agreement from whites and outrage from blacks. Blacks had more tendon and less muscle, giving blacks an advantage in "double-jointedness and general looseness of joints," Kane claimed. Also, blacks "have superior capacity to relax under pressure." Like Braun, Kane said, "perhaps because of a physical inheritance, no black has ever been a swimming champion."

Of course, the theories have had to change from time to time.

Blacks weren't supposed to be able to run long distances. We had a genetic explanation for that too until Africans came to dominate the long-distance races. Suddenly American track coaches have developed an interest in Africa these last few years.

Whites have conceded the physical superiority of blacks because it fits the image: whites still have the brains. Other "geneticists," like coach Cromwell, say that blacks survived in Africa because they were fast and strong. It would never occur to them that it was perhaps the Africans' intelligence, imagination, and creativity that not only let them survive but build highly developed civilizations before Europeans ever heard of Africa. *That* would not fit the image. So we had theorists like Arthur Jensen "proving" that whites have inherently higher IQs.

"All the racial upheaval of the 1960s had taught *Sports Illustrated* was that it's okay to be racist as long as you try to sound like a doctor," Bill Russell countered. His theory of blacks' success: "I worked at basketball up to eight hours a day for twenty years—straining, learning, sweating, studying." *Sports Illustrated* didn't mention small things like that or the social, economic, and political factors involved.

Kareem Abdul-Jabbar forced *Sports Illustrated* to mention the hard work in a Jack Olsen story about him:

> Yes, I was just like the rest of those black athletes you've read about, the ones that put all their waking energies into learning the moves. That might be a sad commentary on America in general, but that's the way it's going to be until black people can flow without prejudice into any occupation they can master. For now it's still pretty much music and sports for us.

Once a black athlete reaches a predominantly white setting, the double standard becomes even more apparent. His acceptance on the court becomes rejection as he walks across the campus or enters the library. What are among Kareem's UCLA memories? Away from the court, he would hear, "Yeah, that's him. He's nothing but a big ———."

If the dominant basketball player of my generation was subjected to this, what must the average black athlete face?

The coach becomes his main white contact, and the court becomes the only home where he is comfortable. But the black athlete feels his coaches discriminate against him and his academic advisers give him different counseling. This may reflect the racism he experiences from them or it may reflect the general distrust of whites. Even well-intentioned acts can be interpreted by blacks as being racially motivated. The same phenomenon, of course, can work the other way.

Over the years, black student-athletes have continued to make the same complaints: subtle racism evidenced in different treatment during recruitment; poor academic advice; harsh discipline; positional segregation on the playing field and social segregation off of it; blame for ills for which they are not responsible. Then there are the complaints of overt racism: racial abuse; blacks being benched in games more quickly than whites; marginal whites being kept on the bench while only blacks who play are retained; extra money for the white players; summer jobs for whites and good jobs for their wives.

To say that most coaches are racist is a great exaggeration. But most coaches, racist or not, were raised on white values in a white culture. The norm for them is what is important for a white society.

Inseparable from that are images—albeit invariably false images—of what black society is and what kind of men it produces. If the white coach accepts these "black characteristics" —and I would believe that most do (just as surveys show most white Americans do)—then he may believe that blacks are less motivated, less disciplined, less intelligent, more physically gifted, raised in a culture bombarded by drugs, violence, and sexuality, more comfortable with other blacks, etc. He may believe those characteristics are a facet of society, or he may simply believe that they are the way God chose to make things. He may recognize himself as racist, one who dislikes blacks because of the negative traits he believes blacks possess. However, more than likely he views himself as a coach trying to help blacks overcome their backgrounds—as a missionary. In either case, he acts on these images and his black players are victimized.

As a missionary, the coach believes blacks are less motivated and less disciplined than whites and will lean heavily on them in practice and in games. He will push them physically, inspire them by any means possible. He will make the black athlete who complains of injury learn to push himself harder, to endure more and more pain.

A racist coach who believes that blacks are unmotivated and undisciplined translates these words into "lazy" and "insubordinate." He may be acting out his hate and want to punish black players for their being black, so he might yank blacks off the court after a bad play, not bring them on road trips, play only a few at any given time. He must show blacks who is boss. John Thompson, the nation's most successful black college basketball coach, told *Sports Illustrated*'s Bil Gilbert why he wants his predominantly black teams to be known as disciplined.

> Undisciplined, that means nigger. They're all big and fast and can leap like kangaroos and eat watermelon in the locker room, but they can't play as a team and they choke under pressure. It's the idea that a black man doesn't have the intelligence or the character to practice self-control. In basketball it's been a self-fulfilling prophecy. White men run the game. A white coach recruits a good black player. He knows the kid's got talent, but he also knows—or thinks he knows—that because he's black he's undisciplined. So he doesn't try to give the player any discipline.

He puts him in the free-lance, one-on-one, hot-dog role, and turns to the little white guard for discipline. Other black kids see this and they think this is how they are expected to play, and so the image is perpetuated.

The missionary coach who accepts that blacks are less intelligent may feel he is "protecting" them by suggesting they first attend a junior college or take less demanding courses to reduce the pressure as they adjust to life in their new society. He may discuss the "adjustments" with the players' professors and get them tutors. As a coach, he naturally looks to his profession for role models for black athletes. How many black doctors, lawyers, accountants, or psychoanalysts is he apt to know? But there are Frank Robinson, Lennie Wilkens, and K. C. Jones. It is not surprising that many black athletes major in physical education or athletic administration.

On the other hand, the racist coach is increasingly suggesting junior colleges to blacks because they can mature athletically there and the coach can watch their skills develop while they pile up enough easy credits to help them slide through their junior and senior years. Harry Edwards calls the junior college phenomenon "the new slave trade." The racist coach doesn't worry about black role models as professionals like doctors or lawyers because he probably couldn't conceive of a black role model in the first place. Black athletes are thus steered into courses on physical education and athletic administration because coaches have a better line on grading in those departments.

The racist and missionary coaches both have a high stake in keeping athletes eligible. After that eligibility runs out, the missionary might, if he has the time (which is not likely) try to help the athlete to graduate. But for the racist, the black athlete becomes invisible. Tutors suddenly disappear, professors suddenly rediscover how to demand more in class, and the student realizes there are no more PE courses to take.

The problems at USC in 1980 highlighted the academic situation of the black athlete. After President Zumberge acknowledged that athletes were admitted on the basis of their physical abilities and often didn't meet the university's minimum admissions requirements, Malcolm Moran of *The New York Times* looked inside the institution. He asked football coach John Robinson what would happen if the university enforced its admissions standards. Robinson quickly responded, "Our team turns white. That's one thing that would happen. . . . If we were to suddenly say, 'We close the doors,' that's almost a racial move. We never faced the problem. We got them in, what do you do with them? I don't think any of us had the understanding or the skill."

It is bad enough that only 51 percent of all USC football players graduated between 1964–77, but Dr. Nathaniel Hickenson, an associate professor of education who studied the black athlete at USC, found that in the same period only 29 percent of the black football players graduated. "My anger is over the exploitation of the black athlete at USC," he told Moran. "There is a philosophy that there is a lessening in the eyes of the alumni if black football players are allowed to graduate."

From the transcripts, Hickenson concluded that most blacks took gut courses. Ethnic studies were probably the only bonafide courses they took, he said. He made particular mention of a course called "Special Problems in Speech Communications," claiming that the class was invented simply to keep athletes eligible to play; they could get from two to ten credits for enrolling. Hickenson said, "I'll bet my life, I'll stake my reputation that at least a hundred black football players in the past ten years have that to show for their time at USC."

In response, Athletic Director Dr. Richard Perry told Moran, "Nat's been using those numbers for a hundred years. I've never checked them out at all. Nat's made a value judgment on a student-athlete that opts not to graduate. I don't remember hearing O.J. Simpson complain about not getting a degree from

USC. It may have been the best thing that ever happened to him."

Is there really much difference between what Jim Bouden of Texas at El Paso told Olsen in 1968 and what Perry told Moran in 1980? Bouden talked about helping the "nigger race." Perry proudly talks about never checking the charges of racial exploitation that have been made "for a hundred years." Never even checking them out! It is hard to comprehend how a college administrator could say it is a "value judgment" to be distressed about a student-athlete who *"opts* not to graduate." Or that the "best thing that ever happened" to someone was not to get a degree.

The racist coach *knows* that only whites are going to play "thinking positions." He wants whites to control the game.

The controlling position in baseball is the pitcher. In football, the quarterback. Everyone loves the smooth, ball-handling guard in basketball. These are the glamour positions that fans and the press focus on. Let the blacks run and jump. The whites are in control; the blacks are still running after them. (Positional segregation will be discussed in depth in Chapter 14.)

When Bill Russell wrote about quotas in professional basketball in the 1960s, whites were shocked. If quotas exist today, do they operate at the high-school and college level?

Stories about quotas are hastily buried when they apply to blacks in sports. But stories about Cleveland's decision to make quotas to include *whites* on basketball teams got lots of publicity.

In Cleveland, there was only 1 white out of 164 players at the city's fourteen public high schools. That prompted Dr. Donald Waldrip, Cleveland's court-appointed desegregation officer, to order each school to carry two whites. However, most whites live in ethnic neighborhoods west of the Cuyahoga River. So the inner-city schools are almost all black.

Jim Chambers, the athletic director of predominantly black JFK High School, told George Vecsey of *The New York Times:*

This order is ridiculous. We had a hundred kids try out
for basketball. Five of them were white. One was the
basketball manager who knew he had no chance. Two
were dropped, one quit right away, and one looked at the
competition and didn't want to be a token. The black kids
don't mind white kids playing basketball. They want the
best team.

As shown earlier, many whites think blacks have advantages
because of their physical attributes. However, Chambers believes otherwise.

Maybe they work harder at it because they can't get a job
in the summer. Maybe a white kid can get a job in a store,
but the black kid is down at the playground practicing
basketball. If the kids earn their uniform, they should keep
it.

Referring to the Cleveland decision, Chuck Cooper, who
integrated the NBA with Nat Clifton in 1950, commented that
"who would have thought that a time would come when this
type of ruling would be necessary?"

In college, players are 68 percent white; head coaches are
more than 90 percent white; assistant coaches are more than 80
percent white. White guards—the control position—outnumber the black guards three to one.

Do college coaches impose quotas so that some whites start?
The evidence seems clear that some do. Many remember that
in 1969 at Notre Dame the predominantly white student body
booed when there were five blacks on the court at once versus
Michigan State. Blacks quit the team, returning only after a
public apology by the student-body president. And this was
Notre Dame, whose president, Theodore Hesburgh, has been a
major figure in the movement for civil rights in the United
States.

At Vanderbilt University in 1978, I met several black athletes
who told me the athletic program and its coaches discriminated

against blacks. I heard that from athletes on many of the campuses where I have lectured. Then in February 1981 Vanderbilt basketball coach Richard Schmidt was criticized by two blacks —Jimmy Gray and Charlie Davis—for benching them. At first, the reason for the criticism was only implicit. But when Schmidt suspended them, Gray let go. He charged the coach with juggling the lineup to maintain a racial balance—a quota of no more than three blacks on the court at any one time. Schmidt denied the charge and threw Gray off the team.

Do coaches get pressured to play whites? Coach Hays quit at Kansas because he didn't want to succumb to the demands not to play four blacks at once. But that was 1964. Lou Carnesseca of St. John's told me he would quit before buckling under to such pressure.

Ken Edwards, now basketball coach at West Texas State, reported that in his days at Portland State, he bent the rules whenever he could to win, but added he did it with the participation and encouragement of the school's academic administration. Edwards reportedly told the *Oregon Journal,* as quoted in *Sports Illustrated,* the bottom line: "What really got to me finally was that one of the administrative people, who is still at Portland State, told me, 'I don't care how you do it, but I'd like to see some more white kids on the floor.' " Before going to Portland, he served as Jerry Tarkanian's assistant, and Tarkanian is one of the NCAA's favorite targets. Bill Walton, the best white player of the 1970s, thinks he knows why. "I can't be quiet when I see what the NCAA is doing to hurt Jerry Tarkanian only because he has a reputation for giving a second chance to many black athletes other coaches have branded as troublemakers," he said.

Georgetown's black coach John Thompson told *Sports Illustrated*'s Bil Gilbert that after he started five black freshmen in 1973, his first year, a white woman called, oblivious to Thompson's color or size (six-ten, 300 pounds). She was angry about a photo in the newspaper showing Georgetown blacks towering over a white teammate. She demanded that coach Thompson stop "abnormal niggers bullying white students." "I told her things were worse than she thought," he went on. "And I was going to send her two tickets to our next game so she could come see for herself, that what she would see would make her blood run cold. I was very sorry that lady couldn't use those tickets. They were for seats right behind where I sit on the bench. I wanted her to get a look at the most abnormal nigger of them all."

The coach is the authority. Athletes don't speak out. This creates problems for all coaches who come up against an outspoken player. When the player is black and not a superstar, he will probably go the way of Jimmy Gray. Only the Bill Russells, Kareem Abdul-Jabbars, and Muhammad Alis can remain because no one can *afford* to let them go.

But remember the heat. I have already discussed the outcry from the press and fans when Russell first spoke up. Then there was Lew Alcindor at UCLA. He said of the press, "They twisted my words and made me look stupid." Once he talked at length about race, Malcolm X, and the future of America. A reporter wrote that he was eccentric and surly and should be sent back to New York.

When he chose not to join the U.S. Olympic team in turbulent 1968, he was called a "traitor" and an "uppity nigger." Listen to him tell Jack Olsen why he chose to work in New York instead of going to the Olympics:

> I was talking to little black kids who are going to suffer because they don't have any examples to model themselves on. I tried to give them some kind of example. They dig basketball, so they dig me. They can relate to me and if I tell them something, they listen. I look at it this way: if I can change ten would-be junkies into useful citizens, turn them onto school and to useful lives, maybe get them started on how to run a crane for $4 an hour, that's the

most important thing I can do right now.... Each of those
ten turns on another ten. ... pretty soon you can see an
end to some of the black suffering that goes on today.
That, in my opinion, is where it's at. By comparison, an
Olympic gold medal is a joke.

Muhammad Ali, who had refused to go into the army, knew
you had to be at the top to speak out if you were black. He said,
"You are only free if you are number one. Otherwise you are
slave."

It's ironic that one of the lawyers who helped him to beat the
system was Bob Arum, who said at the time, "This case proves
that our justice system works—if you have the money and
influence to go all the way." Arum, who helped Ali win his
freedom before the Supreme Court in 1971, now promotes
boxing events in South Africa. Many agree that these matches
help maintain the economic and political enslavement of more
than twenty million black South Africans. And Arum pro-
claims that he is helping South African blacks!

It does not please some white coaches when black youth see
Russell, Kareem, or Ali as role models. So they promote the
sports equality myths. Pure jocks are safe role models. Give
blacks commercials, raise their salaries, hire some black assistants. All these things happened in the 1970s. Have sports been
reformed or pacified? Can blacks speak out today without fear
of retribution?

In the summer of 1978 I traveled to Kutscher's Country Club
in Monticello, New York, to attend the NBA Maurice Stokes
All-Star Game. I spoke to the players about signing a pledge
that they would not compete in South Africa until apartheid in
sports was eradicated. Twenty-two of the twenty-five players
were black. It was very unlikely that any of them would have
been asked to go to South Africa to play. They were all established pros. And they all said, "No!" Explanations varied, but

there was a common theme: to speak out on politics could spell the end of their athletic careers. If this was true in the pros, surely college athletes today—especially black college athletes —who want to be pros will *not* speak out unless pushed to an extreme.

The missionary knows that interracial sex on campus is forbidden even though it may not bother him personally. So he counsels blacks to go with black women.

Howie Evans, the black assistant coach at Fordham, told me of the times when he used to work at a black community center in New York. Recruiters from predominantly white southern schools were coming there to recruit black women for their schools. Those coaches seemed to think they understood the powerful sexual drives of black men so they went out to get them some "safe" women friends from the North.

Missionary coaches recognize the white public's perception of the violent bent of black society so they counsel their players never to start fights. They also believe that blacks want to be together and arrange for separate housing on campus, rooming blacks with other blacks on the road, and encouraging separate social events.

That segregation process starts with the first recruiting trip. A study by Arthur Evans, conducted at Kansas State University, published in the fall 1979 *Journal of Sport and Social Issues,* pointed this out. Most white recruits reported that coaches discussed campus social life with them while most blacks said they did not. Most whites participated in social activities during their visit to the campus. Most blacks did not. Whites were invariably shown around by other whites. Blacks were escorted by either race. Whites reported good-to-excellent social, academic, and athletic experiences on the recruiting trip. Most blacks disagreed on all counts. But they enrolled anyway. The pros were in sight.

*   *   *

The racist coach thinks that all the problems of inner-city life are *caused* by blacks. He believes that his black players use drugs, are oversexed, crave white women, are unable to control their tempers, and must be separated from whites socially.

Thus, if a black player is experiencing an athletic slump, he might be suspected of taking drugs. While drugs seem to be increasingly used by both black and white athletes—some 75 percent of NBA players reportedly take them—coaches rarely publicly talk about white athletes taking drugs.

When J. R. Richard, baseball's best pitcher, slowed down in 1980 after a 10–4 start for Houston, rumors flew that he was on drugs. (That tragedy and its implications will be discussed in Chapter 14.)

The racist white coach will do anything to prevent interracial sex. He uses white teammates to keep tabs on the black men. An administrator at the University of Texas at El Paso, for example, reportedly used to tell their black players to go across the border to Mexico to satisfy their needs.

When I talk to black athletes after a lecture, I try to ask them about this. It doesn't matter where I am—Las Vegas, Los Angeles, Denver, New York, Nashville, or Norfolk—all say there is pressure not to date white women. It doesn't matter how big the star, what era he played in, or whether he was amateur or pro. The rule is clear: don't mess with white women.

The black athletes also tell me the assumption on campus is that they *want* white women more than black women. Not that blacks say they do, but that whites *believe* they do. If a white student wants to sleep with a coed, that's part of college life in the eighties. If a black student wants to do the same, that's the primal animal working out his natural instincts.

Jack Johnson lived with a white woman and was tried under the Mann Act. That was a long time ago.

Yet Elgin Baylor was told not to bring a white coed to a dance at Seattle University and he agreed. That was the 1950s and Elgin was as good a black player as there was.

Junior Coffey was told not to date a white woman at the University of Washington. He refused and never started for his team again. That was the early 1960s and he had been the nation's third-leading rusher at the time. Lew Alcindor stopped dating a white woman at UCLA because both he and the woman were feeling the pressure. He withdrew within himself on campus while increasing his black consciousness. That was the late 1960s and he was probably the most dominant basketball player of his time.

Cleon Jones of the New York Mets was arrested by Florida police who alleged they found him asleep in a van with a white woman—nude. Much publicity followed about the incident but when charges were dropped, it was hardly mentioned. The Mets fined Jones $2,000 and forced him to make a public apology at a news conference in the presence of his wife for soiling the image of the All-American game. Never mind that police said that no crime had been committed. Antimiscegenation laws in Florida are off the books now. They are still on the books of major league baseball. That was 1975 and Cleon Jones once hit .340 and led the Mets to the world championship.

A white coed charged that she was molested by three black football players at the University of Arkansas. Was she crying rape? The three students said it was a "playful act." Apparently a *roomful* of students were present to affirm that not much had happened. But that "not much" still involved not one but three black men and a white woman. That was 1978 and football coach Lou Holtz suspended all three from the Orange Bowl game toward which they had worked all season.

Superstar David Thompson of the Denver Nuggets married a white woman. He said both sets of parents were reluctant to accept the interracial marriage.

Injured in 1979–80, Thompson's career went sour. Rumors of the reasons spread.

I was in Denver at the start of the 1980–81 season. I asked

a white cab driver what happened to the Nuggets the year before? No hesitation. "David Thompson wore himself out screwing that white bitch!" I asked him if he knew Mrs. Thompson or had read anything about her. He sensed where that question came from and got mad. "I don't read about no nigger-loving whores." He refused to take my money. David Thompson had twice been College Player of the Year, had led North Carolina State to the national championship, had averaged 25.2 points per game in his four previous NBA seasons, and had made Denver owner Carl Scheer's life considerably more comfortable by helping to fill the arena with fans. Yet Scheer, for whatever reason, asked David Thompson to pay back part of his 1979–80 salary and publicly take the blame for the poor Denver season. Thompson took the blame, but only loaned the Nuggets $200,000 for two years. Thompson was finally traded to Seattle after the 1981–82 season when it was assumed he had a drug problem. Thompson later admitted to having a drug problem, which may have affected his playing.

How does racial rejection affect black men? Kareem Abdul-Jabbar told Jack Olsen about how he felt after being rejected by a white girl at a dance in New York while he was in high school. I have known him since he was an eighth-grader. At every stage of development he was mature, intelligent, and rational. But on that night he and his friend hit the streets to do damage. They walked toward Fifth Avenue, where they intended to smash store windows, but by the time they got there, they had walked off their rage. Kareem wondered how many were unable to release that rage caused by the granite wall of racial rejection; how many killed or beat up some white person without knowing why they did it?

> That blind rage at Whitey is part of the black condition; all black men reach it; some pass through to a higher plateau of understanding, but some never get out of the rage period and their lives are blighted for it. I understand

them, and I don't turn from them. I once felt the same way
myself.

I remember the reaction of my white fellow graduate students when they read this. They thought it was one of the
scariest things they had ever read. They fantasized that such a
rage could be turned *on them.*

The case involving Quintin Dailey in his last year at the
University of San Francisco has been the most controversial
and most closely scrutinized of all. The case raised issues relevant to all the questions raised about black athletes in this book.
Unfortunately, it offered few answers.

Dailey was accused of raping a white nursing student. The
woman who said she was Dailey's victim seemed to have convinced the public that Dailey was guilty, although Dailey produced several people who cast doubt on her story. His failure
to pass a polygraph test turned the scales against him. The press
began to ask if he would get away with attempted rape because
he was a superstar. Faced with a jail sentence but proclaiming
his innocence, Quintin Dailey chose to plead guilty to a reduced
charge of aggravated assault. As part of the plea, he received
three years on probation. Thus the Chicago Bulls knew when
they drafted him that Dailey would not go to jail.

The Bulls were heavily criticized for picking Dailey in the
first place. But the fires were intensified when he spoke at a
Bulls' press conference. "Nobody heard my side of the story
when it happened," Dailey said. "I really don't want to get into
it now. I have forgotten about the episode. When you've got
other, greater things ahead of you, I can put it behind me. Right
now, it's forgotten."

The national press was furious at what it interpreted as such
blatantly callous and unrepenting remarks. Women's groups in
a number of cities set up picket lines at many Bulls games. In
San Antonio, a fan dressed up as a nurse and let two others do
a mock reenactment of what was supposed to have happened

in San Francisco. It all finally caught up to Dailey. In mid-December 1982, he asked for a leave of absence from the Bulls due to extreme emotional stress. By the spring of 1983, he was reportedly in a drug-rehabilitation clinic.

Even before the public pressure started, Dailey's agent, Bob Woolf, said that what the press had done was "just like a lynching." Was the overwhelming reaction because Dailey was alleged to have tried to force sex on a white woman? Was his guilt so clear that all that followed was justified? Everyone who knew Dailey, whether or not they supported him in this particular case, said he was an outstanding young man who had never been in trouble before. If he really was innocent, why should he have made repentant remarks at the press conference? Even if he was guilty, why was he singled out for such an unrelenting torrent of criticism? Other athletes have been charged with similar or worse sexual offenses and have paid much smaller prices. I honestly do not know the answer, but I keep coming back to the same question: Would the reaction have been the same if the woman had been black?

Missionary or racist, the effects of the actions of white coaches on black athletes on the whole range of issues discussed in preceding sections are not dissimilar. Study after study has shown the devastating consequences to the psyche of a minority person. As long as the act is perceived as being racially motivated—even if it is a well-intentioned act—the end result is the same.

So what should the black athlete do? Should he attend a predominantly black college? After all, black colleges have turned out great pro athletes for years.

Yet black college athletic programs started to decline when the white schools began to integrate. They don't have million-dollar booster clubs to compete with white schools to get star black athletes. Big white schools also offer the lure of bowl games, TV, and a "white education."

Eddie Robinson, the Grambling coach who has the second-best record among active college coaches and has sent 160 players to the NFL, more than any coach in history, explained the situation to the *Boston Globe.* "It would be real hard for me to tell a boy, living in a shotgun house with five sleeping in one room, to turn down a new house, a car, a better job for his daddy. I know it's wrong, but it's hard for a man to walk in another man's shoes."

The Southwestern Athletic Conference, which includes Grambling, Jackson State, and Southern, used to give thirty-five to forty players a year to the NFL in the early 1970s. Six were chosen in 1981. A total of only 18 of the 332 selected were from black colleges.

Pro scout Earl Biederman reflected, "It is much more advantageous for the good athlete with pro ambitions to go to a powerhouse like Alabama."

Could Eddie Robinson coach at Alabama or in the NFL? "I would at least like the opportunity to turn down a job. Every white coach in the country with my tenure has had that opportunity."

Eddie Robinson is black and came along at the wrong time. Yet it is becoming either more profitable or politically necessary to hire some black coaches.

Tulsa hired Nolan Richardson, a black, in 1980 to become the fourteenth black head basketball coach at a major college. Tulsa President J. Paschal Twyman told *Sports Illustrated,* "There was a race factor, to be sure. Tulsa's population is about 11 percent black but we did our homework. We asked around the community and felt out our booster club. We'd been losing for five years, attendance was down, the program was at the bottom, and it was having an impact on our budget. We knew we were breaking some ice here, but we decided to fly with it. We needed to win badly."

Richardson brought four members of his undefeated national junior-college championship team to Tulsa and they won the NIT championship. Some called it another milestone for the black race.

Georgetown, sitting in its own white enclave in mostly black

Washington, had won 296 and lost 302 games between 1947 and 1972. Georgetown needed to win and it needed to relate more to its environment—a black environment. Georgetown president, the Reverend Timothy S. Healy, SJ, told Bil Gilbert:

> There is something about Washington, D.C., that has always reminded me of a cuckoo's nest. The local people make the nest. The cuckoos—the federal people and all their hangers-on—move into the nest. They fly in and out, but their main interests are elsewhere. They don't really care a lot about what they do in, or to, the nest. I think Georgetown has been, to an extent, one of the cuckoos. After the 1968 riots it became obvious that the university's position [being predominantly white and isolated from the black community] wasn't very smart or defensible—socially, intellectually, morally, or empirically. We began making some changes, some statements to the local community that we were going to try to be at least more responsible and useful. I think it's fair to say that hiring John Thompson was one of those statements.

Thompson has won a lot of games and will win a lot more. In becoming the first black coach to win the national championship in 1984, Thompson made many people angry. This was especially true of some media figures. They said he was arrogant, abrasive, and that he kept his team insulated from the public. They said his team was overly aggressive. The attack was prolonged and lasted during the entire NCAA tournament. You could rarely read about Georgetown, on its way to dominate the tournament, without negative personal comments in the articles. It was vicious.

But one had to wonder if we were not hearing the same old tune. After all, Thompson was breaking *all* the molds precast by a stereotyping public. First, he was a big winner with a lot of black recruits coming to the no-longer lily-white campus. Next, these black players were not a free-wheeling, footloose team but instead one of the most disciplined teams in the country. Even more importantly at a time of great negative publicity concerning the academic abuse of college athletes, Thompson's players have one of the highest graduation rates in America. Was there some jealousy involved in the attacks, a hint of "play our game in the middle of the road," of not rocking the boat? Didn't these same scribes used to call aggressive white teams "hustling teams?" Did white coaches like John Wooden get so heavily criticized for keeping the press at arm's length from their teams?

Even if you accept that Thompson's style was a tough one for the public to grapple with, this still doesn't explain the degree of the attacks. The racial issue seemed, once again, to be the factor. While I applaud the few writers who wrote balanced pieces on John Thompson and Georgetown, the others clearly show how far we have to go.

Maybe the black players should attend schools with black coaches. For basketball players, that would be fifteen schools, as of this writing. The NCAA has more than 700 member schools, with approximately thirteen players per team. Therefore, of the 9,000 slots for basketball players, fewer than 200 slots fall under black basketball coaches. The slots are even fewer in college baseball (one coach) and football (two). For the moment, except for a few, black athletes will have to attend predominantly white schools with white coaches.

For now, the black athlete who goes to college is going to have to face all the problems we have mentioned. Academically, the black athlete will enter college at a disadvantage, one artificially maintained because of gut courses and easy grades. He is unlikely to get a degree because once his eligibility expires, so does the school's interest in him.

Athletically, he will have to be the best because otherwise he wouldn't be there. Still, with prevailing stereotypes and blatant racism, he will be scapegoated for feigning injuries, and "dogging it." Coaches will make assumptions about him they would never make about whites. He will receive harsh discipline. He will be pulled out of a game more quickly than whites. He will compete with other blacks for some "black positions" while whites control the game at quarterback, guard, or pitcher. He will face other kinds of quotas as well.

Socially, he will be in an alien world, segregated in student housing, off-campus housing, on road trips, and in bed. He will be a "good man" if he chooses the right way—the white way. But if he does, he separates himself from those who aren't "good men," that is, those who have chosen a black way.

It seems the black athlete cannot win. If, after suffering all these problems, he doesn't get a degree, then why does he subject himself to all of this in the first place?

The answer is simple. He assumes that sports is his way out of the ghetto.

Sport is promoted as the hope of black people. But too often those are empty hopes, blighted hopes. Go into Harlem or Watts and you see the results—black kids going for the hoop, going for the gold. Many cold nights I have come home late and heard a ball bounce against the pavement in a schoolyard as a couple of kids try to see the basket that is dimly lighted by a streetlamp forty feet away. Those kids believe. Work hard here and you will control. Control what? The tap? a rebound? They can make shot after shot and their feelings are positive. These black youth are pacified. They are becoming part of the system, albeit the bottom of the system—right where they are needed. Play, play. If you are good, play till you are eighteen. If you are very good, keep going until you are twenty-two. If you're great, play till you're thirty. But while they may be controlling that missed shot, they slip farther and farther into the pool of unskilled labor. They are forgetting their studies while going up for the rebound.

Unfortunately, this is the same system that "passes" students, including ballplayers, onto the next level without regard to academic achievement. For ballplayers it is just that much easier. They are conditioned that academic work is not necessary; just work on your body. The promise of the pros is the shared dream, no matter how unrealistic.

Fred Buttler is but one tragic example of a man who didn't make it in the pros and is paying the price for not being properly educated. Roger Rapoport wrote about Buttler in *New Times.* Buttler is a classic case of how the athletic-educational complex abuses black athletes.

Fred possessed enormous physical promise when he attended Warren Lane Elementary in Inglewood, California. Coaches at Warren watched as he beat older children in every sport he took up. However, his mother Edna saw that he could not do his schoolwork. She had to ask without success that he be held back a semester in the third grade to improve his reading skills. She questioned school officials when they promoted him to Monroe Junior High School after the sixth grade. She was told not to be so concerned.

He was an immediate football star at Monroe, but he still could not read. He and four other black athletes, who were called the "Hersheys" by the nearly all-white student body, sat in disbelief as they were told they were "just too bright to be in the eighth grade" and, therefore, they were being skipped into Morningside High after the seventh grade. Mrs. Buttler complained to the Monroe administration that it was not fair to send an illiterate to high school. She was patronizingly told "it's the best for Fred."

Edna Buttler watched in dismay as her son accumulated a three-year C+ average at Morningside while never opening a book. There was no need to do so as all the teachers made special "arrangements" for the star football player. At times he handed in blank exams. They were returned with all the right answers. At other times he was given oral exams. Most of the time he didn't have to take any exams. There was no point. He could not read them.

Fred Buttler told Rapoport that the teachers always made

him feel good and gave him confidence that he would make the pros. "No matter how much trouble I had understanding things in class, I always figured I would make a good living playing ball for the pros. . . . Football was going to make me famous. And I knew I wasn't just dreaming because everyone told me I was good." When he graduated from Morningside he had a second-grade reading level—about the same level he had when Edna requested that he be left back in the third grade nine years before.

Although he couldn't read the play book, he got a scholarship to El Camino Junior College. His advisor, Carl Mersola, acknowledged that Fred could not read. Mersola said that the 2 percent minority quotas mandated by the federal government meant "a chimpanzee could come and play football." So Buttler took mostly "activity classes" in physical education and maintained his standing. The cornerback helped lead El Camino to two outstanding years. Fred knew that two more years of college would end with a pro contract.

He decided to attend Cal-LA State. Mersola had to take two days to fill in Fred's complicated admission and grant-in-aid forms. Fred was promised remedial reading help at LA State, but none was there to be had. It did not matter, for he took oral exams and more and more physical education courses. Buttler noted matter-of-factly, "I think some of the coaches were probably happy I couldn't read because that meant I wouldn't waste time on schoolwork since that way I could concentrate on playing for them." The dream continued during his first one and a half years at LA State. He kept up a C+ average and played well. But as his eligibility ran out at the end of the fall semester, so did the great interest and support from the faculty. Suddenly the C+ former football star was a failing student and was flunked out of LA State within months. In the end, Fred Buttler had no degree, no offers to play pro football, and no skills to use for gainful employment. And he still could not read. He is now a factory worker and lives with his mother.

When Fred Buttler was released from jail as charges were dropped after the accidental shooting of his father, he could not find his father's grave because he could not read the signs in the cemetery. The police refused to let him attend the burial. This is Fred Buttler's sports legacy. He is still living with it in America today.

Frank Cuffee faced the same problems but was fortunate to have pulled himself out of it. Frank, who happened to be black, was the first good basketball player recruited by Virginia Wesleyan College. I don't think he started in high school, but at Wesleyan, which had prior to his enrollment amassed a twenty-five-game losing streak, Frank was the best player.

Frank was bright and articulate. We talked a lot. Much of what he talked about was playing for the Virginia Squires of the ABA. I couldn't believe my ears. He was an intelligent young man. Yet he believed that by averaging 17 points a game at Wesleyan, he would have a chance at the pros. I tried to convince him of reality, but he was consumed by his game, didn't study enough, and eventually had to leave school. Only then did he understand.

We stayed in touch. He took control, got a job, and paid his way through another college. The last time I saw Frank was just before I left Virginia. He was working for Greyhound Bus and proudly told me he was just about to graduate. I smiled and was happy. Frank thanked me for all I had done. He told me that he was horrified to see what the police and the press were doing to me, and that the black community was behind me.

Frank Cuffee got back control against heavy odds. Most of his black brothers who get pinned to the backboard don't fall down until it's too late.

A look at the numbers opens our eyes. In 1980, 569,228 kids played high-school basketball. Less than 20,000 played in colleges with perhaps half on basketball scholarships. In other words, almost twenty-nine of every thirty who played in high school never play in college. Only one out of every fifty high-school players gets a scholarship. If the 1978 Eitzen and Tessendorf figures hold, then 32 percent, or approximately 6,400 college basketball players, were black.

About fifty players will join the NBA each year. Thirty-five of those (70 percent) will be black. In other words, the odds against a black college ballplayer making the NBA are 183 to 1. The odds against a black high-school basketball player making the NBA are approximately 11,380 to 1. Jimmy the Greek wouldn't call that a good bet. Yet so many continue to place it with the highest stakes of all—their own futures.

The same figures apply to football. Close to a million play high-school football; some 30,000 play in college, with about 15,000, or less than 2 percent of those who played in high school, receiving scholarships. In a good year, a hundred rookies might make the NFL roster; fifty will be black. The odds on making the pros are 10,000 to 1 for blacks and whites. The emergence of the USFL will improve the odds only slightly—and only if the USFL succeeds. Better than basketball, but awfully shaky.

There are dozens of sports sociologists who can give you percentages and bell-shaped curves to show you why so many blacks play this sport or that, or this position or that. Harry Edwards can do this too, but Harry Edwards is one of these athletes.

Jack Olsen began his *Sports Illustrated* series in 1968 by pointing out the irony that without sports Harry Edwards might not have escaped from the ghetto. "Harry Edwards, out of East St. Louis, Illinois, where he attended various jails as a youth before it was discovered that he could whirl a discus half a mile and San Jose State College offered him an athletic scholarship."

Why isn't Harry coaching instead of preaching the evils of the system? It is because Harry Edwards knows the system. He tries to help the black athlete deal with the system intelligently. He tries to teach reality.

In 1968, Edwards told Olsen, "Black students aren't given athletic scholarships for the purpose of education. Blacks are brought in to perform . . . in most cases their college lives are educational blanks."

Ten years later, Edwards told Roger Rapoport in *New Times,* "Today 25 to 30 percent of the black high-school athletes are functionally illiterate. In junior colleges—20 to 25 percent, and at four-year colleges—15 to 20 percent."

Edwards, in a 1983 article on "The Collegiate Athletic Arms Race," estimated that 65 to 75 percent of black athletes who are awarded athletic scholarships may never graduate. Furthermore, "of the 25 to 35 percent who eventually graduate . . . an estimated 75 percent of them graduate either with physical education degrees or in majors specifically created for athletes and generally held in low repute."

Edwards estimated that approximately three million black youths over twelve place a high priority on a sports career. Fewer than 1,400 blacks play in the NBA, NFL, USFL, or in baseball's major leagues. At most, he estimates 2,400 black Americans make a living in sports—and that includes *all* forms of sports-related employment from receptionist to general managers. Fewer than 500 play in the minor leagues.

The numbers tell an additional story. Fewer than 10 percent of all athletic scholarships go to blacks, less than their proportion in society. Those scholarships are concentrated in football, basketball, baseball, and track. The first two pay for all other college sports combined. In other words, the black athlete, in addition to everything else, helps raise the money to carry the white sports like fencing, swimming, tennis, golf, and lacrosse.

In the end, black college athletes live on a precarious precipice. Suddenly, unless they are the 1 in 12,000 who will make the pros, they are on their way home with nothing to show for their college years except the shame of not having made it to the pros and bitterness and betrayal. For fifteen years they did little else besides perfect the pitch, sharpen the shot, synchronize the pass, and skip the class. The Fred Buttlers are the extreme tragedies. The Frank Cuffees show us hope through individual determination. Both extremes are difficult paths to traverse.

Arthur Ashe, Kareem, and others now exhort young blacks to study to become lawyers and doctors, to develop their minds. But Corporate America doesn't show black youth black lawyers on TV. They show O.J. bolting through airports. Black doctors don't endorse surgical equipment but there are Magic Johnson basketballs and Walt Frazier shoes.

Young blacks may hear Ashe and Kareem tell them to study, but they see the money Ashe and Kareem make from sports. Corporate America does not make statistics on race in sport available on TV or in the newspapers. There will be the occasional item, true, but the items are rare.

But Corporate America does lay out the odds for blacks who are aspiring lawyers. Such odds were highly publicized early in 1981. In 1963, women made up only 3.6 percent of law-school enrollment. By 1981 they represented 33.5 percent. In 1969 (when the American Bar Association began to count by race) the proportion of black law students was 3.1 percent. It reached a high of 4.7 percent in 1977. In 1981 it dropped to 4.4 percent. Worse still, black law-school graduates are not hired by the big law firms. Of the 10,679 partners and associates in the nation's fifty largest law firms, less than 1.6 percent were black. With only 28 percent of the 5,549 black law-school graduates able to get a job with a firm in 1981, the odds on a young black out of the general population doing so are 13,000 to one. Such figures are no aid in attracting young blacks to the books. The picture was dimmer than ever for the 1982–83 academic year when undergraduate black enrollment actually declined from the previous year.

For all too many, that means back to the hoop or diamond. The myth lives on.

In 1968 Olsen wrote in *SI*, "At most, sports had led a few thousand Negroes into a better life while substituting a meaningless dream for hundreds and thousands of other Negroes. It has helped perpetuate an oppressive system."

The only difference today is that more blacks are chasing that meaningless dream. And as each one falls, America's cheap labor pool swells. After the fall, the assembly line looks good.

·14·

The Promised Land

Those among the approximately 11,999 out of 12,000 who didn't make it to the pros have received heavy doses of reality therapy. However, there is still that one. And in the pros the black athlete is finally on nearly equal footing with white athletes. He is there because of his talent.

The pro athlete is financially rich. He does not face the discrimination he knew in high school or college. Perhaps a coaching career looms ahead, or a front-office job will follow after he finishes playing. In any event, if he is exceptional, he will be remembered in the minds of fans and the media.

You can't argue about the money. Agents, players associations, and free agency have resulted in annual incomes that make up for the years of toiling for little or nothing in colleges and in minor leagues.

The racial integration of baseball, basketball, and football has been remarkable. Owners realized that there was an enormous black market that had been untapped prior to the arrival of Jackie Robinson at Ebbets Field in 1947. Movement was slow at first as the waters were tested. The NBA and NFL were integrated in 1950. Ten years after the barriers fell in Brooklyn, the major leagues had only eighteen blacks. The NFL was only

14 percent black and the NBA only 5 to 7 percent. However, the complexion of America's three major sports was very different three decades later when 23 percent of major league baseball players, 54 percent of NFL players, and 70 percent of NBA players were black.

There is certainly no other professional area where blacks occupy such high percentages of the totals.

And blacks have broken into other sports. They are, of course, dominant in boxing and track and field.

Althea Gibson astonished the tennis world when she beat Darlene Hard for the 1957 Wimbledon crown. Arthur Ashe won the U.S. Open in 1968 when he overwhelmed Tom Okker. Leslie Allen captured headlines in 1980 when she became the first black woman since Gibson to win a major tournament. 1983 brought forth two African-born tennis stars for the first time. Blacks have been represented at the top levels of tennis for all three of our integrated sports decades. However, fewer than two stars per decade is hardly dominance.

Pete Brown became the first black man to win a Professional Golf Association (PGA) event when he won the 1964 Waco Turner Open. Charlie Sifford, the first black on the PGA tour, had won the Long Beach Open in 1957 and the Alameda Open in 1960 but the PGA made both events "unofficial." However, Brown was an official winner at last in 1964 when public pressure made it impossible to deny black golfers any longer. Yet, victories for black golfers, like black tennis players, have not been common in the last three decades. Calvin Peete is a new phenomenon.

Barriers fell quickly in the big three sports. In 1966, Emmett Ashford became a major league umpire after a twenty-two-year career. In April 1966, Red Auerbach named Bill Russell as the first black coach in any of sports' big leagues. (John McLendon was hired to coach the Cleveland Pipers in the American Basketball Association in 1961.)

The civil rights movement, the acknowledgment of black

athletic talent, and the owner's vision of a black market have indeed opened the doors in the last thirty years. No matter how far to the right America swings in the 1980s, it is difficult to imagine a decrease in black participation in baseball, football, and basketball. However, increasing racism could easily further delay black emergence in other sports.

Blacks have access to basketball courts, and some parks that can be used as baseball diamonds and football fields. However, they have little or no use of golf, tennis, swimming, and ice-skating facilities. For the most part, these facilities are in the suburbs and are expensive. Also, the socializing that exists almost as part of these sports will further inhibit the acceptance of blacks. Such relationships in country club sports are part of the package. They are not a part of baseball, football, or basketball.

If blacks do use role models to determine what athletic direction they might choose, the choices are surely broader in the big three sports. Black youth will be motivated by the breadth of the examples they see. Five star tennis players in three decades and even fewer golfers do not compare with the 70 percent black NBA. The choices are clear.

So the question becomes how good are the options for the black athlete in baseball, football, and basketball? Is he treated equally in each sport? Is he viewed as the equal of his white counterparts by coaches, the front office, and the fans? Is he paid the same? Are the stereotypes applied to him earlier in his career still assumed by whites? Does he face quotas? Is he limited to playing certain positions because of stacking? Must he perform better than whites in order to stay on the team? Does his fame endure after his playing career? Will he become a coach in the pros or join the front office of his team? Will he be out on the street when his sports career is terminated?

Any serious assessment shows what a short distance we have traveled. To be sure, the numbers of black players have dramatically increased and many have become wealthy. However, what has benefited those few has helped perpetuate the tragedy of so many blacks who reach for the ring only to crash back to the real world without skills. And even those few face racial discrimination in the pros, day after day.

For the black superstars, life *is* secure. Their salaries are equal to white stars. Black superstars have come a long way since 1966 when Frank Robinson, the Most Valuable Player (MVP) in the American League, was offered only two speaking engagements and one TV commercial. (By comparison Carl Yastrzemski, the white 1967 winner, estimated that his extra income resulting from the MVP award was $150,000 to $200,-000.) In 1982, Reggie Jackson was supposed to have made $750,000 in endorsements and speaking engagements.

It is more difficult to tell if salary equality and income from endorsements apply across the board since teams do not reveal the salaries of all their players. Likewise, companies rarely announce the value of the endorsement packages. Irwin Weiner, a well-known agent for ballplayers, said, "When I go in with a fringe player who's white, I can squeeze out a little more money."

Information of salary differentials between blacks and whites has been very difficult to obtain. However, David Meggyesy, the National Football League Players Association Western Regional Director, did a preliminary analysis based on the 1982 NFL season that gives us a clear picture that whites do earn significantly higher incomes than blacks. League-wide, whites averaged $100,730 while blacks averaged only $91,980.

It made no difference whether you played offense or defense or started or were a backup. White offensive players earned an average of $4,970 more than black offensive players. The biggest difference was on defense, where whites took in $11,100 more than blacks ($97,100 to $86,000).

White starters overall made $121,050 compared to $112,880 for black starters. On offense they earned $4,500 more and on

defense a very significant $14,960 more than their black coun-
terparts.

White offensive backups received an average of $87,290 in
contrast to the $78,630 for black offensive backups—an $8,666
differential. White defensive backups made $5,060 more than
black defensive backups.

While Meggyesy's preliminary study has yet to go into the
causal relationships of these figures, his memo to the NFLPA's
Board of Player Representatives in May of 1983 went to the
heart of the matter:

> Consistent with this historical pattern of racial discrimina-
> tion, a similar pattern exists today regarding players sala-
> ries. Simply put, in the NFL, black professional football
> players earn less than their white counterparts. Numerous
> theories have been presented as to why racial discrimina-
> tion exists in the NFL. These theories are beside the point;
> the real issue is that that racial discrimination does exist,
> and that it must be eliminated.

It would appear then that, at least in football, the salary
differential is great below the superstar level. A case could be
made that the black superstar has not only been allowed to
make big money both in salary and commercials, but that it is
to the advantage of the owners for this to happen. Reggie and
O.J. seem to be everywhere. Such special cases are then used to
anesthetize the public. In fact, the big changes in these areas
affect only the most visible blacks.

There still are situations where black pros, even when they
are superstars, are viewed differently from whites. Some blacks
are accused by white teammates, management, and fans of
being lazy—of dogging it.

Wayne Simpson is a case in point. In 1981, everyone was
talking about the sensational start of Fernando Valenzuela.
Forgotten was the year of the then twenty-one-year-old Simp-

son in 1970. He won 10 straight and 13 of his first 14 games for the Cincinnati Reds. Among his victories was a one-hitter. He was an All Star at twenty-one. However, over the next nine years he averaged only 4 wins a year, complaining of incessant pain in his arm. Team doctors said nothing was wrong. Sparky Anderson, the Reds' manager, was quoted as saying "Simpson's problem is mental." Another black man dogging it.

But Simpson kept on pitching with pain by taking cortisone shots. Then in May 1978, under a doctor's observation, Wayne Simpson tried to throw a few pitches. His hand grew cold, white, and numb. The doctor called for an emergency operation to prevent the loss of the hand. Simpson had four bypass operations in the next year and still has almost total disability in his right hand.

When he was finally examined by doctors who had no stake in keeping him in the game, it was revealed by Simpson that "over the course of my pitching career, I had rubbed out an entire artery." Referring to his two sons, Simpson told Ira Berkow, "when the time comes, I'd be crazy not to tell my two boys that sports isn't nearly as glamorous as it seems." It was a hard way to learn. He is still learning. He had to sue to attempt to get workmen's compensation from the teams he pitched for. As of the writing of Berkow's article he had not received it.

Houston's star pitcher, J. R. Richard, may be the worst victim yet. He was in the midst of his best season in 1980 with a 10–4 record, 119 strikeouts, and a league-leading 1.80 ERA. He had struck out more than 600 batters in his previous two seasons. He had not missed a turn in the starting rotation in five years. His highest ERA in those five years was 3.11. He had won 20, 18, 18, and 18 in his last four full seasons. There were few if any better pitchers in baseball.

On June 17, Richard complained of "deadness" in his arm and sat out until June 28, when he was knocked out by Cincinnatti after only 3½ innings. The media attack began. It alleged that Richard was lazy, a loafer. It speculated that he might be into drugs. But he pitched better on July 3 (six innings, three hits, two runs) and in the All-Star Game, which he started (two innings, one hit, three strikeouts). Then he lasted only three innings against Atlanta on July 14. The media attack intensified even as Richard went on the disabled list. Hospital tests discovered a clot but doctors said he could pitch under supervision. Then he had a stroke during his first workout and nearly died.

The critics were silenced. Enos Cabell, the Astros third baseman, told Bill Nack of *Sports Illustrated* that the criticism would not have come down if Richard had been white. "We always knew we had to be better. There is a difference." Carolyn Richard, J.R.'s wife, lamented to Nack, "Black and big, a big star. . . . Other guys had problems on the Astros. Ken Forsch [a white pitcher] was out a whole half of a season. [Nolan] Ryan hasn't been pitching to his ability. I've never seen a player dragged through the mud like this. It's something we'll never forget. Never."

Charlie Sanders of the Detroit Lions was chosen as the tight end on the NFL's "team of the seventies." He had been selected for the Pro Bowl seven times and caught 336 passes in ten years. He hurt his knee on a preseason play in 1976 but continued to play on the advice of team physicians. On the game day, doctors had to wire his knee, shoot it with electrical charges, and have his leg heavily wrapped. The pain was enormous, but he played. The media printed stories saying coaches thought Sanders was a hypochondriac. In November 1977, he went to see a specialist in Toronto, who performed an arthroscopy to discover that the bone "was completely rotted out."

Sanders asked Ira Berkow of *The New York Times*, "Why wasn't I given an arthroscopy earlier, or why did people refuse to believe I was in such pain? I don't know." He discovered that Lions physicians had withheld medical information from him. One of the Lions' physicians told Berkow, "Sometimes it's not good to tell a patient everything . . . you wind up scaring the patient needlessly." Unlike the Astros, the Lions have not apologized. In fact, they appealed a workmen's compensation award to Sanders of $32,500 cash plus $156 per week for the injury, but the award was settled out of court and Sanders was hired as a part-time community relations worker for the Lions.

These are the cases of black superstars. Grumbling about average black pros is incessant. The difference is that the average black pro who grumbles can be let go.

There has been considerable publicity given to athletes taking drugs in pro sports. NBA executives, for example, estimate that 40 to 75 percent of the players use cocaine and 10 percent use free base, a heightened form of cocaine. A five-day binge on free base can cost between $2,000 to $12,000. Whites are too smart for that, according to the image projected by the press. The junkies are black.

It didn't seem to surprise anyone when Pete Rozelle suspended four players—all blacks—prior to the 1983 season for cocaine use. Yet no one believed that Pete Johnson, Ross Browner, E. J. Junior, and Greg Stremrick were the only users in the NFL. The drug-related convictions of Kansas City baseball stars after the 1983 season shocked many. Yet we knew there were many others.

Simon Gourdine, the former NBA deputy commissioner, wondered whether the furor caused by the drug revelations was racially motivated. He told Jane Gross of *The New York Times,* "if someone chose to, they could have concluded that 100 percent of the black players were involved with drugs. Anytime there are social problems like drugs or alcohol, the perception is that it's black players involved. That concerns me." The size of the fine and then the suspension of LA Dodger reliever Steve Howe—a white—gave hope that Gourdine's projection is not totally accurate.

In September 1983, the NBA and the NBA Players Association took a strong stand on drugs. Starting at the end of 1983, any player known to be distributing or using drugs would be banned from the NBA. With an estimated 75 percent of the players using drugs, it will be difficult to see how this ruling will be effectively and equally enforced. However, if it works, it could be the model for other leagues. And cleaning up the players' acts would also help countless youth who see them as role models.

When it comes to taking out aggression through sport, there is a difference for black athletes. The white athlete can act out his aggressive impulses against other whites or blacks. The black athlete can do the same with other blacks. However, he approaches a dangerous line when he considers hitting a white man. He knows the price could be too high and may have to further repress these feelings.

Many stories have been told of the restraint displayed by Jackie Robinson when he broke into baseball. He turned the other cheek so often that some men thought him saintly. Larry Doby, the American League's first black, told Jack Olsen what it was like in those days:

> When I think of things the way they were, I wonder how we did it. I remember sliding into second base and the fielder spitting chewing tobacco juice in my face and just walked away. I walked away. They'd shout at you: "You dirty black so and so." I didn't have a fight until 1957. Charlie Neal had one in Brooklyn about the same time. I guess we celebrated our independence.

During the same era, Bill Russell's white high school coach in Oakland told his all-black team to keep cool since, "the second there's any trouble everyone is going to blame you, whether it's your fault or not. You'll be guilty . . . and everyone will claim it's a riot."

While there has been a change in the black athlete's freedom to defend himself, distinctions still exist.

Incidents of black versus other blacks or Latins on the playing fields were treated disinterestedly. On August 22, 1965, for example, Dodger John Roseboro, one of the league's first prominent black catchers, was seriously injured when the star pitcher of the Giants, Juan Marichal, hit him over the head with a bat, causing serious injury. Roseboro sued for $110,000 but settled for $7,500 out of court.

In a case of comparable brutality, Los Angeles Laker forward Kermit Washington, a six-eight black man, was involved in a fight with two white Houston players. It broke out between Washington and seven-foot Keven Kunnert in a December 9, 1977 game. Washington then hit six-eight Rudy Tomjanovich so hard that he broke his jaw and fractured his skull. Tomjanovich sued the Lakers and received $3.3 million, $600,000 more than his lawyers requested! The Lakers appealed, and prior to a decision, an out-of-court settlement was reached for an undisclosed but presumably lesser amount. Still, that type of fine has to have a numbing effect on future fights. But one wonders why Roseboro got $7,500 and Tomjanovich $3.3 million.

One could argue that Roseboro was not hurt as seriously as Tomjanovich, who missed the remainder of the 1977–78 season. However, he returned the following year to average 19 points. That was *prior* to the jury's staggering award, so there was little doubt about permanent damage totally ruining his career. Was there any thought in the minds of the jurors that a black man who viciously hit a white man in public must pay dearly for his sins? Was the ruling to make other blacks return to "turn-the-other cheek" to survive?

Kareem Abdul-Jabbar went a long way toward answering this question in *Giant Steps,* his autobiography. Kareem witnessed the fight and saw it as Washington, enraged by Kunnert's punching him, swinging wildly in self-defense at the oncoming Tomjanovich. Kareem was restraining Kunnert, and Tomjanovich, coming from behind, was trying to do the same with Washington.

Kareem discussed the NBA's response. Kunnert was not disciplined at all. Washington was fined $10,000 and suspended without pay for 26 games. "What that said to me, and to all black players in the league, was that if somebody white punches you out, you play defense and hope that the refs will try and stop it at some point. If not, just realize that the NBA needs white players to keep the white fans interested and the arenas filled and the networks on the line. Count on no support from the people who run this business."

Washington was told that the league owners forced Jack Kent Cooke, the owner of the Lakers, to trade him, as they would not tolerate Kareem and Washington on the same team. Kareem had hurt Kent Benson, a white rookie center, earlier in the season. Kareem noted, "Here were two extremely powerful black men who had both severely beaten white players, and the owners wanted us separated because they would not have us intimidating the rest of the league. That's hard to prove and easy to deny, but I fully believe it."

Much of this is a matter of speculation. Other questions in the three major sports are not so open to speculation. One is the matter of quotas, which continue despite denials. Another related issue is that of the need for blacks to perform better than whites to remain in the pros.

As we've seen, NBA management denied quotas existed when Bill Russell first exposed them in the 1960s. They were denied again in 1980 when the league took action against Ted Stepien, the new owner in Cleveland who proclaimed, "I think the Cavs have too many blacks, ten of eleven. You need a blend of white and black. I think that draws and I think that's a better team." He sent black star Campy Russell as a gift to the Knicks. He dumped black guard Foots Walker, who was third in the league in assists. He obtained undistinguished whites Mike Bratz and Roger Phegley in trades. He offered his budding superstar Mike Mitchell (black) to San Antonio for Mark Olberding (white). In only his second year, Mitchell had averaged 22.2, shot 52 percent, and led the team in blocked shots. Olberding averaged 10.5, his best in five seasons. But San Antonio reportedly nixed the deal because Olberding was their only white starter.

Ironically, Mitchell eventually went to San Antonio for Ron Brewer and Reggie Johnson, two blacks, while Olberding ended up in Chicago along with Dave Corzine in the Artis Gilmore trade. In spite of losing two white regulars, San Antonio managed to begin the 1982–83 preseason with five white players on the squad.

No matter how badly coach Stan Albech's management might have wanted white starters, the fact is that the five whites had a combined career-game average of only 6 points per game each, compared to the nearly 14-point average of the seven blacks on the preseason roster. The likes of Mike Bratz, Paul Griffin, Roger Phegley, or Rich Yonaker were not ready to shake up the NBA. The career of Rich Yonaker is a case in point. He was drafted in 1980 in the third round after averaging 3.7, 5.7, 6.8, and 5.9 during his four-year collegiate career at North Carolina. His NBA average for 1981–82 was 3.3, yet he was still on the 1982–83 preseason roster. None of this should be surprising since San Antonio is one of only four cities cited in the 1980 census as showing an increase in the percentage of whites since 1970. Its black population was less than 5 percent.

Joel Axelson, the director of operations for the NBA, objects and calls the charge of quotas in the NBA "total garbage." He told Gary Meyers of the *Daily News,* "I never heard of a personnel decision made on the basis of black or white. They don't make decisions on that basis—99 percent of the clubs are looking for people to win games."

However, Lenny Wilkens, who was one of the very few black pro coaches in all pro sports, said, "The unwritten rule is that there should be a minimum of three white players on each team." Larry Fleischer, the counsel to the NBA Players Association, as reported by *Sport* at the end of 1978, said simply, "There are a number of players in the NBA who are on teams not because of their ability but because they are white."

Is there a system in the 70 percent black NBA to regulate the number of whites per team? In spite of the denials, the twenty-three official preseason team rosters submitted prior to the 1982–83 season reveal some convincing evidence. Fourteen of the twenty-three teams listed at least a 25 percent white roster. The nine exceptions included Atlanta, San Francisco, Houston, New York, Philadelphia, and Washington—all of which have large black populations, running from 25 up to 61 percent. Still, most sought whites in the draft since crowds are predominantly white. The nine teams with the most whites include Boston, Dallas, Denver, Phoenix, Portland, San Antonio, and Seattle.

It is even more interesting to look at the 1982 college draft. Fifteen whites were chosen in the first three rounds and selected in the official *NBA Register* as "promising newcomers." Of those fifteen, twelve or 80 percent were chosen by eight of the nine teams who did not have at least a 25 percent white roster. New York, Philadelphia, Washington, and Kansas City took two whites each in the first three rounds. A glance at the statistics of these newcomers makes one wonder if the teams were selecting for increased strength or for adding players who might join the already existing pool of marginal white players in the NBA. Four of the fifteen had career averages below 10 points per game including one drafted by Houston who had a college-career average of 3.0! Only four of the fifteen averaged more than 14 points per game. Utah selected Mark Eaton early in the fourth round after he averaged 1.8 points per game at UCLA, where he played a total of forty-one minutes in his senior year.

Is it plausible that this is an accident? If it is, how else can you explain that Seattle, which has a high percentage of whites on its basketball, baseball, and football franchises, drafted Bill Hanzlick of Notre Dame in the first round in 1980? Hanzlick averaged 4.1, 3.7, 8.7, and 7.5 in his four years of college basketball. Seattle has one of the smallest black populations (46,755) of all the major U.S. cities. It needs white players and it gets them.

Quotas aside, there is no way to argue against the charge that blacks must perform better than whites to remain in the NBA. Front-office people deny this, but candid white sports personalities do not. Al McGuire noted, "If a white and black player are equal, I think the white player would get the edge in time played and pictures in the program." Former Knick white superstar Dave DeBusschere said simply, "The white guy has a better opportunity." The numbers don't lie. All figures that follow come from the 1982–83 official *NBA Register.*

To be sure, there are genuine white stars like Larry Bird, Alvin Adams, Bill Walton, Dan Issel, Jack Sikma, Scott Wedman, Kiki Vandeweghe, Kelly Tripuka, and Tom Chambers. There are other fine white players like Paul Westphal, Tom Owens, Swen Nater, Billy Paultz, Ernie Grunfeld, Mark Olberding, Rick Robey, Chris Ford, Bobby Jones, Steve Mix, Kevin Grevey, Mitch Kupchak, Dave Robisch, Kyle Macy, Kevin McHale, Kent Benson, Mike O'Koren, Jim Paxson, Jeff Ruland, and Kurt Rambis, among others.

But a look at who the NBA teams carry is revealing. Of the four whites on the preseason roster of the 1982 champion Lakers, three had career averages under 7 points. This was true of both whites listed by Golden State. Five of the six shown on Portland's roster averaged under 5 points per game. Five of the six whites for Dallas had career averages of less than 9. Statistics like this hold throughout the NBA with only a handful of exceptions like Boston, Denver, San Diego, and Philadelphia.

In fact, New York, Utah, Denver, San Diego, and Philadelphia were the only teams in 1981–82 whose white players had collective career-scoring averages greater than their black teammates. The average career-scoring average for whites in the league is 9.3. For blacks, it is 11.1. As Enos Cabell said about baseball, "There *is* a difference."

And blacks dominate the top of the league. There were only four whites among the twenty-four chosen for the 1982 NBA All-Star Game. In 1981–82, nine of the top ten scorers were black as were eight of the top ten in rebounds and field-goal percentage. The top ten in assists were all black. In 1980–81, blacks held the top ten positions in scoring, field-goal percentage, and assists. In 1979–80, blacks had nine of the ten top positions in scoring, field-goal percentage, and blocked shots plus a clean sweep again in assists.

The prospect is bleak for owners who might want whiter teams. Only 27 percent of the first-round draft choices in the 1970s were white. Of the fifty Associated Press first-team All-American selections in the 1970s, only thirteen were white.

So as more blacks come into the league, owners have to retain the marginal white ballplayers in order to maintain the desired percentage of whites. Black athletes have claimed that this was the case for many years. It is no different today.

In spite of the fact that blacks in the league outnumber whites by almost three to one, white players with five years' experience in the NBA and who averaged under 8 points per game actually outnumber blacks in the same category by nineteen to sixteen. Black veterans averaging more than 8 points outnumber whites in the same category by seventy-two to twenty-eight. Measured on a statistical basis, marginal whites have a better chance of becoming "veterans" than marginal blacks by almost four to one.

Sports critics agree that the reason quotas are most frequently mentioned in basketball is that positional segregation in a five-man game that is almost seventy percent black is impossible. While the guard position in college is overwhelmingly white dominated, no position in the NBA is. Height in basketball is the key determinant. The whole range of a player's skills are on display when he is on the court. Without the ability to control the number of blacks by making them compete for the same positions, it is suggested that the same has been accomplished in basketball through quotas.

However, the fans apparently believe that there has not been enough control. While attendance in baseball, football, and hockey has soared since 1976, it has declined in basketball. Baseball sold 8 million more tickets in 1980 than in 1976 (up 26 percent); the NFL sold 2.3 million more in 1980 than in 1976 (a 21 percent increase); 2 million more hockey tickets were sold during the 1979–80 season than in 1976–77 (up 24 percent). But the NBA tickets sales for 1980–81 were down by 8 percent over the previous year and were less than they were in 1976–77. The frustration of fans with player strikes reduced attendance in baseball in 1981 and football in 1982–83. But race seemed to be a primary factor in the NBA.

A fan at a football game can hardly tell who is black and who is white under all that gear. But the fan can be virtually certain that the quarterback, Mr. All-America, is white. In baseball, the players are so spread out on the field that a racist fan would not feel overwhelmed by hordes of blacks.

But in basketball there is no way to hide black bodies glistening with sweat. Ten could be concentrated in a twelve-square-foot area. *That* is too much for some.

A survey of Philadelphia fans during the 1980–81 season confirmed this. Philadelphia had the best record in the NBA and had Julius Erving, the league's most exciting player. But the survey was taken by the Philadelphia *Daily News* because the 76ers were bringing in only 55 percent of their capacity and ranked only ninth in total attendance. Fifty-seven percent of 955 responses agreed that "a white audience won't pay to watch black athletes." Julius Erving agreed. "I would like to say that race is not involved, but that would be naive."

The Celtics have always had at least one white superstar. Now it is Larry Bird. The Celtics sold out 95 percent of their seats, compared to 57 percent in Philadelphia. The teams were fierce rivals and had nearly identical records. Yet, on a percentage basis, the Celtics outdrew the 76ers by almost 40 percent. Knowing the formula, they made Larry Bird the highest-paid player in the NBA and made Kevin McHale the fourth highest-paid player prior to the 1983–84 season. As outstanding as McHale is, he is not the NBA's fourth-best player. Bird is close to the best.

With the exceptions of Los Angeles, which won the 1982 NBA championship, and Milwaukee, which won its divisional title, all the league teams that had an average attendance of more than 70 percent of capacity had at least three whites on the team. You couldn't buy a Knick ticket in New York when it had white superstars Bill Bradley and Dave DeBusschere to blend with Walt Frazier, Earl Monroe, and Willis Reed. With an up-and-coming young, but all-black team, the Knicks could draw only 63.4 percent of capacity in 1980–81. It did not seem coincidental that the Knicks chose white players in the second and third rounds of the 1982 draft.

If you are among those who agree that the NBA needs a quota system since it is "too black," then look at major league baseball, which has the smallest percentage of blacks of the three major sports. All figures are taken from the 1983 *Who's Who in Baseball*.

Only 19 percent of major league players are black Americans —a decline from the 1960s. If you include black Latin Americans, then blacks make up a total of 23 percent. Are black baseball players evenly distributed through a quota system? Twenty-two of the twenty-six teams in the majors had seven or less blacks (nineteen teams if you include black Latins). The number seven is 23 percent. Is it an accident that more than 75 percent of basketball and baseball teams conform to the overall percentage? It would seem hard to believe that the distribution of blacks and whites could be so if it occurred by chance.

Statistics would seem to show that blacks in baseball have to perform even better than those in basketball vis-à-vis their white teammates. Let's take a close look.

A veteran is defined as anyone who has played in the majors

for five years. All figures are career averages. While the percentage of black veterans (seventy-nine) to white veterans (sixty-eight) is higher, a black has to be better than the white to last that long. Only 21 percent of black veterans had career batting averages below .261 while 46 percent of whites did. Only 4 percent of black vets hit below .240 compared to 17 percent of the whites. Sixty-six percent of black veterans had lifetime averages above .270 in contrast to the twenty-seven percent of whites who hit that well. Forty-four percent of black veterans had better than a .281 lifetime average juxtaposed to only fifteen percent of whites.

The figures hold steady if you include all players in the 1983 *Who's Who in Baseball* with more than 100 at bats. Ten percent of the blacks hit above .300 compared to only two percent of the whites. Forty percent of the blacks batted .281 or better while only fourteen percent of the whites did. Sixty percent of the blacks had career averages above .270 while seventy-five percent of the whites had career averages below that.

Any realistic analysis must conclude that blacks outperform whites in baseball *by far*. It goes on—black Latin American ballplayers also outperform white Latin Americans. Only 4 percent of the black Latins have career averages below .241 while 31 percent of the white Latins do. As Hispanic markets open up, the recruitment of Latin American ballplayers increases. But once again, the color of their skin plays a part in their chances to have a lengthy career.

The story for pitchers is the same. Nearly twice as many blacks as whites have career records above .600 (18 percent versus 10 percent). Twenty-nine percent of black pitchers in the league had more than 100 career victories versus only seventeen percent of the white pitchers.

In terms of the pitchers' career earned-run averages (ERAs), considerably more blacks than whites (30 percent to 20 percent) have ERAs below 3.20. Almost three times as many whites as blacks (31 percent versus 11.7 percent) have ERAs greater than

4.01. Whereas 16 percent of white pitchers have career ERAs greater than 4.41, no blacks do. Consistently, black pitchers have lower ERAs. They are better, and they have to be, for it is next to impossible for black pitchers to play major league baseball *unless* they are excellent black pitchers.

Do blacks dominate in baseball as they do in basketball? The answer is clearly yes, especially considering that barely one out of five players in baseball is black, including black Latins. In 1983, half of the top twenty hitters in the National League and American League were black. Among home run leaders, five of eleven were black, as were six of the ten leaders in runs batted in and runs scored. Eight of the ten leaders in hits were black.

Unlike basketball, the chances of baseball becoming "whiter" are excellent. According to a 1978 study by James Curtis and John Loy, the percentage of blacks in baseball went from 10 percent in 1960 to 16 percent in 1968 and 27 percent in 1975. However, only 19 percent were black Americans in 1983, rising to 23 percent if black Latin Americans are included.

The number of minor league teams has decreased rapidly in the 1970s as college baseball has taken up more of their role. By 1982 the number of leagues had declined from fifty-nine in 1949 to seventeen while the number of players in the minors had declined from 9,000 in 1949 to only 3,300. In 1970, blacks used to make up 30 to 40 percent of the players in the minor leagues. By 1975, the minors were only 15 percent black. This reflected several things. First, since many of those blacks who sign contracts are more talented than whites, they move up to the majors faster. Second, some more are going to college on scholarships. A third, less tangible factor may reflect racial tensions in big cities. Most scouts are whites who may not only dislike blacks generally but are also reluctant to go see blacks play in the inner cities.

But don't look to the colleges with any hope of seeing more blacks playing baseball. While more black baseball players are going to college, the numbers are still small. In 1979 and 1980 combined, only one black made the *Sporting News* baseball All-American team. Since the proportions of college players selected in the baseball draft has risen from 40 percent in 1971 to 67 percent in 1982, the prospects for blacks going to the majors is even dimmer.

Not much has been said about professional football. Are there quotas? Are blacks also outperforming whites there? It is harder to tell since football as played in the NFL is almost totally segregated by position.

I was living in Denver when the Broncos drafted Marlin Briscoe from the University of Omaha in the late 1960s. He was drafted as a defensive back in spite of the fact that he was a star quarterback in college. Injuries compelled the Broncos to play him at quarterback. He passed for 3 touchdowns in his first game. The following week he was on the bench watching the woeful Broncos fall behind 14–0. He was sent in and they won 21–14. He didn't play in the next game. When the regular was injured, Briscoe started and passed for four TDs in a victory. That was their last win but in two of the final three losses Briscoe passed for more than 200 yards. In his five starts he did this four times. At the end of the season, Briscoe was released and never played quarterback again. That was my first introduction to the word "stacking," or segregation by position.

Is it true now in the NFL? Using the twenty-eight NFL 1983 team media guides, the statistics are overwhelming. On offense, 99 percent of the quarterbacks were white; 97 percent of the centers, 77 percent of the guards, and 68 percent of the tackles were white.

The patterns are more pronounced today than they were in 1968 when a white player told Jack Olsen:

> It's not very complicated to figure out. The play starts right in that cluster. . . . Those three guys and the quarterback are it. It doesn't make a damn bit of difference what

the other seven players do; if anybody in that tight little cluster screws up, that's it. The play is dead. Now, how can white coaches, with all their built-in prejudice about the Negro, assign positions like that to black men?

On the other hand, 88 percent of the running backs and 77 percent of the wide receivers were black.

Sociologist Jonathan Brower did a survey of coaches and asked them how they would characterize the three positions dominated by whites. They used the following words: intelligence, leadership, emotional control, decision making, and technique.

The defensive position that shows the most meaningful statistical difference by race is cornerback (92 percent black). The words used by coaches for the black-controlled positions of running back, wide receiver, and cornerback were: strength, quickness, and instinct.

There are no black coaches in the NFL. If the white coaches hold traditional racial beliefs, then player assignments could easily be made according to race. The table on page 228 was compiled from veterans listed in the 1983 media guides and demonstrates the patterns.

A 1975 study of NFL players by Eitzen and Sanford shows that as their careers developed from high school to college to the pros, blacks were increasingly represented in reactive positions and increasingly underrepresented in control positions. Not only stereotyping by coaches, but also self-selection by some black athletes who assess their chances of success exacerbate the problem of positional segregation. As black athletes mature and see what happens to the Marlin Briscoes, they may choose to change positions.

Lee Ballinger, in *In Your Face,* elaborated on what happens in football. In 1974, Joe Gilliam was named as starting quarterback for the Pittsburgh Steelers. He led them to a 4–0–1 record and first place in the AFC Central Division. Gilliam was

POSITION	WHITES BY PERCENTAGE	BLACKS BY PERCENTAGE
Offense		
Quarterback	99	1
Running back	12	88
Wide receiver	23	77
Center	97	3
Guard	77	23
Tight end	52	48
Tackle	68	32
Kicker	98	2
Kick-off returner	18	82
Defense		
Cornerback	8	92
Safety	43	57
Linebacker	53	47
Defensive end	31	69
Defensive tackle	47	53

benched because the Steelers were "weak offensively." The facts that their points-per-game average was better than 75 percent of the teams in the NFL and that they were in first place in the division were irrelevant. What was relevant was that Joe Gilliam was black.

In 1976, James Harris became the NFC's leading passer after never being given the opportunity to play quarterback for Buffalo. After helping to win twenty of the twenty-four games he started and being named Most Valuable Player in the Pro Bowl, James Harris was traded for future draft choices.

Such examples have to teach black high school quarterbacks that they should try out for other positions. Actually, Briscoe, Gilliam, and Harris were fortunate. Most black college quarterbacks drafted by the NFL are switched to other positions without ever getting the chance to prove themselves at their natural position. This is not to say it is impossible for a black to make it at quarterback; however, it is very unlikely as the 99 percent white figure shows.

The offensive team is clearly the most visible in the minds of fans. It is interesting to note that of the twelve of twenty-eight NFL teams with a majority of blacks, eight had more total whites on offense than blacks. Sixty-five percent of the whites in the NFL play offense; fifty-six percent of the offensive players are white while sixty-two percent of the defensive players are black. Do the clubs do this for fans who want to recognize more white faces?

Baseball has its own positional segregation. The pitcher and the catcher are central to every play of the game. Of the fifty-eight catchers listed in the 1983 *Who's Who in Baseball,* none were black Americans. Seven percent were Latins. Only 6.6 percent of the 296 pitchers were black. Another 7 percent were Latins. It should not be surprising that these pivotal "thinking positions" are held mostly by whites. The people who cover second base, shortstop, and third base are also considered to be in thinking positions. Blacks make up 21 percent of second basemen, 11 percent of shortstops, and 9 percent of third basemen.

However, first basemen and outfielders mainly react to other players. Outfielders need quickness and instinct. Not as much skill and training is considered necessary to hold these positions as the others. Eighty-four percent of all blacks listed as offensive players were either first basemen (19 percent) or outfielders (65 percent). In spite of being outnumbered in the league by almost five to one, blacks have numerical superiority over whites in the outfield (seventy to sixty-eight).

The positional segregation has gotten worse over time. In 1960, there were 5.6 times as many black outfielders as pitchers; in 1970 there were 6.7 times as many. By 1980, it stood at 8.8 times as many black outfielders as pitchers. The total percentage of black pitchers and catchers had declined since the late 1960s.

According to *Who's Who in Baseball* for 1983, the positional breakdown is as follows:

POSITION	WHITES BY PERCENTAGE	BLACKS BY PERCENTAGE	LATINS BY PERCENTAGE
Pitcher	86	6.6	7
Catcher	93	0	7
1B	55	38	7
2B	65	21	14
3B	82	5	13
SS	73	11	16
Outfield	45	46	9

Sports sociologists have written at length on the question of why positional segregation exists in baseball. James Curtis and John Loy have done some of the best work in the early 1970s. But their studies were done when the overall proportions of blacks to whites were substantially increasing. However, now the overall proportion is at best stabilized. The sport is no longer "opening up." It never opened up at the central positions. According to Harry Edwards, management did not want to yield these positions to blacks because of the high degree of leadership responsibilities and outcome control associated with them.

Denials of racism are made by both general managers and social scientists. I cite the following lecture given at the University of Rhode Island during a two-week course on "Race and Sports." Participants included Harry Edwards, Roscoe Brown, Willis Reed, and myself.

Then there was Dr. Edward Hunt, an anthropologist from Penn State. As reported in the Kingston *Evening Bulletin,* he talked about the many physiological differences between blacks and whites. Above all else, the key for performance for the doctor seemed to be what the eye color of the participant was. He explained that studies have shown that the brains of dark-eyed people have more pigmentation than the brains of blue- or light-eyed people and such pigmentation affects the transfer of nerve impulses to the brain (translation: dark-eyed people don't think fast). Needless to say, most blacks are not blue eyed.

As a result, he said, "blue-eyed people are self-paced while dark-eyed people are interactive . . . reaction time of dark-eyed whites and blacks is better than those of light-eyed whites." (Translation: dark-eyed people are quicker and more instinctive, while light-eyed people have emotional control, discipline, and intelligence.)

All of this, according to Hunt, explains positional segregation and why blacks dominate certain sports. If Frank Sinatra only knew. "Old Blue Eyes" could have been a great pitcher or quarterback, but not much of an outfielder or defensive back. In basketball he could shoot fouls better but not field goals. He wouldn't have been much of a boxer but could have played with Borg and McEnroe. I wonder what would happen if Larry Holmes had an eye transplant. Would he become a quarterback? In the end, it all depends on the same thing—one's skin color and the racism that brings forth.

The search for white superstars will be most intense in any sport such as basketball where the numbers of blacks are highest. The perennial search for the Great White Hope in boxing is also well known. White promoter Bob Arum has been mining white South African fighters in his efforts to find one. Black promoter Don King reportedly said: "I'd run through the jungle and fight a lion with a switch to get a good white fighter." South African Gerrie Coetzee proved to be inept in his first two WBA title shots, then won in an unprecedented third try late in 1983. Many believed Gerry Cooney to be the man—before he fought Larry Holmes.

In 1978, Calvin Griffith, the owner of the Minnesota Twins, shocked everyone when he spoke to a Lions Club in Waseca, Minnesota: "I'll tell you why we came to Minnesota in 1961.

It was when I found out you had only 15,000 blacks here. Black people don't go to ball games, but they'll fill up a rassling ring and put up such a chant it'll scare you to death. . . . We came here because you've got good, hard-working white people here." Many understood what Griffith was saying. Whites understood he wanted to make more money. Blacks understood he was a racist. Rod Carew was the star of the Twins. He has been baseball's most consistent hitter for twelve seasons in a row, with a .300 or better average and a .333 lifetime average. Although Griffith later apologized and said the statements were taken out of context, Carew said, "I refuse to be a slave on his plantation and play for a bigot." He was traded to California.

It is no small irony that after Jackie Robinson blacks were let into sports largely to increase attendance. Thirty years later they are being restricted again because it is perceived that they are hurting attendance. How far back the pendulum will swing is open to question.

Professional black athletes are sophisticated enough to know that they will face the same pressures in sports that other blacks will face in society. At least they take comfort from the money they have made and from their fame that will endure over time. When their careers are over they think they can, perhaps, approach the general manager for a job coaching or in the front office. Perhaps.

I remember the day my father was elected to the Basketball Hall of Fame. It was one of the happiest days of his life. There was no reason to doubt he would be selected, yet the fact of election was nevertheless a proud moment, and my father went to the ceremony with joy.

When Bill Russell followed Bob Douglas as the second black man elected to the Hall, he refused to go to the induction because of the racism in the sport. It made one think. That was 1974. Blacks were already dominating basketball and yet there were only two black men in the Hall of Fame. Abe Saperstein, the white owner of the Harlem Globetrotters, went in before Bob Douglas.

I assumed that the controversy created by Bill Russell would move more blacks into the Hall quickly. Between 1974–80, twenty-two whites and five blacks were chosen. That made a total of 102 whites and 7 blacks. The other blacks were Elgin Baylor, Tarzan Cooper, Wilt Chamberlain, Oscar Robertson, and John McLendon. Amazingly, McLendon was chosen as a "contributor" and not as a coach. He won 522 college games, was the first to win three consecutive national titles (NAIA, 1957, 1958, and 1959), and was the first black pro coach. The NBA is 70 percent black. The Basketball Hall of Fame is 94 percent white.

Emlen Tunnell, the great New York Giant defensive back, was the first black elected to the Football Hall of Fame in 1967. Willie Davis, defensive end for Green Bay in the 1960s, was the fifteenth black chosen in 1981. George Blanda, the ageless quarterback and place kicker, was also enshrined in 1981. He was the ninety-fifth white. The NFL is 54 percent black. The Pro Football Hall of Fame is 86 percent white.

The National Baseball Hall of Fame is in Cooperstown, New York. Jackie Robinson was appropriately the first black inducted. That was in 1962. Eighty-six whites preceded him. His induction didn't exactly open the floodgates for blacks. Up to 1981, the only modern-day blacks chosen have been Robinson, Roy Campanella, Roberto Clemente, Ernie Banks, Willie Mays, and Bob Gibson. The Baseball Writers of America select those chosen few. In 1979, twenty-three members voted against Willie Mays, who hit 660 home runs, had 3,283 hits, and played in twenty-four All-Star Games. Nine blacks have also been chosen from the Negro Leagues in separate elections and are housed in a separate (but equal?) room. Baseball is 23 percent black; the Baseball Hall of Fame is 91 percent white if you include the Negro League stars, 96 percent if you don't.

*   *   *

Who knows sports better than the athletes who play it? It is natural to think that one could transmit the skills and knowledge accumulated over the course of many years of playing to young players. Many athletes have dreamed of this. Black athletes have also dreamed of it. They want to become managers and coaches.

That dream had barely begun when Olsen interviewed Larry Doby in 1968. The number of blacks in the major leagues had only just started to rise. Doby, of course, was the first black allowed into the American League. In 1968, he hoped to be the first black manager. He said, "Wouldn't it be a shame if baseball waited until the ball park is burned down before it stepped in and did the right thing." In 1968 Jim Gilliam of the Dodgers was the only black coach. There were no black managers and only a handful of blacks in the front offices. Many whites thought having blacks in such positions would be bad for publicity. Others thought blacks weren't smart enough. Many didn't want blacks to be in charge of whites.

Doby added, "Black athletes are cattle. They're raised, fed, sold, and killed. Baseball moved me toward the front of the bus, and it let me ride there as long as I could run. And then it told me to get off at the back door."

Doby was suddenly hired as a coach by Cleveland after the article appeared. Was he hired to prove he was wrong or to co-opt him? It must have hurt when Frank Robinson was hired by Cleveland in late 1974 to manage the team for which Doby was coach. There was a lot of talk about which black man would be chosen as the first black manager. Speculation centered largely on Gilliam, Doby, and Hank Aaron. White writers wrote for years and at length about which blacks might be qualified to manage while white owners hired white manager after white manager.

So Robinson managed Cleveland in 1975, 1976, and then was fired in early 1977. Under his guidance, the Indians had their best two-season record in ten years. Yet he was let go early in the next year. The image of a black boss was just too tough. Before he was canned, Robinson had a highly publicized argument with Gaylord Perry, his white pitching star. The next day a sign was hung at the ballpark: "Sickle Cell Anemia: White Man's Hope."

Larry Doby was finally hired to manage the White Sox for the tail end of the 1978 season. It was hardly a real chance.

Henry Aaron seemed certain to be the next black named as manager in 1978 when the incumbent manager of the Atlanta Braves was fired during the season. After all, he had just broken Babe Ruth's all-time home-run record in spite of death threats, racial harassment, and the need for police protection. It seemed that some whites couldn't stand to see a black break the greatest record of the greatest white superstar of all time. But Aaron seemed the natural choice to become manager. In fact, he was traded to Milwaukee. He told Phil Musick, his biographer:

> The owners seem to have gotten together and decided that certain men—certain white men—should be hired and rehired no matter what kind of failures they've been . . . as soon as they're fired by one owner, they're hired by another.
>
> Baseball is no different than stagnant water. The Negro has progressed no further than the field. Until we crack that area, there is no real hope for black kids coming into sports. We're greats on the field for twenty years, then they're finished with us.

Late in 1980, Maury Wills, the former great Dodger shortstop, was hired by Seattle. Frank Robinson came back when the Giants hired him for the 1981 season. 1981 marked the first time two black managers were working simultaneously. When they met for the first time in 1981, *The New York Times* duly recorded it as an historic event. It was good that they did because Wills was fired only 24 games into the season.

It should be noted that Wills and Robinson were the only two of twenty-six major-league managers with Hall of Fame credentials. If you are black, you have to be better. If you are black and want to manage, you better have been a superstar. Robinson was one of twenty-six managers in 1983.

There were some 123 coaches in the major leagues in 1983. Of the 123, 110 were white.

Opportunities for blacks as managers in the minor leagues and in college are even fewer. Kansas State was the only Division I school with a black manager in 1983. Front-office jobs are just as scarce.

There were three black coaches leading NBA teams as the 1982–83 season began. Paul Silas was in his third year at San Diego and was the only black NBA coach with a losing record. Lenny Wilkens had coached for ten years and was with Seattle. He had a winning percentage of .541. That was the fourth best record of anyone in the NBA with a tenure of five years or more. Al Attles had coached for thirteen years and had a .531 winning percentage. That was the sixth-best coaching record in the NBA. Once again, blacks had to be better. Both Silas and Attles left at the end of the season. The hiring of K. C. Jones by Boston left two black NBA coaches at the start of the 1983–84 season.

Look at the graveyard of black NBA coaches. Bill Russell was the first coach in 1966. In his two reigns with Boston and Seattle his record was 367–249 for a .595 percentage. Those black coaches with bad records never got second chances. They include Earl Lloyd in Detroit and Elgin Baylor in Utah. In fact, Wilkens is the only black to lose with one team and be hired elsewhere. Yet many whites like Larry Brown, Gene Shue, Dick Motta, Connie Fitzsimmons, Tom Nissalke, and Kevin Loughery were instantly rehired after failures.

What about other black coaches? Ray Scott was fired by Detroit one year after he was named coach of the year. He had a .523 percentage. K. C. Jones was fired by Baltimore a year after he led them to the NBA finals. His three-year record was 148–91, for a .629 percentage. It took almost a decade for him to be hired again when he joined the Celtics in 1983. The Celtics have been by far the most consistent in hiring black coaches with Russell, Tom Sanders, and K. C. Jones. While this would seem to contradict Boston's emphasis on white players, in fact it may show that in this case race plays no real part.

In Willis Reed's first year of coaching the Knicks, they rose above .500 and made the playoffs for the first time in four years. He was fired after fourteen games in his second season. Reed told the *Sunday Daily News:*

> To be let go without a shot, though, is very disappointing. If you don't do the job, that's different. But when you do and show signs of continued improvement, that makes it hard to take. . . . It's really tough on a black coach. I do believe some of what happened to me was racial. But that's something you learn to live with because you must cope with it every day.

When he couldn't get another pro job, he took an unpaid assistant-coaching job with St. John's in 1980–81, then accepted the job at Creighton. But still no NBA. Even if blacks *are* better, they still might not make it. The winning percentages of Scott, Jones, and Reed were .523, .620, and .510, respectively. Nine of the twenty white head coaches at the helm when the 1982–83 season started had *worse* records than any of these.

The 1982–83 NBA guide showed only four of the thirty-six assistant coaches as black. The percentages go down when you discuss black college coaches.

The situation in football is even worse. A report commissioned by the NFL Players Association was released late in 1980. It revealed that there were no black head football coaches and only 10 black assistant coaches out of 225 in the NFL. In

1983, there were still no black head coaches while 27 out of 269 assistants were black. The NFL is 54 percent black. Ninety percent of its coaches are white.

Dr. Braddock, who headed the Johns Hopkins research team studying race as a factor in the NFL, reported:

> Whether direct or indirect, it is evident from our data that race has been a limiting factor in the career mobility of blacks. If recent trends are taken as valid indicators of blacks' future prospects in the NFL, then these prospects do not appear to be very bright.

No research team was really needed to recognize that fact for pro football. College football, however, is in a self-congratulatory mood these days after Wichita and Northwestern became the first major colleges to hire black head coaches. College baseball had only one black as head coach at a major college (Kansas State) at this writing. While some acknowledge these hirings as a beginning, the percentages are still dismal.

The following chart shows the coaching breakdown in the three major professional sports at the close of the 1983 baseball season and at the start of the 1983 football and 1982–83 basketball seasons:

	HEAD COACHES			ASSISTANT COACHES		
	BLACK	WHITE	% WHITE	BLACK	WHITE	% WHITE
Baseball	1	25	96%	13*	123	90%
Basketball	2	21	91%	4	32	89%
Football	0	28	100%	27	242	90%
Totals	3	74	96%	44	397	90%

*Includes Latins

Everyone went into a flurry when Jim Rice, the Boston Red Sox' star hitter, called their front office racist in a July 1978 story in *Sport.* Writers rushed to the defense. This, after all, was the city where outspoken Bill Russell was hired as the first black head coach. Temporarily forgotten were more recent events in the city where white students and parents were physically attacking black students in South Boston who were being bussed to integrate the schools. That had never happened in an integration case in a northern city before.

But in the front office of the Red Sox? Jim Rice was just another ungrateful nigger. Why, if it weren't for sports . . . Rice was in the midst of hitting 46 home runs, batting in 139 runs, and hitting .315 for the year. In his six full seasons through 1980, he *averaged* 33 home runs, 110 RBIs, and batted .307. If he was hitting .250 he would have been playing in Pawtucket after the *Sport* story. But he was Jim Rice, so the media had to defend the front office rather than campaign to get rid of him.

In the specific case of the Red Sox, you have to wonder why in 1980 this same front office had only one black man on the roster—Jim Rice. Because of the Red Sox, Boston has long had the reputation as one of the most racist sports towns in America. The Sox were the whitest team in baseball in 1980, a dubious distinction they still held in 1983. But Boston should hardly be singled out for criticism when you look around the three major professional sports. In fact, despite having a predominantly white team, the Celtics have had more black coaches than anyone.

The executives and members of the front offices in charge of professional sports in America are whiter than white. All the information that follows has been derived from the 1980 publications of the individual teams in all three sports.

A black man, Simon P. Gourdine, the former NBA deputy commissioner, didn't become the commissioner although no one doubted his talents. Gourdine himself said, "If sports ever has a black commissioner, it will be in the NBA." Note he did not say *when,* he said *if.* No black man has been president, or vice-president, or . . . Gourdine is no longer with the

NBA. He was not replaced with another black as some had expected.

Cecil Watkins, also black, was the NBA's assistant supervisor of officials. Watkins is now referee development administrator, too, but it should come as no surprise that there are few black NBA referees (five of the twenty-seven total) for Watkins to supervise. Or that there are only eight blacks out of a hundred in the NFL and only one in major league baseball. Comments made by ex-umpire Art Williams, now a bus driver in California, were readily ignored. As reported by *Sporting News* in 1978, he was disgruntled after he was let go by the National League. After all, he had to deal with Al Barlich, consultant to the National League on umpires and not with sympathetic Cecil Watkins. Williams said, "They're letting me go because I'm black. They're bringing up another black umpire and they don't want to have two when the American League doesn't have any. I'll never work for Barlich again. . . ."

So the NBA had two blacks in the thirteen posts in the NBA league office in 1982. Progress? Perhaps, but it is certainly not a great leap forward for blacks. Look around the NBA. Wayne Embry was vice-president of the Milwaukee Bucks. Arnold Pinkney was an executive in Cleveland. Al Attles was not only the coach of Golden State but was also sports' first black general manager. Progress? The NBA's great leap forward is like Chairman Mao's—an abject failure. These were the totals! There were 121 whites listed as executives (presidents, vice-presidents, board chairmen, general managers, etc.). Embry, Attles, and Pinkney were the only three blacks. That was a total of 2.4 percent in 1982.

There were 300 people listed as administration and staff for NBA teams in that season. Larry Doby, unable to manage in the major leagues, was the Nets' director of community relations. Will Robinson held the same post in Detroit. Wayne Scales was Portland's director of promotions. There were only nine others in the rest of the league. Fourteen NBA teams had no blacks listed as administration/staff. Zero! The league had 12 of 399 or a total of 4 percent.

Segregation applied even to the sportscasters (chosen by management). If you live in New York you have seen Butch Beard doing the Knick games; in Chicago you have seen Norm Van Lier and Kenny Mac; in Washington it has been James Brown; and in Portland Steve Jones. In nineteen of the twenty-three NBA cities there were no black sportscasters. Of the fifty-five sportscasters, five, or 9 percent, were black. Perhaps this represents progress compared, for instance, to the 4 percent of the nation's newspaper writers who are black. But it does not when compared to the black percentage in the NBA.

Of the total of 544 listed in all categories combined, 29 were black. That's 5.3 percent, less than half the proportion of blacks nationwide when the proportion of blacks in the NBA is some 650 percent greater than the national proportion.

The NBA is probably trying to balance its image as an all-black league by overwhelming us with white faces in other sections of their media guides. Maybe they are even hiding some black faces in lesser positions to do this.

What about the NFL, which is not perceived as all-black and has no such image difficulties? Buddy Young was director of player relations for the NFL Office until his tragic death late in 1983. Paul "Tank" Younger (San Diego) and Bobby Mitchell (Washington) were assistant general managers for their respective teams. They were the only 2 executives out of 117 working for NFL teams. That's .016 percent in the NFL, which was 54 percent black in 1983.

There were 452 people listed as administration/staff for NFL teams. The following black men were listed as scouts for their teams: Rosey Brown (Giants), Dick Daniels (Washington), Bob Hill (New Orleans), Lawrence McCutcheon (Rams), Ralph Goldston (Seattle), Bobby Grier (New England), Otis Taylor (Kansas City), Charles Garcia (Denver), Clyde Powers (Baltimore), Milt Davis and Elbert Dubenion (Miami). Paul Warfield was director of player relations for Cleveland. Frank Gilliam had the same post for the Vikings. Darryl Stingley was executive director of player personnel for New England while Bill Nunn, Jr. (Pittsburgh) and Jackie Graves (Philadelphia) were assistant directors of player personnel. Ronnie Barnes was head trainer for the Giants; Sid Brooks was equipment manager for San Diego; Willie Alexander was a career consultant for Houston; Claudia Smith was director of public affairs for New England; and Ted Chappelle was director of security for Cleveland. Only thirteen others were listed as assistants, receptionists, or secretaries. That is 32 of 452, making a total of only 6.6 percent for blacks—barely one-tenth of the number in the league. Of the twenty-eight teams surveyed in 1983, nine had no blacks in this category of administration/staff; ten others had only one black; six others had only two. The LA Rams with four out of fifty had the most.

Combining all categories of executive, head and assistant coaches, and administration/staff, as listed in the 1983 team media guides, there were 879 posts, 61 (6.5 percent) of which were held by blacks. It was a stark picture for future employment prospects for ex-black football players.

If black professional athletes entertain any ideas of staying on with their teams after their playing days end, they should look elsewhere. The door is shut tight for blacks. Very tight.

What are the "retired" black athletes going to do? What are their marketable skills? Roscoe Brown, president of Bronx Community College, estimates that only 20 percent of the NBA players have college degrees. Less than 10 percent of major league baseball players have degrees. The NFL Players Association 1982 survey showed 65 percent of their players did not receive degrees. The employment records of former athletes is hardly encouraging.

Everything is compounded for the retiring black athlete. It doesn't matter whether you are Bill Russell, Jackie Robinson, Bob Gibson, Hank Aaron, Ron Leflore, or Tony Oliva, all of whom wrote books when they retired. A black player out of uniform looks like any other black to most whites. A cop might back off once he sees the driver's license, but until then any athlete is just another black face.

There are, of course, extreme examples of what happens to former pro athletes who suddenly find themselves facing double- instead of triple-figure incomes. Bill Robinzine chose to take his own life. A small but growing number have had to turn to crime. Broke, with no professional training, former star running back Mercury Morris began dealing drugs. Now he faces fifteen years in prison.

Morris was among the one in nearly 12,000 who made it to the pros. Many of the others who "made it" soon will join the 11,999 who didn't. Back on the streets, they will have to decide what they will do. For most, the options are slim. Corporations no longer need to hire blacks to fill quotas. The Equal Employment Opportunity Act, introduced in Congress with the approval of the Reagan administration, would prohibit the use of quotas to increase the hiring or school enrollment of women and minorities.

Team owners use blacks just as corporations use them in factories. Maximize their utility and then discard them. In the meanwhile, the athlete has devoted most of his life developing the skills necessary to become a pro player. Because of that, he is not likely to become a surgeon, a lawyer, or an intellectual leader. When his career is over, his standard of living is likely to decline.

If sports are ever to live up to their promise as harbingers of racial change, then the press must tell us about the fates of all the Fred Buttlers as well as the Magic Johnsons. And we must learn about the deeds, and not just the statistics, of multifaceted men like Paul Robeson, Bill Russell, and Kareem Abdul-Jabbar if blacks are to avoid the trap of a life of playing sports alone as youth and being forced to work as unskilled labor forevermore. Everyone needs a role model to help draw out and build his natural talents. Even though I came from a secure middle-class background, I still needed one and was lucky enough to find him in my own home. When poverty makes success seem a far-distant goal, children need so much more than a helmet, a glove, a bat, or a ball. Creatively used, sports can help the process of total education. Tragically, the truth is that for blacks today, even considering the important exceptions, sports helps to mire most blacks in the quicksands of ignorance that only perpetuates their poverty.

· Conclusion ·

Sportswriters have trumpeted the positive sides of sport while rarely examining the negative. The premise of this book is that sport is a reflection of society, that it reflects both the positive and the negative. This book attempts to counterbalance all of the writings about the joys of sport with a critical look at the less than positive side.

Since completing the body of the text, I spent two weeks in Angola with an American basketball team, experiencing some of the best that sport has to offer. With no diplomatic relations between the countries and five years of virulent rhetoric spewed from both Washington and Luanda, it was hoped that this basketball tour would soften the rhetoric and make way for better relations.

The American team, coached by Lou Carnesecca, was chosen from the Big East Conference. The players—eight blacks and three whites—did not know what kind of reception they would get from the Angolans in light of the prevailing hostility toward America in Angola. Their concerns melted away as they ran onto the big court of the Citadella arena in Luanda. Fifteen thousand Angolans cheered wildly for the team, which marched out behind the American flag. The flag had never been flown in Angola before. It was a stirring moment for everyone. A total of 75,000 came out to see the games as much for the political as for the sports importance. Our players learned about Africa and Angola and the Angolan players learned about life in America. Both teams transmitted their messages to their own people through the large press coverage the tour received. If I had become overly cynical about sport, this experience tempered those feelings and reminded me what a positive force it can be.

There is little doubt that sport has the potential to deliver significant outcomes for individuals, teams, nations. Whether or not sufficient reforms will occur that will enable us to make the myths of sport into realities is another question.

The 1968 Olympic protest, followed by campus protests, sensitized even hardened sports administrators and owners to the reality that some changes had to be made. But all they offered were higher salaries for the pros, and greater inducements, both academic and material, for the college players.

Owners and administrators weren't challenged. The glare of the stadium lights made it hard to see the horror of the ghetto surrounding the stadium. Things were getting worse in sport and, of course, in society. We were a society content to grow a little fatter each year. However, as the economy soured and times grew worse, people suddenly were resisting the draft, protesting U.S. involvement in El Salvador, U.S. support for South Africa, and campaigning for a nuclear freeze. Professional athletes were striking and scandals seemed to be behind every athletic department door. Digger Phelps shocked America when he said good college athletes were receiving $10,000 a year. My father cited that same figure twenty years before. Why were we shocked in 1982? We have known about the problems all along. But will we do something about it now? I have my doubts.

Americans have always looked for the positive and have tried to ignore the negative in sport. That is why each new scandal brings cries of anguish but rarely brings change or acknowledgment of root problems. Today's scandal quickly becomes tomorrow's aberration. The patterns of the 1980s show that the average American is still ready to blame the victim for his problems.

The foremost condition for meaningful change is to recognize the need for change—that is, we must face up to the problems in sports. This book is particularly concerned with race so my proposals focus on the plight of black athletes, but many apply across the board to all athletes.

Unfortunately, no one is in the position to propose changes that would totally eliminate racism in sport. Since sport free of racism can only exist in a society free of racism, it is more realistic to suggest changes that would ease the problem of racism in sport by giving the athlete a better understanding of and, thus, more control of his own destiny.

As has been shown, little has changed for today's black athlete since sports integration began with Jackie Robinson. That fact makes it both more exciting and, consequently, more frightening for some to contemplate substantial rapid changes.

Changes have always emanated from current conditions. In the late 1960s, campus-wide protests provoked athletic protests under the inspiration of the likes of Harry Edwards and Jack Scott. There is now no such protest on the horizon. However, the media, especially in its more recent role of watchdog and informer on the inner turmoil of the sports world, may prove to be a catalyst for necessary change.

Changes must come about at all levels to have the desired effects. At each level, it is the importance of the role of education that is the key. Everything that happens to the athlete after his career ends depends on what knowledge and skills he has obtained while playing on the field or court. We can't realistically expect that individual and institutional racism will change quickly. Therefore, the emphasis must first be on exposing it and then teaching young athletes to deal with it. Preparing them for the nonathletic job market is most crucial.

Parents who have pushed their children into sports without comprehending what they (their children) are embarking on must be made to see things more clearly. If every Pop Warner or Little League team would have a meeting with parents prior to the start of each season, motives, goals, and expectations of both children *and* parents could be explored. Facilitators for these meetings would have to have had some training to elicit those responses that would be most helpful in seeing behind the scenes. The facilitator could bring in the importance of education and discuss racial factors if they exist at that level of play.

With the controversial adoption of Proposition 48 (mandating minimum standards on precollege test scores in order for athletes to be eligible in the first year), the NCAA has helped focus attention on the education of high-school athletes.

As we've seen, academic standards for high-school athletes are probably the least rigorous of all levels. High schools have little motive to prepare their athletes educationally. If more were embarrassed by star athletes not being able to play for a year, then perhaps they would feel the obligation to prepare them better.

It is ironic that the presidents of many predominantly black colleges and universities opposed Proposition 48 as being discriminatory against black athletes. Proposition 48, which will go into effect in 1986, requires that any Division-I freshman athlete must have a "C" average in eleven basic courses and have scored either 700 on the Scholastic Aptitude Test (SAT) or accumulated a score of 15 on the American College Test (ACT). The 700 standard predicts a 50 percent graduation rate at Division-I schools.

The black academicians opposing Proposition 48 were joined by civil rights leaders like Jesse Jackson and Ben Hooks. Some of the objections were justified. First, it is widely accepted that such tests as SAT and ACT are culturally biased against minorities. The fact that the special committee of the American Council of Education, which conceived of Proposition 48, had no representatives from black schools is a major slap in the face of American black higher education. Yet, the critics also said that the new Proposition 48 standards were arbitrarily high and were a means of reducing the number of black athletes at predominantly white institutions. Having witnessed and studied the craving to win of athletic departments at such schools, I cannot agree with the latter objection.

Fortunately, Harry Edwards had the courage to stand up once again as a seemingly solitary voice arguing forcefully that, if anything, the new standards were too low and undemanding. It was necessary for someone as respected as Edwards to step forward. High schools have to have some standards and Proposition 48 is a start.

If it forces high-school athletes to take their studies more seriously, it will not only help those who actually continue to play in college but also those who aspire to do so but never make it beyond high school. As stated earlier, an average 1 of every 12,000 high-school athletes makes it to the pros. For more than 11,000 of the 12,000, the athletic career ends in high school. If they don't have some skills by their senior year, then they almost certainly face a menial job or, worse, they could become one of the 55 percent of black youth who are unemployed.

But Proposition 48 attacks the problem only at the high-school level. It does nothing for the athlete after he or she gains admission to college. By the time they are there, most scholarship athletes, especially black ones, are sure that the pros are in sight and academics are even less important than in high school. It is the moral obligation of the university to ensure that they obtain a real education.

Any experienced academic adviser realizes that the transition for an ordinary student from high school to college is difficult. It is more difficult for an athlete, due to the time demands imposed on him; it is most difficult for the black athlete who quite possibly has arrived with less developed academic skills as a result of the star syndrome and institutional academic neglect in high school.

One way to reduce the controversy surrounding Proposition

48 is to eliminate freshman eligibility altogether so that all athletes can make the transition. Given the proper advice and adequate time to grow into their new environments, athletes would begin the second year on a more equal footing with other students. This proposal is not meant to suggest a return to "freshman" basketball and baseball teams. The freshmen would have no athletic obligations that year although they would receive full financial support. This would increase costs to universities since they would be forced to carry more scholarship athletes on the varsity. However, this should not be a significant burden, if financed by dramatically increasing athletic revenues.

The question of financial support of athletes in general and black athletes in particular is a sensitive one. Most fans don't realize that current sports scholarships are awarded on an annual basis. Black athletes, taught from childhood about the financial insecurities of blacks in a white society, are particularly vulnerable to this rule since they have to fear the wrath of white coaches or administrators more than white athletes. Any serious reforms for athletes must include the guarantee of the chance to complete their education within a reasonable period. It would include a five-year guarantee—as a minimum —with extensions if academic problems developed directly as a consequence of their sports participation. Thus, the athlete would be certain that if he was sufficiently motivated, additional tuition and fees would never stand in the way of obtaining a degree.

Two other rule changes by the NCAA could help both white and black athletes. Both are favorites of athletic departments. First, red-shirting of athletes should be banned. The goal of all athletes and athletic administrations should be identical in this regard; that is, that every student try to graduate in four years. To deliberately prolong this process for athletic purposes should become a violation.

Second, the transfer rule should be eliminated. As it stands today, very few athletes consider transferring to another school because they would have to sit out a year from sports competition. This rule is particularly unfair to the black athlete who frequently finds himself in an uncomfortable social environment or faced with a coaching staff he can't deal with adequately, and wants to transfer to another college. The coach holds all the cards now since the athlete who leaves pays a high price in terms of competition. While the average college student can and does transfer easily, the athlete is trapped. The situation has to be almost unbearable for him. To be at all fair to the athlete and his future, the transfer rule must go.

All of these rule changes—eliminating freshman eligibility, red-shirting, and the transfer rule as well as guaranteeing financial aid throughout the duration of an athlete's college career —will help the athlete when he is in college. Proposition 48 will help prepare him in high school. But selecting a college is very difficult. How can the athlete recognize the type of coach who might want him to help his team so badly that he would bend the truth about the school?

Harry Edwards, among others, has suggested a solution that would be unpopular with colleges with things to hide but would benefit the prospective student-athlete tremendously. Each athletic department would have on record, as certified by the university president, an academic summary statement of all athletes at the school. The summary, done sport by sport, would include what the students are majoring in, grade-point averages, and the graduation rates of student-athletes over the previous five or ten years.

Furthermore, the academic summary statement could anonymously compare the high-school records of each of the school's athletes with their university performance. The latter might help a high-school athlete see where he might fit into the equation. It might also be valuable to categorize the students by race so that if the prospective recruit is black he will see if there are academic disparities between different racial groups at the school.

The prospective recruit would be given this summary statement at his first point of contact with the school so that he could have a headstart in determining what kind of future he would have there.

Before proceeding, I must state that I agree with those who say that athletes deserve special treatment. Part of their being enrolled is an obligation to give the school literally thousands of hours of their time during their four years of eligibility. Their time brings the school entertainment, prestige, and, frequently, handsome revenues. To argue against special treatment for athletes is naive and irresponsible. However, what I mean by special treatment is the assurance of academic preparedness and not exemption from such preparedness.

I would break down the special on-campus responsibilities of the school into creating the best possible social environment and, concurrently, the best possible academic environment.

Under the former category, more black coaches, assistant coaches, sports administrators, and academic advisers should be hired. As demonstrated, little has been done to increase these numbers beyond a handful of head coaches and a few more assistants.

Second, each academic year should begin with a week-long seminar for all athletes and coaches. Experts should be brought in along with former athletes to discuss in depth the whole range of problems faced by today's student-athletes including academics, drugs, and future careers either as pro athletes or as ordinary citizens. In terms of race, it would be critical in such sessions to face all the issues honestly and directly. Black former athletes should meet with players and coaches. The discussions should deal with all the racial issues, both related to and unrelated to sports.

Having worked in Norfolk, Virginia, which is a major navy port, I became familiar with a series of controversial race-relations seminars that navy personnel had to attend in the 1970s under the direction of Admiral Elmo "Bud" Zumwalt. In discussions with the participants I saw three different reactions. The hostility of racist whites remained unchanged. Those whites who had little contact with or knowledge of minorities but did not bear hostility were the most affected. They began to understand the origin of racial stereotypes and to grapple with them positively. Blacks saw clearly what they were up against with the racists and saw some hope with the other whites. Mostly, they clearly comprehended where they stood in a primarily white institution and, thus, knew better what they had to do to successfully cope with the obstacles they would face. I believe the same type of program could help within college athletic departments and certainly merits a chance.

Finally, an ombudsman in the president's office should be appointed to objectively hear the grievances of all athletes toward their coaches or athletic administrators. Hopefully, this would operate preventatively and diminish tensions rather than increase them. The ombudsman would have to have the respect of key athletic department people without being so close to them as to lose objectivity.

Under the all-important category of academic environment, there must be several modifications of the current situation at most schools.

It must begin with the admissions process. Every athlete should gain admission according to the same criteria as all students. This would put them on an equal footing from the start.

Proper academic counseling is crucial. As it stands today, some 75 percent of those athletes who do graduate leave having majored in physical education or other sports-related subjects. Counselors must advise athletes of the limited value of such courses and attempt to direct them to a variety of others to see both what they are interested in and what their career options would be if they pursued a particular major. The counselor should have an in-depth academic profile of the student-athlete that indicates where his strengths and weaknesses lie.

A full-scale study program should be constructed. Athletes should be able to schedule their classes to end two hours prior to practice so that they spend those hours each day studying together. Special tutors and remedial experts, where necessary, should be available to work with the athletes during this and other time periods.

These are all basic proposals designed to give the student-athlete a fighting chance to succeed academically and are realistically adoptable by the universities.

However, being realistically adoptable doesn't mean they will be adopted. The NCAA has proven ineffective in enforcing academic standards. The recent interest evinced by college presidents in changing this gives some hope. But there must be more—a better way to induce the universities to act.

The best suggestion I have heard came from Jack Scott, who proposed that athletes' academic progress should be a basis for the acquiring and maintenance of a university's accreditation. With the institutions' overall academic integrity on the line, the university or college would have no choice but to establish the necessary programs that would ultimately lead to giving all athletes, black and white alike, the chance to obtain a useful education beyond the sports field. In turn, when such sports careers end, the athletes would be more prepared to control their own fates in the job market. In turn, the effects of racism would be diminished.

Whether in sport or in society, no rational people wants to admit it is racist. Our authority figures are used to mask the reality. Athletic directors, the police, the FBI, and the press explain to us that the obvious forms of racism are less than obvious.

My own experience with the police and their accusations is a modest example. I have tried to show in the preceding chapters how irrational the arguments of the police and medical examiner were. But the local press ran with them and I believe that the vast majority of white people from the area still believe them. Isn't that more comfortable than to think that violence can be directed at a college professor, even an outspoken one? Or that South Africa was involved in so small a matter? Clearly it is.

We must recognize that in some substantive ways blacks are actually worse off in society today than they were thirty years ago. And, as has been shown, blacks are as bad off in sports today as they were before the so-called athletic revolution began in the 1960s.

In the 1960s it took blood and death to make us wake up to and effectively challenge racism. It took the courage of Tommie Smith and John Carlos in Mexico City to force us to examine racism in sport. The authorities claim, "These things don't happen anymore." Without the upheaval and violence, we have become apathetic as a people.

But violence has shown signs of reemerging. Forty-seven percent of blacks surveyed in 116 cities in 1980 said racial violence against blacks had occurred in their local community in the previous twelve months.

All of this is exacerbated by the fact that black Americans had their expectations raised by civil rights victories in the 1960s only to have them dashed in the 1970s. The frustration, disappointment, and anger of young blacks are reaching a new peak. This is true of the black athlete carried by educational institutions for his or her athletic prowess until eligibility expires. It is equally true of the many black students socially promoted through American public schools. The result is the same—a lack of learned skills forces the black to become part of the vast sea of unemployed youth or to take up unskilled and low-paying jobs in the secondary labor market. The athlete at least has memories to go with his resentment. But those memories ultimately aren't very useful on the street.

Fifty years ago, my father was thought of as a "nigger lover" when he and his teammates played against black teams. Thirty years ago he was even more of a nigger lover when he brought Nat Clifton up to the Knicks. Twenty years ago I was called a nigger lover when I brought my black friends into our almost all-white neighborhood. For most of my adult life I have been a nigger lover to some because of my work in the civil rights and anti-apartheid movements. Now my son Joey is a nigger lover to others who hate his father or hate him because he has so many black friends in school. Where will it end? *Will* it end?

I am frequently asked how a family man can stay in the struggle and take such risks as I have already been subjected to in the past few years. It is precisely because I am a family man that I continue. In my thirty-seven years, I have never once felt totally free. No matter how good my personal and professional life might have been, no matter what short-term accomplishments might have been achieved, I have never been and can never feel totally free myself as long as others aren't. I want Joey and Chamy to know that freedom so I continue to join the thousands of others working for that freedom.

When I joined the civil rights movement in the 1960s I was somewhat of an oddity as a white. When I joined the anti-apartheid movement in the late 1960s, I was an oddity as a white American working on an international racial issue. I worked for two and a half years for the World Conference of the United Nations Decade for Women on the issue of Southern African women. When I was hired I was informed that other than for my race, sex, and nationality, I was perfect for the job.

But that is precisely the point. Problems of race relations aren't only the problems of blacks, women's issues aren't only the problems of women, restrictions on Africans affect people other than Africans. All such issues are ultimately human rights issues to be solved collectively by blacks and whites, men and women, Africans and non-Africans.

I have chosen sports as the vehicle through which I can best contribute to challenging racism. This vicious form of hatred has poisoned our people and artificially divided the human family far too long already. White America can no longer call the problem of race "the Negro problem" nor treat it with benign neglect. No form of neglect of racism is benign. White America needs to take a profound look at itself, understand what it has allowed itself to become, and work collectively as well as individually to initiate the transformation.

A close examination of sport can help us to confront the broader societal problems. If, however, we choose to continue ignoring the signs around us, then we may be forever doomed to our current self-consuming fears of one another. This time, promises must be kept.